FLORIDA STATE
UNIVERSITY LIBRARIES

JUN 2 6 2001

TALLAHASSEE, FLORIDA

AGAINST ECONOMICS

For Antara, Indrina, Malini, Anjana – and Cory Leigh: provenance of my passions, (hapless) legatees of my cares.

Against Economics
Rethinking Political Economy

RAJANI KANNEPALLI KANTH

Ashgate
Aldershot • Brookfield USA • Singapore • Sydney

© Rajani Kannepalli Kanth 1997

All rights reserved. No part of this publication may be reproduced, stored in a retrieval system, or transmitted in any form or by any means, electronic, mechanical, photocopying, recording or otherwise without the prior permission of the publisher.

Published by
Ashgate Publishing Ltd
Gower House
Croft Road
Aldershot
Hants GU11 3HR
England

Ashgate Publishing Company
Old Post Road
Brookfield
Vermont 05036
USA

British Library Cataloguing in Publication Data

Kanth, Rajani K.
    Against economics : rethinking political economy
    1. Economics
    I. Title
    330.1

Library of Congress Catalog Card Number: 97-71456

Reprinted 1999

ISBN 1 85972 610 0

Printed in Great Britain by Biddles Limited, Guildford and King's Lynn

Contents

Acknowledgements vii

Introduction: Against Economics 1

Part I Economics and Epistemology: Marxism, Realism and Beyond 9

1 Critical Realism: The *Nouvelle Critique* 11
2 Against Eurocentrism: Prolegomena to Liberation 31

Part II 'Development' Studies: Retrospect and Prospect 51

3 Theory and Policy in 'Development' Studies: An Overview of the Mythology of 'Progress' 53

Part III Arguments in Political Economy: Old and New 73

4 Economic Theory and Arms Expenditures: A Resumé of Issues 75
5 Sraffa, and All That: A Retrospective on Some Foibles of the Cambridge School 103
6 Why England Led the Way: Clues to a Critique of Eurocentrism 110

Part IV Classical Economics: Myth and Reality 121

7 The Ricardian Rigmarole: From Policy to Paradigm 123
8 The Parson and the Plutocrat: Toward Restitution 143

Part V Revolutions in Economic Theory: The Parameters of Paradigm Shift — 161

9 The Eclipse of Ricardian Ideas: A Primer on Paradigm Shift in Economics — 163

Part VI Otiose Controversies in Marxism: Against Orthodoxy — 191

10 The Falling Rate of Profit: Clarifying a Conjecture — 193
11 The 'Asiatic' Mode of Production: Eclipse of a Notion — 200
12 The 'Transition' to Socialism: In Dubious Debate — 211
13 Beyond Marx: *Contra Theses on Feuerbach* — 226

Part VII New Horizons: Against Patriarchy — 229

14 Feminist Horizons: Toward Cultural Revolution — 231

Postface: Rethinking Political Economy — 239

Bibliography — 246

Acknowledgements

This book ranges freely across the canvas of economics, that imperial affliction of the modernist temper, in the small hope of posing a challenge to rethink the innate misery of its squalid speculations, trapped as they are in the hoary paradigm of scarcity (and *work*) that demands the restless labour(s) of the many in favour of the rank luxuries of the few. The years of febrile cogitations that underlie its rather simple message had best not be wished upon anyone else, for the waste of a sensual life is, verily, the saddest of all human sacrifices. Yet, these cheerless lucubrations, on the deep-rooted banalities of economics and economism, were not entirely conducted in dire isolation, leastways not all the time; and the few who gladdened the pensive heart during the unbelievably long sojourn deserve to be noted.

In the order in which they come to mind, I wish to mention the following who, one time or other, in their own singular – and unknowing – ways, lightened the burden: Noam Chomsky, Roger Owen, Robert Heilbroner, Paul Sweezy, Sathyanarayana Raju, Harry Magdoff, Roy Bhaskar, Bill Brugger, Mark Blaug, Svend Hylleberg, Paul Hanson, Tony Lawson, Ali Shamsavari, Wolfram Elsner, Peter Skott, Paul Auerbach, Peter Bell, Steve Fleetwood, Geoffrey Harcourt, Kamal Chenoy, Sanat Kaul, Janeen Costa, Shikha Dalal, James Ryan, Sudipta Kaviraj, C.P. Bhambhri, Tony Brewer, Shaun Lovejoy, and (always) – Cory Leigh.

Thanks are also due to the kindly folk staffing the Avebury imprint, led by Sarah Markham, and including Valerie Polding, Anne Keirby and Jacqui Akkouh, who accommodated my endless interrogations about form and format with forbearance beyond any call of duty. Closer to home, Ms Marianne Tange, and the many student computer buffs of the Economic Institute, tried to tide me over the unyielding idiosyncrasies of computers, diskettes, and documents (and other such mysteries of cyberspace); but all success here is owed to the gracious Ms Pat FitzGerald who smoothed out all the remaining ruffles.

A little learning is a dang'rous thing;
Drink deep, or taste not the Pierian spring:
Alexander Pope

Introduction: Against Economics

1

At least since Ricardo's time, economics has specialised in airy, inane model building, basing its vapid 'discoveries' putatively on the verities of inspired introspection, deductively mapping the dismal universe of human action, in the material sphere, in its own dark, dim and dubious light. The absurdities of this specious 'methodology' notwithstanding, the so-called 'hypothetico-deductive' approach has since become the dominant way in latter-day economics, of which neoclassicism is the most prominent, if not only, representative. It is high time, however, that this dissembling philosophy of tendentiously vacuous abstraction were put paid to, and genuine economics knowledge – available, if at all, only in some thoughtful strands of economic anthropology – placed, finally, in an empirical, contextual, and historical setting. In contrast to the canny shrewdness of untutored businessmen, traders, hawkers, hucksters, buyers, and sellers, the world over, who 'do' economics on a daily basis (and without the insufferable affectation of the economist), that still sustains an invaluable, if untapped, trove of practical information in the material sphere, academic economics knows next to nothing about the real workings of the 'economy', outside of its self-indulgent models, dioramas, and daydreams. In this sense, had economics taken cue from the *oeuvre* of Adam Smith rather than Ricardo, perhaps we might have experienced some slight modicum of real knowledge in the contemporary economic domain, instead of the facile and shallow truisms generated by the stultifying irrealist axiomatics of 'mainstream' economics taking cue greedily from Ricardian antics as egregiously displayed in the class struggles of early nineteenth century England.

This work is a call to jolt critical political economy out of the long sleep induced by the disingenuous hallucinations of Ricardo, and his illegitimate progeny of neoclassicists. However, ironically, this call is possibly already too late; for the damage has gone on for far too long, and run far too deep; the very *materialism* (in no other frame could living life be rendered inanimate by being equated to other 'factors' of production) of standard economics (and Marxian economics as well) is now an unassailable obstacle to understanding human behaviour in the material sphere, which is anything but autonomous from other allied areas of societal endeavour. Materialism was a bold *modernist* effort at severing the critical links between the economy and the larger matrix of *culture*; it fails, however, quite spectacularly (paralleled, somewhat, in the case of the collapse of Soviet socialism, itself modelled aridly on the (failed) promise of more and better goulash for the masses), on a daily basis, as evidenced in the routine rebuffs to the scientistic predictions of economists provided by the recalcitrant empirical facts of the economic life, despite the strenuous effort invested, within the dour kingdom of capital, in *compelling* asocial, acquisitive behaviour on the part of all and sundry. In this context, it is necessary to remember that all human social action takes place in a domain of irreducible cultural values: as such, economics has, for over two centuries, put the theoretical cart (but as a useful blinder) unsplendidly before the empirical horse; time the long-suffering horse were given a much-needed respite.

A 'science' based on prognostications about individual behaviour can only sink swiftly in the quicksand of individual variance; the individual is always 'free'; only aggregate behaviour is more 'predictable', for being more 'orderly' – but never on the basis of *individualist* assumptions. As such, neoclassicism – as Keynes well understood – swallows its own epistemic tail quite regularly (and, apparently, to its own immense satisfaction). Curiously, the more false its premises, the greater has been its meretricious passion for exactitude (and the gleeful embrace of the paraphernalia of quite gratuitous, and ill-used, mathematics), and its emulous craving to don the apparel of the natural sciences. Indeed, so ingrained is this disingenuous ardour that it is always more acceptable, in economics, to be *precisely wrong* than to be vaguely right. The 'maximisation' assumption, for instance, is preferred for conferring accurately calculable outcomes in the theoretical domain rather than accepting the simple ontic truth of the essential variability of humans in all spheres of societal conduct. An increase in price, *ceteris paribus*, of any commodity, for our marginally concocted 'consumer', can induce all manner of real reactions in any serious observational context that may or may not include the 'rational' response legislated by economic theory; and still economics pursues the chimera of calculable rigour in the desultory schema of human behaviour.

To rethink economics is merely a prelude to repudiating its despotic, self-fulfilling hegemony (for it is not merely an abstract ideology of materialism; it is the master tool of *forcible transformation* of the world in its craven image); today, as in the yesteryear of nineteenth century classical economics, *economics is simply the crown jewel of the ideology of capitalism*, nay *modernism* (of which even 'socialism' was/is only a temporarily vanquished aliquot part). As currently organised, economics is far more than merely an epistemically sterile muddle – posing a dire threat to human civility and social amelioration, as it infuses its noxious vapours of *crass materialism, unmediated greed, and amoral calculation* (the biblical heroes were right to rail against the money-changers: indeed conventional economics is simply the debased, and debasing, world view of that shiftless order), into the ingenuous schema of societal institutions. As such, the trustees of the very possibility of civilisation are those ready now to root out the menace of the economic 'point of view', lock, stock and barrel, from social discourse. Only pre-capitalist cultures, the eternal cradle of human values, overrun materially by the tyrannical phenomenology of implacable greed (where property is deified and people devolve into chattels), carry the innate *spiritual* strength to resist its deleterious effects (appropriately enough, the United States, with the least burden of such a heritage, is the one formation most rabidly committed to its nostrums); no wonder that the most serious challenges to the mind-set of modernism today come not from any 'socialist' or 'radical' rebellion, but from the defiant cultural stances of ethnic, cultural, and religious revolt gathering steam, however slowly, in both North and South.

The papers in this volume concern themselves with the internal dynamics of the economics world view to an extent perhaps quite unwarranted: the point, lest it be lost in the idle ephemera of sterile debate, is not to criticise economics endlessly, *but to dispense with it altogether*. We have, simply, no need either for economics or for economists; the world did immoderately well without them in the past – the future, if it is possible at all, will be free only if stripped of its treacherous corybantics. Humans, *contra* the prejudices of social science, are *tribal* – i.e. convivial – entities, not the putatively 'social' creatures (of ideological fancy) trapped within the alien societal (and ideological) forms of *modernist* 'state' and 'society'; and the greatest enemy of conviviality, grace, and civility – the ineradicable reminders of a paradise lost – today, is this corrupt, cash-based, market-oriented, economic point of view. These matters were well understood (and passionately pilloried) in the classical period (as with Mandeville's *Fable of the Bees*) of the birth of the discipline in the capitalist Enlightenment; but the protesters were, for the large part, silenced by cannon, co-option, and chicanery. Today, on the brink of genocidal and commercial wars, dire planetary involutions, and environmental disasters, it is likely that the current generation(s) of the global victims of the institutional artefacts of 'economics' will rise again in dauntless number to reject its pharisaic philosophy of Mammon. The needed epistemic break with the modernist Enlightenment will then have been fully achieved; it would then be only fitting that the highest form of postmodernist critique of the modern era is only one that hearkens wistfully back to premodernist intuitions of care, consideration, and coexistence.

3

Today, economics – *a self-referential language game with zero representational efficacy* – lives within a carefully constructed ideological fence designed to keep manifest reality at bay; within that well-endowed perimeter, its principal efforts lie in the flourishing cottage industry of turning commonplace, trite, axiomatic truisms ('law of demand', the 'free rider' problem, 'public goods', etc.) into formalised, 'mathematical' statements whose degree of difficulty is inversely correlated with relevance, realism, and meaning. As such, *economics says nothing that people engaged in the ordinary business of life don't 'know'*, but gains the misleading semblance of dignity only because it is expressed in a language foreign to many (indeed, I venture the hypothesis that, if the world were all forcibly taught mathematics, up to at least college level, economics would swiftly take to recasting its liturgy in some suitable archaic, dead language: *mathematics, in effect, serves the same ideological function, in economics, that masses in Latin served the priesthood of the church)*. A lifetime spent studying this form of systematised self-deception is a lifetime spent wallowing in mindless idiocy: in fact, most economists, of this bent, *are* idiots, from whom not one meaningful (let alone novel) insight about the world could be, even forcibly, extracted.

I have often wondered what the 'Nobel laureate' (of whom there are, already, an indecent few) in economics sees in the mirror every morning that assures him (yes, it is a male club), deep beneath the mask of bad faith, that he is indeed deserving of that high accolade (one would think he were ahead, qua economist, simply to be supported at the public expense, year after year, with no quid pro quo to speak of!!). If the amorality of the economic mindset had not completely wiped out any sense of even the mildest shame or mortification, perhaps he would realise, in all humbling modesty, that even the most naive graduate student in anthropology 'knows' more about the nature of plural values inhabiting this earth, and its diverse cultures, than he, at his Nobel-winning best; and yet, by grace of the logic of the forces of Mammon, the student of anthropology, if he is any good, is assured only of driving a cab, late in his career, while our Nobel laureate, like the rest of the chosen mandarinate, will smirk lifelong all the way to his bank(s), and back (too bad society is apparently powerless to impose a system of tithes, as a sort of wages of shame, on the income of these high priests, so the lay congregation benefits a trifle from the cumulating blessings of this self-seeking church of egregious gluttony).

In field after field, the neoclassicist agenda – *designed to pre-assure the myth of near-perfect market self-determination under a regime of laissez-faire* – and its slash and burn ideology, have rendered barren and desolate, the variably opulent pockets of the empirical world. In the 'theory' of demand, the object is merely to suggest that the demand curve has a negative slope: in the theory of supply, to demonstrate the positive slope of the supply curve (so as neatly to produce, taken together, the required effect of a stable 'equilibrium'); in production, the smooth, twice differentiable production function (with returns to scale left conveniently up to the theorem to be 'proved'), that also betrays the incidental felicity of scattering distributive largesse according to marginal productivity; in trade, the notion that, despite recalcitrant realities, rich or poor, weak or strong, we 'all' benefit from trade; in industrial structure, that, despite near-total local and national market power of the megacorp, 'competition' is alive and well and catering to consumers; in welfare theory, to suggest that minor distributive adjustments (preferably without state intervention, along the lines of the so-called Coase 'theorem'), can 'produce' satisfactory equity and distributive justice, in spite of the rank exploitations and inequalities of profit-led production; and, in all economic behaviour, that rational maximisers are the dominant species in the economic world (behaving in ways that make the world more handily determinate, and predictable, on first principles alone, for the know-nothing economist).

Sad to say, for every such Big Lie in economics, there will, only too soon, be a Nobel laureate grandee standing in sure, but surly, guard. In a methodological sense, it were as if, in a hopelessly n-dimensional, non-linear physical world, the physicists were to exclusively and endlessly fabricate simple linear 'models' (because calculations become, Oh so much easier!) inside hermetically-sealed laboratories, in the hope that one day, in all guilty abashment, the universe (realising its error) would reswitch itself to assume the correct posture prescribed for it. Better still, rather than investigating the real properties of the moon, the economist as physicist, looking deliberately away from it, prefers to 'assume' a certain structure, and properties, for it; indeed, so perfect would this artificial moon be, that it would rotate just as often round the earth as the economist believes to be 'rational' (i.e. beneficent for capital). No other 'science', *other than an ideology blessed with state power, could dare to suggest that, vis-à-vis its canonical 'theoretical' prejudices, reality is ever-exogenous and empirical facts permanently anomalous*! The truth needs be bluntly stated: the economics emperor, and his (yes, it's a *masculinist* enterprise) overflowing, and overfed, legions, have been starkly butt-naked for aeons; time we, its long-suffering dupes, gulls, and victims, sounded the bugle and sent them scurrying back to the cave to rethink their own arabesque hallucinations again.

4

The simple, inexorable, and universal antidote to the premises of neoclassicism, is the ever-present reality of that ineffable matrix of values we call 'culture'. Its philosophy of materialism, which even a critical tradition like Marxism shares wholeheartedly, is antithetical to the very notion of culture since it legislates *universal* (Hobbesian) human attributes ('more is better', etc.) in the face of the opulent variance of cultural norms. On this score, every economist, including Nobel prize winners, must of necessity fail Anthropology 101 as a matter of course (in fact, failing would have to be a sort of professional *requirement*). At any rate, it is culture – and its close correlate, morality – that now stands, like the rock of the ages, against the squalid pretensions of materialism; small wonder that the mightiest rejection of European, anti-humanist metaphysics of profiteering comes today not from any secular, liberal movements (all but co-opted into the logos of corporatism), but from Islamic (i.e. religious) forces the world over (some day to be joined by similar, *affective* movements world wide). Not a 'revolt against reason' as the CNN mind-set loves to portray it, but a revolt against the perversions of rank materialism and venality; for all its raw violence and apparently inflexible intolerance, the Islamic revolution is yet a struggle to define a tribal lifeform within a womb of a collusive, cooperative and conciliatory, set of *moral relationships*. The many victims of the European Enlightenment – women, minorities, tribals, etc. – in restless, inchoate effulgence, are stirring, apparently at long last, to shake off its venomous coils.

Social knowledge is *contextual*, never general; individuals are variable, cultures even more so: as such, the idea of a social science is an audacious exaggeration (the corporate need for information and *control* necessarily disregards this elementary precept, insisting on a purely make-believe 'social science' that is always a masquerade for social policy). The alien societal forms ('nation', 'state', etc.) delivered by modernism are all inherently collapsible (as easily witnessed both in Bosnia and the ex-USSR), built as they are, paradoxically perhaps, on the *immaterial foundations of materialism*; *contra* the puerile fantasies of 'social contract' ideas, the social – or rather, the *tribal* – form is not a contractual union striking a sort of negative 'balance of interests', but a positive *balance of affections*. The twenty-first century might yet see to the further unravelments of these artificially, and materially, fabricated societal forms, and the inexorable return to sentimental and affinal bondings, that characterise the very species being of the human animal. In that era, economics will expire, albeit with the same lack of grace with which it announced its rude and rough entry into the European firmament. We can only hope – against hope – that it yet leaves, in its inevitable trail of extinction, a still habitable social and natural world.

5

This book is an open invitation to the awakened, and the just awakening, to actively struggle to extirpate the menace of economics and economism, and to complete the much-needed epistemic 'break' with the Eurocapitalist Enlightenment, that dire harbinger of the Age of Vandalism, and the blight of the convivial world, for far too long. Of all forms of repressive desublimation, the *despiritualisation of reality* (which Max Weber was to call the 'disenchantment of the world'), and the *desensualisation* of social ties, has been the most devastating to the human psyche; and economics has played the dominant role, since the Scottish Enlightenment, in the ensuing debasement of affective relations (within its manifest of depravity, the economist is able, and willing, for a price, to calculate 'optimal' – even 'socially' optimal – 'levels' of everything, from murder, to mayhem, to pillage and rapine of peoples, and the environs; what is the price of an American life? The makers of the autodestructive Ford Pinto are alleged to have 'rationally' set it at less than about $11 – the cost of repairing the faulty tanks – or so ...). If the sordid is with us now, as our daily, inescapable, moral condition, it is to economic ideology that we must pay fealty; even were a more adequate political economy not to demand the end of economics, the very mildest of human aesthetics would so require it.

The societal life-form is a forever-open crucible of creative innovation; it is, necessarily, 'unbounded', and free (it is this uncontrollable urge for freedom that is anathema to corporatism, and its cumulating, confiscatory logics of control and domination); and *freedom is the morality of the human species*. No branch of economics, neoclassicist or Stalinist, can withstand a moral critique of this nature (while they can easily dispose of a materialist revolt). To rethink political economy on these lines can only be the sybaritic prelude to inviting the banished wards of human sensuality – sentiment, affection, love – back inside the forbidden garden of human exploration of the virtually limitless alternative forms of cultural creation. Moral critiques, not being debatable, are, not debasable; one states the moral principle, and moves on; not all the ICBM's in the world can scathe its invincible armoury – not all the gold in Fort Knox can buy out one single sentiment in it. However, as sentient beings, even in this rarefied domain, we are vested with the signature of choice; only if we so choose, can reason (once again) be led by (more sympathetic) affections; the paradigm of 'work', by play; politics, by domesticity: alien social ties by kinship, and so on. Science, economics, even societal organisation, have all been part of the masculinist, predatory, appropriative, hierarchical, possessive, divisive, and destructivist agenda for far too long; they may yet be pacified by the embrace of the ever-present university paradigm of *femininity*, that for aeons has, ever so silently, pointed the way to a human emancipation.

It is within this immanent feminine principle of *hospitability to all living creatures*, that we may yet embrace the Gandhian ideal of nonviolence (or what I term *revolutionary pacifism*) as a mode of convivial living involving both self-determination and self-provisioning. The rational, materialist, stupefaction of Thanatos may yet be exorcised by the sibylline stirrings of Eros – *the simple, sensual tie between all forms of life* – whose excision is at the very base of the modernist malaise; it is possible to step off the treadmill of inveterate production and insatiable consumption required by the alien *paradigm of work*, its mythology of permanent scarcity, and its consumptive ideal of the gluttonous slave (second only to the voraciously omnivorous slave-driver) as the very pinnacle of human evolution. And, in this emotive (re)construction of Utopia (merely a form of *rediscovery* of a lost idyll), it is only fitting that, as the poet and the prophet have had it for centuries: *all you need is love – not economics.*

Part I
ECONOMICS AND EPISTEMOLOGY:
MARXISM, REALISM AND BEYOND

1 Critical Realism: The *Nouvelle Critique*

1

It is a remarkable index of the existing distance between models in economic theorizing, Marxist or neoclassical, and the social object that they claim to either describe, explain, or predict, that few questions are ever addressed to the realist content of their suppositions.[1] Even when these contending paradigms engage each other, rarely is attention directed to what Max Weber might have called 'fundamental assumptions';[2] instead, energy is usually dissipated in struggling over the attendant policy implications or the mechanics of the theoretical apparatus, without an examination of the infrastructure of suppositions upon which the edifice actually rests. Premises being taken as given, the struggle then is joined either over matters of internal consistency or over the policy directions indicated by a model. But 'models', more likely than not, tend on average to be true to their own presumptions, and thus the data and ideas they generate are similarly constrained by their initial assumptions; accordingly, debates between paradigms turn out to be quite generally frustrating, with neither side convinced at all of the arguments of the other.[3] Historically, this problem has been raised in the manner of Kuhn[4] as the problem of 'incommensurability' between different schools, without of course any clue as to how such problems can be adjudicated or surmounted. More than occasionally, this very real problem as been 'resolved' in the manner of the post-Althusserians, suggesting that social truths can only be relative, and therefore than science is only a form of social partisanship where one declares at the outset one's article of faith and then joins the fray, presumably against similarly-endowed antagonists.[5] In various degrees and in various guises, this very Weberian idea has, as well, had the sanction of some mainstream writers, such as Myrdal, Schumpeter, etc.

The alternative to this perceptual relativism has been the positivist[6] tradition, whether amongst the Marxists[7] or the mainstream. In their domain, facts are alleged to speak for themselves without filters or assistance from theory, with the scientist usually defined as a passive sensor objectively recording reality, with little causal interaction between scientist and the object of study. In standard positivist discourse, the neutrality of the scientist and the scientific enterprise is taken as given, with the world conceived of as a closed system such that invariant regularities can be both perceived and recorded. The monism and absolutism of positivism, coupled with an ingenuous naivete about the social nature of science, have turned it usually into an ideology that does not recognize ideology as a thing-in-itself, whether in support of Friedmanite discourse (Friedman, 1953) or Stalinist dogmatism. Wedded to a narrow empiricism confined to an examination of surface phenomena (and epiphenomena), positivism has, quite notoriously, denied itself the need for a search for generative mechanisms or even for any desire for providing explanations for social phenomena, with prediction being defined as the more instrumental, and inclusive, function of science.

At one level, therefore, social science seemed caught in a bind, between the Scylla of relativism an the Charybdis of positivism, between a denial of the objectivity of knowledge and the dogmatic assertion (without proof) of the neutrality of science conceived in empiricist fashion. At another level, a very definite polarity reigned between individualism and collectivism as approaches towards the study of social phenomena, this duality referring not so much to matters of epistemology (as in the relativist/absolutist dichotomy), as to ontological issues. Neoclassical theorizing, for example, in almost all its forms, has relied upon the atomized individual as the unit of social action and behaviour, in the manner of methodological individualism à la Popper (1962), seeing society as only the plural of the individual, with pre-given motives gratuitously ascribed to *homo economicus*, conceived as a universal historical subject, regardless of space-time referents. At the opposite end of the pole was Durkheimian sociology (Durkheim, 1964)[8] reifying the social and imposing collective determinations on individual spheres of social action; variants of institutionalism and Marxism were prone to use this organicist and positivist model by way of a counterweight against the heroically 'free' individual of neoclassical exaggerations. While the one model denied social agency (or 'interdependencies', as they might be called), the other reified it, leaving the human being a passive object of history. The 'enlightened' Marxist occasionally tried to reconcile the antimony between these two opposed views by trying to link them 'dialectically' (Berger, 1967) – implying that socially predetermined individuals nonetheless were able to react back and change society – succeeding only in reaping the errors of both models, retaining both voluntarism and reification rather than disposing of these twin errors of social formulation.

Organized social science – economics included – found itself in the prison of these apparently irreconcilable dichotomies with disputes routinely falling into the premeasured no man's land formed by this implacable rivalry. This is not to gainsay unorthodox efforts to break out of this moribund state by way of imaginative excursions, the work of Bachelard (1970; see also 1968)[9] and Feyerabend (1978), for instance, in the direction of science as a matter of psychology and science as a matter of little consequence, respectively. While both these non-conservative departures from mainstream views have had considerable influence on recent discussions, neither perspective has been able to dislodge completely the central divides in science as already identified, for reasons that themselves belong to the area of the philosophy of science. The failure in these corrective visions is perhaps best located in their weak ontological visions of the nature of society, something that transcendental realism – as reflected in the work of Roy Bhaskar (1989) – seeks to set right. As a vital new paradigm in the human sciences, Bhaskarian realism seeks to resolve the classical antinomies that have divided social science by offering a vantage point from which both individualism and collectivism can be corrected, such that neoclassical theory can be convincingly refuted, while orthodox Marxism and Stalinism can equally be rejected in favour of the original insights in the classical Marx, insights into the real ontology of societies, on whose irreducible basis alone we can hope to construct efficacious categories to explain and understand the dynamics of social existence. In what follows, in stages, the realist vision is described, encapsulating the varied intellectual moments of the *oeuvre* of Bhaskar.

2

Realism itself, as a recurrent tendency in social philosophy, has had many varied referents. In its simplest form, realism asserts the independence of the objects of scientific discourse from the activity of science and the scientist. In this general sense, any perspective can bear the realist title for simply asserting the independent existence of the disputed entity in question, be that a universal, a material object, a proposition, etc. Consistent with this formulation, scientific realism is validated when we can demonstrate that the terms of the discourse are believed to possess real referents – independently of the theorizing. Actually, however, it is unnecessary to demonstrate that the scientists actually believe in that proposition, so long as it can be shown that their behaviour lends credibility to it. This much, of course, did not require a Bhaskarian elucidation, being a readily identifiable position even if its significance has usually been underrated. The specific Bhaskarian supplement to this is in his bold theorizing of a metaphysical realism, an elaboration, in his words, of 'what the world must be like prior to any empirical investigation of it and for any scientific attitudes or activities to be possible' (Bhaskar, 1986, p. 6). In this rendering, epistemologies must be both bound and referred to ontology; for realism is seen not as a theory of knowledge or of truth, but of *being*. This is critical, for now both empiricism and rationalism can be rejected for defining being in terms of the very human attributes of experience and reason.

Stated differently, what is being maintained is that every theory of knowledge presupposes a theory of the objects of knowledge, i.e. a theory of what the world must be like for knowledge to be possible at all. This priority of ontology rejects the post-Humean idea (which Bhaskar terms the 'epistemic fallacy') that ontological issues may always be transposed into an epistemological key. Of course, it is not being asserted that knowledge can be reduced to being, for that would be to subscribe to the 'ontic fallacy', something equally to be avoided. Epistemology provides us with the transitive dimension in our studies of the world around us; ontology demands, on the other hand, recognition of the intransitive dimension of reality, a reality that predates and preexists this, without need for a human world of perception and experience. The sciences, especially the social ones, have been guilty of the taint of anthropomorphism, centring the universe on human attributes as if – as in the Christian view – it were all designed so as to be perceived by the sovereign human subject.

Transcendental realism – to use the term favoured by Bhaskar – involved a careful recognition of the various parameters of the transitive and the intransitive in the social study of society. It necessarily involves the following predicates: an *ontological realism* implying that society is an intransitive, knowledge-independent, irreducible, real object of scientific knowledge; an *epistemic relativity* in the transitive domain, suggesting that knowledge about the social object cannot but be socio-historically limited and constrained; and the possibility of *judgmental rationality*, implying that, nonetheless, despite epistemic limitations, it is possible to sort the true from the false in the competing claims to knowledge. Additionally, Bhaskar posits a metacritical dimension allowing for a self-relexive scrutiny of all the philosophical and sociological presuppositions presumed by the discourse, a metacritique being defined as a logical procedure seeking to identify the 'presence of causally significant absences in thought', or, in other words, to identify what 'cannot be said in a scheme about what is done in the practice into which the scheme is connected' (Bhaskar, 1986, p. 26). Bhaskar claims neither uniqueness nor certainty for his approach, but hopes to show, nonetheless, that it is 'demonstrably superior' to the various irrealist accounts in fashion today, the proof of the pudding resting entirely in the eating of it.

The central idea behind transcendental realism is the decisive importance of an ontology of the real for the practice of science. But the real is far from being the flat, 'empirical' terrain beloved by positivism, for the very first recognition is one of *ontological depth*, i.e. a recognition of the multilayered stratification of a highly complex, differentiated reality. It is this ontological reality of a layered universe that demands that knowledge move, necessarily, from manifest phenomena to deeper or anterior levels of phenomena, the search being one of locating generative or causal mechanisms within the triple layering of reality, within the domains of the *real*, the *actual* and the *empirical* (generally collapsed into one in positivist discourse, or denied independent legitimacy as with the subjective idealists). By way of illustration, the principle of gravity is irreducibly located in the intransitive realm of the real; it is actualized in the falling apple; and then, should a perceiving subject be proximate, becomes part of the empirically-constituted experience of the latter. But nature is not, as in the vulgar positivist view, always so transparent (nor is the observer gifted only with a guileless innocence); in fact, contrary to Hume, constant conjunctions are only rarely visible in nature (if nature were easy to 'read' there would be little need for a 'science' of nature) but need, in fact, to be recreated in the laboratory. The point being made is a powerful one; causal laws (the real) are ontologically distinct from patterns of events; and events (the actual) are similarly distinct from experiences (the empirical). Positivist empirics is therefore guilty of two category mistakes: of reducing causal laws to constant conjunctions of events (confusing powers with their exercise), and the latter to experience, thereby making the real a property of the empirical, rather than the other way around. Gravity, as a property of the real, operated even when its several actualizations remained unperceived or uncomprehended by human subjects; it would, accordingly remain operational even in a non-human world stripped suddenly of all human experience.

Transcendental realism asserts the non-identify of thought and being, of the objects of the transitive and intransitive dimensions. In so asserting this, the Bhaskarian realist denies empiricism for limiting the concept of the natural order to what is given in human experience; it also denies idealism for seeing it as a human construct. For realism, the cognitive possibility is determined by the nature of the (independent) object (for it is humanity that is the contingent phenomenon in nature, and knowledge a cosmic accident). The 'forlornness' of the universe, as Heidegger saw it, acquires in Bhaskar, thereby, an important scientific legitimacy.

3

The implications of transcendental realism for economic theory, although varied and complex, are quite decisive. As mentioned early on, neither neoclassical theorizing nor conventional Marxian economic theorizing can escape unscathed from the implicit critique immanent in the realist framework.

In fact, it could not be otherwise, considering that realism is a devastating refutation of positivism, and positivism – in various referents – has tended to cut across both of these major schools in political economy. Upon subjection to realist scrutiny, it becomes quite apparent that positivism, while purporting to be a method for science, is actually a fairly sophisticated ideology for science, wherein Bhaskar conceived of its (historical and functional) necessity – despite its readily identifiable errors.

Bhaskar argues that, while positivism is a theory of the nature, limits and unity of knowledge, it, surprisingly, is not a theory of its *possibility*, because scientific knowledge is apparently seen as quite an unproblematic affair for, within it, there is no serious contemplation of its own limitations and possibilities. Besides being a theory of knowledge, it presupposes a very definite ontology of societies, whether or not it is aware of such presuppositions. It is the enduring weaknesses, if not outright error, in this ontology, that renders positivism defunct and irrelevant as a sane method for science. For the positivist posits, implicitly, an ontology of closed systems and atomistic events coupled with the perception of the scientist as a passive sensor and recorder of pregiven, unmediated facts – derived from constant conjunctions – rendering social knowledge an individual attribute. Positivism entails, as already seen, double reduction: causal laws are reduced to constant conjunctions, and the latter foregrounded in individual experience; reducing causal laws to events and events to experience positivism fails to locate the independent intransitive existence of causal laws, while at the same time failing to recognize human experience as a social product and knowledge as a social production (compounding the error in ontology with an error in epistemology). In the words of Bhaskar (1989, p. 51), positivism 'can sustain neither the idea of an independent reality nor the idea of a socially produced science'.

In so doing, positivism gainsays the transience of historical knowledge, the hierarchy and differentiation within reality and the transformational nature of society; further, positivism ignores the possibility of causal interdependency between scientific subject and social object – the transitive dimension – aside from overlooking the fact of the openness of social systems where invariant regularities simply need not occur, barring chance. Reifying and naturalizing 'facts', positivism effectively dehistoricizes them; fetishizing science, it fails to see science as a social production; reducing knowledge to human experience, it humanizes nature while simultaneously – for its monism – naturalizing society. Being at once ahistorical and asocial, it fails to account for both scientific change and any transition in the 'facts' that it so very dispassionately brings to light.

It is this very ontological inadequacy that dooms methodological individualism, that near kin to positivism, which maintains that facts pertaining to social phenomena are reducible to facts about individuals, are indeed explained by the latter. In this extraordinarily alienated view, army becomes just the plural for soldier, and society the plural of the individual; in his crushing refutation of this mistaken methodology, Bhaskar points out that any advertion to motives or rules for the individual always involves reference to irreducibly social predicates. Thus, writes Bhaskar (1979, p. 35), 'a tribesman implies a tribe, the cashing of a cheque a banking system'; micro statements cannot simply be added up to form coherent macro situations, the logic of the latter cannot be derived from the former. A singularly telling example offered suggests that, in all simplicity, the garbage collector's reason for collecting garbage is not the reason, usually, that society wants garbage collected; similarly, a soldier's motive for joining an army might have little to do with the rationale for the existence of such an institution. The logic of the whole is quite apart from the logic of the parts.[10]

Even more strongly, realism challenges the ascription of rationality and maximizing behaviour to the sovereign 'free' individuals. As Bhaskar writes (1979, p. 37), 'to say that men are rational does not explain what they do, but only at best ... how they do it'; so, in trying to explain everything, the assumption of rationality explains nothing, being only an a priori attribution without explanatory content, failing only as grand tautology, casting no light whatsoever on actual empirical behaviour.[11] In this light, neoclassical thinking is only a normative theory of efficient action recommending 'a set of techniques for achieving given ends', rather than a social science, for it arrives only at a pre-given praxiology under the delusion of generating a (spurious) sociology. In this regard, the grand collation of mistaken agendas consecrating the triple alliance between positivism, methodological individualism and neoclassical motivational ascriptions, could only constitute a blueprint for a colossal default in the search for a science of economics, a default guaranteed almost a priori by this straightforward denial of the real ontology of societies in general, and capitalism in particular. The articles of doom are underwritten by the double error in neoclassical theorizing, the disastrous coupling of an empiricist epistemology with an individualist ontology of society.

Within a realist matrix, revealing the ontological inadequacy of the triad formed by positivism, methodological individualism and neoclassical 'assumptions' about *homo economicus* is indeed simple enough. But the power of the realist critique goes even further, for it is not content simply with demonstrating inadequacy; a true critique, as per Bhaskar, needs to go beyond falsification and demonstrate the conditions for the necessity for the persistence of the false paradigm, i.e. to reveal the ideological intent or content of the intellectual system in question. To designate a system of ideas as 'ideological' requires us, in terms of our alternate theory, to: (a) explain most or all of the phenomena covered by it; and (b) to explain additionally significant phenomena not covered by it; then (c) to account for its historical genesis; next, (d) to indicate the conditions for its reproduction and their limits; and finally, (e) to locate its present function.

The social function of positivism, then, in the words of Bhaskar (1989, p. 61), is to 'conceal the historically specific structures and relations constituting sense-experience in science'; by naturalizing facts – converting social objects into things – positivism effectively dehistoricizes them. First atomizing and then reifying social 'facts', the positivist account induces, aside from its monism, a fusion of the world with experience (in its empirical realism), and the reduction of knowledge to experience. Infusing certainty into scientific knowledge imparts a legitimacy to the scientific status quo, while reducing it to common empirical apprehension lends validation to the postulates of 'common sense'. The unmistakable presentiment sanctioned by positivism is that things are as they appear, as they seem (Bhaskar sees in this concession to common sense the possibility inherent in positivism of justifying the status quo, regardless of 'whatever and wherever that is'). In this regard, the very denial of the notion of a possible disjuncture between appearance and reality – i.e. the absence of a theory of ideology – makes the enterprise itself profoundly ideological. Positivism, in its denial of the transfactual, independent existence of the scientific object, in its denial of science as a social production, in its limitation of the world to the range of human sense-perception, in its denial of the validity of the cognitive claims of other social practices besides itself, functions and the 'limit form of empiricism' – as an ideology *for science*.

Similarly, neoclassical assumptions universalize for all times one possible set of behavioural characteristics, arguing, à la Hume, that 'mankind is much the same in all times and all places', a comment that flies in the face of the most trivial discoveries of modern social anthropology. The real irony in this anti-historical stance is that positivism, originally with Comte, purported to be a theory of history. The conceptual world of positivism is flat for the lack of differentiation in reality; the real world is stripped of all its concealed or opaque mechanisms, of its ontological subtlety, of deceptive appearances, of powers and potentialities of which we might be unaware, consisting only of 'the passing flux of experience, as described by common-sense', a closed system ruled by constant conjunctions; its shallowness matched only by its everyday accessibility. August Comte, of course, had been quite forthright about the political intent of positivism (which he considered a deterrent to the negative – meaning critical – philosophy of the Enlightenment): in his words (Comte, 1893, pp. 37–8), '... the positive spirit tends to consolidate order, by the rational development of a wise resignation to incurable political evils ... A true resignation – that is, a permanent disposition to endure steadily, and without hope of compensation, all inevitable evils ... '.

4

Transcendental realism offers a penetrating critique not merely of neoclassical pretensions, but also of vulgar Marxism and some aspects of Marx's own intellectual predilections, for the critique of positivism is not a chariot that may be arrested at will. The critique of Marxism, similarly, takes the form of pointing to enduring ontological inadequacies in the Marxian schema which render some of its suppositions invalid. Central to a critique of Marx is a rejection of the 'material base/ideational superstructure' metaphor, an important element of both Stalinist and non-Stalinist discourse, the main difficulty here traditionally being the unsuccessful effort to reconcile the thesis of the relative autonomy of the superstructures with the idea of their determination – in the last instance – by the base. The metaphor itself provides the inspiration for the two common errors plaguing Marxian discourse, these being: (a) super idealism, where the superstructure is completely emancipated from the base (as in Althusser, 1971; see also Gerratana, 1977 and Hirst (1976, p. 396) where science is totally autonomous); and (b) reductionism, where the superstructure is simply an epiphenomenon of the base (as with Lukacs, 1971; see also Stedman-Jones, 1971, where science is an expression of it). The very notion of a base/superstructure disjunction allows for the errors of theoretical idealism and economic reductionism. Bhaskar's suggestions for a restructuring of Marxian discourse are of critical interest. He argues that there is something very misconceived in the traditional Marxian manner of lumping together all ideas, indiscriminately, to form a bloc termed a superstructure, as distinguished from a 'material' base, for, quite simply, even purely economic activity necessarily has an inalienable ideational component (all activity, economic or otherwise, necessarily carries with it the presumption of some conception carried by the agent as to what and why he/she is doing). The Marxian error in this regard may be located quite unmistakably; Marx provided a decisive critique of the Hegelian error of positing the autonomous existence of the ideal (aside from arguing for the primacy of the material over the ideal), but the Hegelian thesis can hardly be inverted: there can be no grounds for arguing for a purist autonomy of the material in social existence, for the material sphere is inextricably bound up with ideas – to the extent that we are speaking of human society. It follows, then, that the distinction between base and superstructure, as originally formulated, is false and misleading, specially so in the hands of immature and rash Marxists eager to apply instant formulae to the diversity of history.

The suggested alternative procedure then, closer to the inspiration of Marx if not the letter, is to conceive instead of different (multiple) ideologies associated with different practices, these different and varied practices having autonomous 'bases' of their own. Different ensembles of practices generate their own rationalizing ideologies; in this view, then, religion is a real social practice with its own justifying ideology enjoying a real autonomy from other practices such as politics, despite the fact of linkages, connections and homologies between them and other ideologies. The material conditions for the reproduction of these practices may still be traced to the social economy that sustains all social life; but this is not to imply any determination of the practices themselves. The point is of extraordinary significance for Marxian theorizing: ideational structures are not reflexes of an all-determining material 'base' – in fact the idea of a material determination is devoid of content altogether. Away from the stasis of a fixed 'base', Bhaskar offers the dynamics of social practices as the ultimately 'determining' agency, for ideologies bear determinant links with practices.

At the next remove, Marx's ideas come in for castigation on account of their flirtation with elements of positivism (the Marxian critique of idealism, so thoroughly made in *The German Ideology*, was never followed through with a similar critique of empiricism, despite many apprehensions of the importance of the latter critique) – the idea of 'laws of motion' so cheerfully repeated by generations of Marx scholars. Again, law-like regularities are only characteristic of *closed systems* (the assumption of positivism) but society, being an *open system*, is not subject to such immanent 'laws'. Much of the non-historical accounts in *Capital*, for instance, need therefore to be dropped (including the scenarios of anticipation of an indeterminate future, such as the visions of communism and the 'withering away' of the state, etc.), for there Marx comes close to fetishizing economic categories with a kind of naturalism (the cost of trying to subvert the classical economics from within) that simply cannot be sustained given the ontology of societies. 'Laws' such as the 'falling rate of profit' simply cannot be taken as such, and it is small wonder that Marxian economists – armed with econometrics, that special tool of positivism – operating in that area are such devotees of positivist methodology in practice. The point can be made quite simply; prediction, in an open system, is virtually impossible (which is why neither Friedmanite neoclassicals nor positivist Marxians have ever displayed anything but a sorry record in this regard). The social sciences – at best – can only aspire to explanation, not prediction, for social life has to do with meanings, and meanings can only be understood, not measured. So, precision in meaning assumes the place of accuracy in measurement (as an a posteriori arbiter): to quote Bhaskar (1979, p. 59), 'Language here stands ... to social science as geometry stands to physics'.

All in all, then a good bit of Marxian baggage gets jettisoned, having to be trimmed: (a) in the light of ontological realities of society; and consequently (b) in the light of a methodology appropriate to (a); the tremendous content gain for Marxism despite this radical surgery is in the salvation – beyond criticism – of its central insights into social life at the cost only of abandoning unsustainable flourishes that do violence to reality. The sophisticated Marxian will now have to accept the fact that social phenomena are conjuncturally determined, requiring explanation with respect to a multiplicity of causes, with no place for either determinism or historicism, social life needing to be grasped as a totality, a totality whose configuration is continually changing. The different moments of this totality will need, of course, to be asymmetrically weighted, 'primed', as Bhaskar puts it, 'with differential causal force' depending on the issue in question. Truly, then, realism encompasses Marxism and surpasses it as a genuine critique would and should.

5

As a competent methodology in the social sciences radically current in its apprehension of the discoveries of modern-day philosophy of science (something that neither neoclassical economics nor conventional Marxism can lay claim to), it would seem as if transcendental realism would need no further justification, no other strengths with which to parade its potency as a devastating critique of the ruling pretensions in social science. But Bhaskarian realism offers more than a sedentary methodology of science; it offers also a perspective on human emancipation that is solidly based on the underlabour of science. 'The philosophers,' complained Marx in a well-known statement (in Marx and Engels, 1970), 'have only interpreted the world; the point, however, is to change it'. For too many Marxians, this declaration has led to the denigration of the cognitive enterprise, flinging themselves into the struggle for change, perhaps, at some cost in terms of missed cognitive apprehensions. Realism strongly insists on the view that science is, ipso facto, revolutionary or emancipatory in that it helps to pierce the necessary veil of illusion that envelops social practices. Thus, for Bhaskar, no a priori, subjective declaration of the emancipatory agenda is needed as a preface to science, for science itself, if taken seriously and carried through, counteracts ideology and provides enlightenment. By a similar token, even work preceded by reactionary motives can unwittingly serve emancipation, provided the scientific programme has not been wantonly abridged in the process.

Of course, the emancipation that science provides is of a cognitive nature, and, as Bhaskar frankly conceded (1979, p. 112), 'dissonance not liberation may be the immediate result of enlightenment'; and this dissonance could just as easily lead to revolutionary activity as to plain and simple 'despair'. There is a logical gap, Bhaskar reminds us (contrary to the chiliastic hopes of many a Marxist) between 'knowing and doing', and no science can – logically – lead an individual from one to the other. Although this very well-founded scepticism is a sane counsel for caution, nonetheless Bhaskar argues for the general emancipatory potential of explanatory knowledge which 'increases the range of real (non-utopian) human possibilities', swinging the balance of the 'argument' against the status quo. In this respect, the dominated and exploited classes, peoples, etc., are deemed to have (should have?) an interest in knowledge as a necessary condition for emancipation. In keeping with ontological realism, Bhaskar is careful to preclude any necessary scenarios of liberation. Unlike the fancies of some forms of Marxism, knowledge may not be either a necessary nor a sufficient condition for social change.

6

By any token, transcendental realism poses a real challenge to the long reign of positivist intuitions (be it logical or empirical positivism) in economic science, whether of the Marxian or neoclassical variety. It does so in each case by explicitly denying the possibility of making arbitrary ontological assumptions (something ruled as a methodological virtue in Friedman and a practical inevitability in Max Weber) in a social science. It does so in each case by denying that an *adequate epistemology* is possible upon the basis of an *inaccurate ontology*. The rather desperate – though not necessarily waning – Ricardo-Robbins[12] tradition of arguing for an economics based only on a radical apriorism of inspired introspection is likely to meet, in this critique, rather fatal objections to its clumsy pretences. On the other hand ultra-empiricism, or the 'instrumentalist' variant of mainstream economics, is likely to see its positivist rudder flounder quite hopelessly – at least on a logical plane – in the face of its own revealed myopia and counter-factuality. In this respect, it is important to remember that transcendental realism provides a correction and a critique both to ruling epistemologies and the ontologies they conceal. Neither positivist-inspired moniom nor its obverse, a plural neo-Kantian hermeneutics, live up to the ontological demands of social reality. *Monism* fails for not recognizing the transitive dimension in social science, the causal interdependency between subject and object in the social production of knowledge; *hermeneutics*, for all its correct emphasis on the *verstehen* idea, implying that in social life we are always dealing with a pre-interpreted reality, nonetheless fails to come through for its misapprehension of the intransitive dimension of society; in other words, the presence of causal interdependence does not contradict the possibility of the existential intransitivity of the social object of investigation. Put in Bhaskar's words (1979, p. 60), '... although the processes of production may be interdependent, once some object exists ... however it has been produced, it constitutes a possible object of scientific investigation. And its existence (or not), and properties, are quite independent of the ... process of investigation ... even though such an investigation ... may radically modify it'. The point, made against both positivism and hermeneutics, could not be clearer: the human sciences can be sciences in 'exactly the same sense, though not in exactly the same way', as the natural ones. Realism, therefore, demands a series of necessary modifications in the nature of economic theorizing, specially with regard to the nature of 'assumptions' made about the human units of analysis, with respect both to intentions and activities, for both predicates of purpose and action need to be derived from a legitimate specification of the matrix of social relations in which they arise and exist; motives can neither be ascribed nor assumed – they need to be derived, in all their defying complexity – from the structure of social relations within which their meanings are realized. Stated simply, the challenge to neoclassical theorizing consists in demanding that it gets its anthropology right (and its political sociology) in a real world of unequal strata, power differentials, exploitation and unequal access. Even apologetics needs be based, it would seem, on sound conceptions of the social order. This vital ontological correction reveals both the strength and the limitations of the realist challenge; for realism does not – perhaps cannot – provide a substantive economic theory, although it can point to the construction of a stable scaffolding upon which such a social economics (the very term 'economics' itself betraying an irrealist fragmentation of the unity of social life) may be erected. At this stage, at any rate, realism offers more a critique than a complete reconstruction of economic categories; but it is a critique that shares little of the wishful thinking common to both Marxian and neoclassical visions, basing itself instead on logically and empirically sustainable propositions.

The foregoing necessarily implies that the ruling currents are unlikely to be displaced by the sheer strength of the logical critique of realism; for the great strength of paradigms – as tested in my own work on Ricardo (see Kanth, 1986) – has less to do with logical rigour than to conformity with the ruling perceptions of order. In that respect, realism is unlikely to supplant – except at the fringes – the main body of erroneous doctrine, the kiss of realism leaving asleep (but not undisturbed) in dogmatic slumber the wayward princess of mainstream political economy.

The mechanics of paradigm-shift have to do with material, not logical truths (see Kanth, 1985, pp. 157–87). But, though socially and materially inspired, paradigms in social theory still need to shore up their logical apparati. It is in this regard that the realist challenge will impose enormous strain on the main corpus of economic theory by way of the requirement for readjustment of its defences. The monist variant of positivism, in qualified retreat ever since the hermeneutical tradition launched its critique of naturalism, may well be further sequestered by the realist assault. However, it is likely that the neo-Kantians[13] – within the ruling orthodoxy – might be the early beneficiaries of this waning of positivist influence. Similarly, at a different pole a cautious institutionalism (see Samuels, 1988) might receive a renewed lease on life, since they were among the first to recognize indeterminacy and overdetermination in social life, bringing them a step closer to accurate ontological apprehensions than either the neoclassicals or the vulgar Marxists. In this respect, realism can probably only register vicarious triumphs, as it helps prod social thinking to closer approximate the domain of the real. To use a metaphor drawn from Bachelard, it will be a while – if ever – before the nocturnal philosophy of realism can overshadow the diurnal practice of positive science: a pity – but then again the owl of Minerva was never intended, perhaps, to fly at dawn.

7

The proof of any system of ideas in the social sciences must lie in its application; indeed, it could not be otherwise given that social science exists primarily in the domain of *praxis*, for all its silver-laced abstractions and flights of rhetorical fancy. And scientific realism would be but a barren, bastard creation if it could not reap a richer harvest than the many rival orthodoxies extant in the field of social explanation today. By way of illustration, I wish to point to my own study of Ricardo, in desperately abbreviated form, as a case study (serving to unmask the real historical Ricardo) exemplifying the tenets (and yields) of realism as applied to an examination of a rather prosaic subject in political economy, illuminating the real agenda of the most misunderstood, and misinterpreted, of all the classical economists: David Ricardo. It will be seen that the world has harboured a mismeasure of Ricardo's preoccupations, having been befuddled by aprioristic epistemological readings into misconstruing the true ontology underlying Ricardian realities.

Ricardo has received no dearth of scholarly attention from the economics profession, historically speaking, but with a significant boost to his notoriety accorded, of course, by Sraffa's postwar writings that have indeed made of 'neo-Ricardianism' a respectable term in some sections of economic discourse, with something of a cult following in England, Italy and India (aside from sympathisers virtually everywhere). However, before Sraffa, as it were, opened up yet another paradigmatic reading of Ricardo (the 'neo-Ricardian' manifesto) in the '50s and '60s, we have had two great enduring traditions that defined Ricardo (though antagonistic to each other) to the world for some three-quarters of a century: the Marxian and the neoclassical, respectively. Each, in splendid disregard of the real Ricardo and the original Ricardian agenda, was to dissolve the subject within its own sulphuric solvents of prefabricated ideology. For the Marxians, stated simply, Ricardo was the last (great) step of English political economy, in the ascendant since at least the time of Petty, carrying the labour theory of value as far as their bourgeois class sympathies would allow them (but not, obviously, far enough!), until Marx stepped in to relieve them of their misery in the one fell swoop of Volume One of *Capital*. Marx's treatment of Ricardo is thus full of both filial reproach and admiration: if only Ricardo has grasped the theory of surplus value! – if only, in other words, Ricardo's agenda were the same as Marx's!

The neoclassicals, equally, were to peruse Ricardo through their own marginally biased vision: Schumpeter, a great neoclassical on value theory, no matter what his deviation on other issues, praises the analytical machinery of Ricardo, his 'model-building' penchant (something, incidentally, of appeal to the Marxians as well), while bemoaning, simultaneously, the entire exercise as a great 'detour'. If only Ricardo could have grasped the marginal utility idea, what a great economist he might have been! But where Schumpeter was content to leave the issue with a lament, Hollander has recently stepped in to argue that Ricardo was always located precisely within the Walrasian general equilibrium world of supply and demand, and hence in the unbroken tradition leading to Walras and Jevons, his labour theories being only a simple misrepresentation on the part of subsequent scholarship. And thus Ricardo is made out to be a great (crypto) neoclassical, only erroneously perceived as otherwise by tendentious scholarship.

Whether in its Marxian or in its neoclassical variant, this unpardonable sin of *grid* readings has been the very bane of 'histories' of economic thought, where the ancients are not accorded the simple dignity of having preoccupations all their very own, and unmindful of our altogether too current class struggles. Contrary to Marx, the so-called tradition of classical economics was not groping blindly (and unsuccessfully) for the grail of surplus value; and *contra* neoclassicism, the classical economists were not 'mistaken' and deluded in their work for not having stumbled upon the marginal calculus of utility. Political economy has always been a *policy* science and the policy problematic of each age, each generation (even within the general epoch of capitalism) is necessarily somewhat different, being conjuncturally determined by developing realities. Even at a casual perusal, then, it is clear that Smith, for instance, dealt primarily with the issue of *production*, Ricardo with *distribution*, and Jevons with *exchange*, the accumulation process calling attention to different *moments* of crisis in its evolution: each is a different object of analysis, located in a different phase of historical time, and bearing a differing weightage placed on an elucidation of the concept of value, distribution, etc. Indeed, even our (spurious) genealogies in the history of thought betray only our own preoccupations, and the hoary ideological axes we grind: for the laissez-faire capitalist, matters will have to begin with Smith; for the labour theorist it will have to be Petty, and so on.

The point could be neither simpler nor clearer: the real Ricardo has never been studied with any care in either of the two grid perspectives just noted, his agenda having never been clarified, his ideas never sifted for their connections with his preoccupations, his policy mission never defined, his intellectual stratagems never placed in context. The realist lesson is loud and clear to all but the doctrinaire: Marxism and neoclassicism have devolved into present day epistemologies ever seeking to reconstruct, in retrospect, a bygone ontology, recreating not the historical Ricardo located in specific time and place and purpose, but an academic Ricardo, a model Ricardo, who may then become the ahistorically dubious vehicle of our own contemporaneous struggles: the real, *intransitive* object of science (David Ricardo, Esq.) is forgotten, for never having been studied – instead, we are crafted a new scientific object, the *transitive* object of our loaded attentions, the Ricardo of our fantasies. Needless to say, the late Mr Sraffa, too, has followed in this regrettably well-worn wake of forging a valiantly fictionalised character in his own right.

8

So, who was the real Ricardo then (as opposed to Marx's Ricardo, Schumpeter's Ricardo, and Sraffa's Ricardo!)? The answer, in the nature of things, can only be historically located; for social theory can hardly be comprehended outside of its historical provenance. So it is to the modalities of English social history that we must of necessity turn, for they were the grist to this gifted financier turned political economist (who, a life of toil being denied, dabbled in many diversions, from chemistry to geology and, even – at one point – economics!): the Napoleonic Wars, French commercial policies, the Bank of England's responses, the trade situation, labour and agrarian unrest, and so on.

It was, however, the great French debacle at Waterloo, whose significance and prospects for England Ricardo appreciated as no-one else, that brought this talented stockbroker to the fore of policy formation (having first established the necessary plutocratic credentials by securing inner membership of a select band of 'loan contractors' serving to fund Pitt's adventurous financial policies); thereafter, his parasitic financial past notwithstanding, he was to identify himself with – and lead – policies favouring industrial capital. Protected from any personal financial worries, Ricardo was left free to play the part of statesman for the capitalist class as a whole. In effect, therefore, the Ricardian agenda was historically set by the parameters of the completion of the English bourgeois revolution, ongoing since the mid-seventeenth century – and never had captainship of industrial capital been invested in a more tactical intellect. The Ricardian period, as will become obvious, was determinately situated between Waterloo and the repeal of the Corn Laws of 1846.

1815 was a year of moment in the evolution of English capitalism; with Napoleon sent into retirement at Waterloo, the long run struggle between England and France for world mastery had just been decisively settled. But as yet unsettled was the domestic battle between corn and cotton, or landlords and manufacturers, respectively. Looked at from the viewpoint of industrial capital, as Ricardo wantonly chose to, there were only three major obstacles standing in the way of England's becoming the workshop and foundry of the world: (a) the Poor Laws, as amended in 1795, for impairing capitalist work incentives; (b) the Corn Laws, for impeding the import of cheap corn, and for preventing a consequent foreign demand for domestic manufactures; and (c) the Reform Question, for a 'parliament of landlords' as yet checked the growing pretensions of manufacturers to state power. A cursory examination of Ricardo's interests, struggles, and interventions (considered important enough by him to warrant purchasing a seat in the Commons), reveals the splendid class logic of his political endeavours, and the special words of his impressive championship. In Parliament, he championed the manufacturing interest consistently on all three issues; and outside Parliament, where the writ of the Ricardians ran even larger, in his major tract, the *Principles* of 1817, he made out (or so he imagined) an almost foolproof theoretical case against the Corn Laws and the landed order. In this struggle, the inspired slogan of laissez-faire served to delegitimise landlords, the Corn Laws and the Poor Laws, while attendantly strengthening the economic and political interests of the manufacturers. In short, Ricardian laissez-faire stood for the dictatorship of industry over agriculture, of cotton over corn, of industrial capital over all, and of capital accumulation over all other priorities.

Ricardian theory, then, was guided by the prior dictates of policy; and his paradigmatic pedantics were all enveloped by the Great Advocacy. The so-called Ricardian model endeavoured, unsuccessfully, to tie general economic stagnation to straitened conditions in agricultural production, such that the Corn Laws and their landlord patrons could both be depicted as ruinous to the general interest. His 'theory of distribution' – to elevate, gratuitously, a hasty, practical concoction – his tortuous gropings for the invariable standard, and his attachment to a simple labour theory were all born of this need to set up an airtight theoretical case against the specific political economy of protectionism enacted by the landed oligarchy, still anachronistically wedded to the idea of a social compact between rich and poor, master and servant. Curiously, it was Malthus – the otherwise insufferably retrograde apologist for the landed interest and the lifelong political antagonist of Ricardo – who fully understood logical fallacies inherent in the spuriously rigorous Ricardian model – although to no real avail. For Ricardo succeeded where Malthus was to fail, despite his dramatic empirical and logical failings, because manufacturers triumphed in practice over the expiring political economy of the late aristocracy. However irrefutable his relentless critique, Malthus was not to obtain a hearing – for he was at the losing end of history, of policy, of class affiliation; on the other hand, when every Ricardian policy initiative had ultimately triumphed, with the repeal of the Corn Laws in 1846, Ricardian 'theory' itself suddenly became defunct and bereft of purpose, dying a natural, unmourned death soon after. A Ricardo after 1846 served no end whatsoever, and the model, literally, became useless and slid into disrepair. Indeed it could not have been otherwise, for his was a pseudo-science, spawned by advocacy, protected by bizarre intellectual feints, and nurtured by patronage and power.

So this was the *real* Ricardo, the political champion of an emergent industrial capitalist order. His theories were makeshift, his analytics spurious, his value theory purely instrumental, his empirics almost nonexistent. And yet, for reasons all their own, both Marxians and neoclassicals have elevated Ricardo's topical, policy-inspired 'theoretical' pronouncements (methodological fictions in the main) to the status of general, even 'abstract' theories (Sraffa, of course, taking this tendency to its logically absurd limits; this is a well-worn track in economics, however: witness Keynes, for instance, promoting his employment policies, born of the Depression, into a 'General Theory' of this, that, and the other!), thereby creating an entire domain of Ricardo criticism that misses its target with an almost epic, if wasteful, grandeur.

In this particular instance, it becomes clear that when judiciously employed, the realist approach can uncompromisingly strip away epistemological illusions nurtured of speculative ideology, referring all such fabrications to the acid test of ontology. I believe that my Ricardo story helps to dispel countless myths about Ricardo built up over the last hundred years within the ruling epistemologies by simply according the true ontological subject – David Ricardo – the dignity of his own personal policy agenda within a clearly specified material context. In so doing, several realist postulates are vindicated: epistemic relativity, ontological specificity, the intimate connections between theory and policy, and the close kindred between science and class struggle (i.e. science as part of social praxis). Made clear also is the *radical difference between the real object of science, and the scientific object* – and the need, always, to be guided, in our investigations, by the former rather than the latter. In all of this, of course, we are merely concurring with the true facts of history, whether we nominally term the approach historical materialism or critical realism. If the latter project occasionally illustrates, as in this Ricardo criticism, that Marx himself, as often as not, did not follow his own methodological discoveries, then so much the better for the interpretive science that he, along with Engels, so enterprisingly founded. At its most promising, I venture, critical realism dares to apply the tenets of historical materialism to Marxism itself, a task apologetically neglected for far too long, and by too many, in the domain of critical studies.

Notes

1 The Friedman variant of positivism actually went to the extent of denying any need for a realist scrutiny of assumptions on the doubtful grounds that predictive efficiency neutralizes any errors in the prior specification.

In fact, in what Samuelson characterized as the 'F-Twist', Friedman almost implied that predictive accuracy was related, in a simple fashion, to the degree of irrealism of the assumptions. For a discussion of this issue, see Blaug, 1980, pp. 103–14.

2 Max Weber's explicit directives on method are to be found in Weber, 1949. A more contemporary discussion is available in Giddens, 1971.

3 The Capital Controversy between the two Cambridges might well be treated as a case in point. For an engaging account, see Harcourt, 1969.

4 Kuhn, 1970; for a fuller statement on the Kuhn debate, see Lakatos and Musgrave (eds), 1970.

5 For arguments in this vein, see Hindess and Hirst, 1975. Not dissimilar is the orientation of Cleaver, 1979.

6 On the mainstream tradition of positivism, see Kolokowski, 1972. For a discussion of positivism in relation to social theory, see Giddens (ed.), 1974; as regards economics, see the Friedman classic *Essays in Positive Economics* (1953); also Coddington, 1972; in the area of philosophy, see Ayer, 1952. As for classical Humean sources of positivist and many neoclassical utilitarian ideas, see Hume, 1748 and 1886.

7 In the Marxian variant, the revisionism of the Second International, some aspects of Bolshevik thinking, and of course Stalinism, represented Marxism as an empirical science of social engineering. See, in this regard, Neurath, 1973; also see Bukharin, 1926 and Plekhanov, 1972. More recently, the work of John Roemer and Jon Elster is illustrative of this tendency, given in their embrace of analytic philosophy.

8 For a more current appraisal, see Giddens, 1971.

9 For the Bachelardian influence on Marxian views, see Lecourt, 1975.

10 In striking consonance, Keynes argued the case for the paradox of thrift. In fact, much of Keynesian economics is based on the rather simple – yet important – proposition that a macroeconomics may not be constructed as a simple extension of micro propositions. It is in this regard that Keynesianism is a step closer to realism than the neoclassical system it tried to criticize.

11 The theory of consumer behaviour is a good example of a completely axiomatized deductive system unable to predict (surprisingly, given the emphasis placed on prediction as a necessary function of science) virtually any case of empirical consumer behaviour, although ready to 'explain' – post factum – any given instance of behaviour. Stated simply, the law of demand boils down in practice to the proposition that anything is possible: quantity demanded may rise, fall or remain stationary, given an original change in price. All these disparate behaviours may subsequently be titled as 'rational', depending upon the premise used to justify each instance separately. In this case, the attribution of 'rationality' to all possible behaviours makes the concept a caricature.

12 An excellent discussion of this and other methodological controversies in economics may be found in Blaug, 1980.
13 The neo-Kantian writ runs large upon contemporary theory; see Winch, 1958; in economics, see Myrdal, 1959 and 1970. For a placement of the *verstehen* tradition in social science, see Outhewaite, 1977.

2 Against Eurocentrism: Prolegomena to Liberation

1

The time is perhaps ripe now, at this juncture of the near-total triumph of the capitalist mode, and the apparent capitulation of the erstwhile 'socialist' bloc, to re-examine the corpus of 'science' that capitalism has arrogated to itself, not least in the form of 'economics'. It should be obvious that not only is capitalism defended today as the best of all possible worlds[1] (it being usually taken for granted that the matter is now empirically resolved beyond contention, in a Darwinian mode of argument, à la the so-called Alchian Thesis[2]), both politically and economically, but also as the only system guaranteeing plural values alongside the rigour of a positive, objective science that is universally applicable. In fact, the so-called 'scientific' world view is often blithely equated with the European capitalist revolution historically, as though the Egyptian, the Indian, and the Chinese, to speak only of a few non-capitalist, and/or extra-European, scientific traditions, never existed.[3]

Perhaps this much was to be expected; after all, since Europeans had pretty nearly conquered the world, they had earned the 'right' to rewrite history on their own, self-congratulatory terms.[4] And that is, in fact, exactly what happened. However, success in this sphere was not entirely univalent for the votaries of capital, given the emergence, coeval with the European conquest of the world, of a European working class movement whose most famous, if not always most faithful, representative was to be Marxism. The Marxist, generally, did not question the fairytale of the capitalist Enlightenment as the great European boon to humankind, but she did suggest that, in many regards, this revolution was inadequate, incomplete, and indecent. For its part, Marxism claimed to have achieved a sort of *sublation* of capitalist philosophy, being ready in its own way to go beyond it, though carefully building on its preexisting foundation. Thus Marx visualised his political economy as fulfilling the failed promise of the Ricardians, that is as completing a 'search' process (for the holy grail of surplus value) begun, supposedly awkwardly, by Petty, Smith and Ricardo.[5]

Perhaps the best document that illustrates the critical ambivalence of Marxism vis-à-vis capitalist modes is the *Manifesto* (Marx and Engels, 1968), which is, astonishingly, as much a ringing paean, celebrating the capitalist revolution in lyrical terms not even approached by capitalist ideologues in their most zealous moods, as a critique of it. Accordingly, in all dialectical, if dubious, relish, Marxism celebrates the accomplishments of capitalism prior to rejecting it (the rejection itself being an inescapable verdict imposed by historical 'forces' immanent in the womb of the order) as an inadequate social formation.

The burden of my critique here is to show that there is little in capitalism (or in erstwhile 'socialisms', for that matter), and the crown jewel of its hegemonic ideology – 'economics' – that warrants any such celebration; and that *human emancipation demands the almost total rejection of European capitalist institutions ('science', and 'economics', included) if we are to survive as a (decent) human species in a hospitable ecological environment.* I will also argue that this is not merely an *argument*, in a rationalist mode (where *debate* is the end-all), but a vital *moral* imperative (where *deeds* count for more) as well. Finally, I will, however summarily, evaluate the claim of realism to have set right the agenda of science and (socialist) emancipation on a philosophically sound footing.[6] Given that this paper is written for an *economics* readership (may their tribe decrease!!), many of the examples, and some arguments, are taken from that arena, to the neglect of the many other (and vastly more interesting) dimensions of social life.

2 Science

Too often, in intellectual discourse, we take meanings as given. And quite often, for that reason, we capitulate unwittingly to the ideological kernels that inhabit the domain of words, to the disarming spell of everyday 'reverie' as Bachelard (1968) so very eloquently put it. Science is one such word that has been sacralised by capital (as much as by its socialist enemies), its myriad profanities notwithstanding. Even Marxists and anarchists, generally contemptuous of most conventional social contrivances, nonetheless genuflected readily, and uncritically, before this vengeful goddess – if only for needing its blessed anointments for the easier dissemination of their ideas.

The capitalist revolution separated the state from the church (at least formally). It immediately conjoined the state with the new deity of science, however, thereby giving this new tradition a power boost that put it almost beyond the reach of social discipline.[7] The mythology of religion was soon to be replaced by the mythology of science, as science itself blessed the state and sacralised the world view(s) of capital. Physics led the way in this beatification of formal knowledge (Newton being the ruling demiurge in this cosmos), and physics-envy naturally was to become the obvious bane of all the sciences, economics being no exception.[8]

Stated simply, science, in economics at least, became identified with quantification per se, with qualitative analyses sinking into a low second place as inferior (if not wholly irrelevant) modes of analysis.[9] The apparent rigour of mathematics[10] was recruited avidly by neoclassicism to justify and defend its truistic, axiomatic, and almost infantile, theorems that deeply investigated but the surface gloss of economic life. Indeed, for the longest time, Marxists (in the US) had to live in the academic dog-house for not being familiar with matrix algebra, until keen (if not always scrupulous) Marxist minds, with academic tenures at stake, realised the enormous (and inexpensive) potential of this tool for restating Marxian ideas in formalised language and instantly acquiring the gloss of high science, the latter-day pundits of repute here being Roemer in the US and Morishima in England, who were of course soon emulated by a host of lesser lights to whom this switch in language alone promised hours of (well funded) computerised fun and games.

Of course, all the formalisms did not advance a critical understanding of the *organon* of Marxian system, and its many difficulties, one iota; but it did succeed in generating grudging respect for the Marxist by the even more facile and shallow savants of neoclassicism. The enemy was being forced to speak their language; capitulation could not be far away.

The point should be clear; henceforth, the aura of science would perforce hallow all social projects deemed necessary by (and to) the governing elite. Mathematics could now step in in place of traditional forms of mumbo-jumbo to keep the lay audience in a comfortable trance of mystification – from which it was hoped they would (and need) never awake. *And yet the facts of social life have always stood in truculent, if silent, testimony against this meretricious scientism.*[11] Indeed, to ask the questions, what is economics a science of, and what qualifies it as a scientific discipline, is to invite a revelatory education into the inherent charlatanism of economic ideology. The issue here is not so much the validity of economic theory (problematic enough in any economic discourse), but rather its deceptive wrap of *scientism*. The fact is that even if economic theory were true, and its 'science' valid, in some acceptable sense, *it would still represent only one manner of interpreting the myriad facts of social life*; and it would not, ipso facto, have the right to impose its special discernments, such as they are, on other traditions by force.

In simple terms, science is only one tradition amongst many, with no epistemic prior claim to apodeictic knowledge; it succeeds in capitalist society not because of any demonstrable cognitive superiority but because, with the blessing of state power, it has managed to rig the game in its favour, monopolise research funds, and drive its competition out of the market. But it is time, indeed, that its erstwhile competitors were resuscitated and revived and generally brought back into being, so science can (as in medieval times) learn all over again to humbly *work* to prove its platitudes, rather than to simply pontificate from the commanding heights of power and privilege.

3 Economics

What is economics a science of? Interestingly, diverse intellectual traditions have provided diverse answers. For Smith, economics was the science of the *production* of wealth, for Ricardo *distribution*, for Jevons *exchange*, etc., faithfully reflecting the various historical moments of capitalist evolution in Britain,[12] and their own location within it. Contrary to the selective emphases in the foregoing, and speaking more generally, economics is simply an examination of all those varied moments of the economic life. But how shall we study such 'systems'? Mainstream economics, classical or neoclassical, has approached the 'economy' wearing the raiment of the very select premises of capitalist society, i.e. with the specification of self-directed, Hobbesian, individuals armed with material passions, seeking requital only in a deluge of privatised consumption.[13] *All the realist problems of mainstream economics can be traced to this fundamental epistemic error, of supposing 'maximising' behaviour (apart from assuming it to be 'rational') to be unmediated by cultural norms.*[14] Indeed, we can ask some rather simple questions at this stage which help underscore the gross vapidity of the discipline. Firstly, how do we know these highly select behavioural traits to be true (even within its own domain of market society)? Secondly, how do we know them to be *universal*? Economics, of course, has customarily argued these postulates by *assumption*, through the fable of 'inspired introspection' as in Ricardo's choice parlance.[15]

This is, surely, a fantastic feint. One can now assume economics truths to be self-evident and move on, which is in fact what economics did, and still does, with someone like Friedman (1953) 'methodologically' (i.e. *spuriously*) placing these alleged axioms securely beyond critical reviews.[16] Few sciences, other than wholly sham ones like economics, could dare to make such incredible claims! But economics is the ruling ideology of the capitalist system, embodying its flagship *logos*, so to speak, and so it can do just that, with impunity; indeed, with its highly specious pretensions being sacralised by the wholly gratuitous bestowal of a Nobel Memorial prize. Thereby, one tendentious way of *interpreting*, and apologising for, the economic society of capitalism, can now come to be seen as the only, axiomatic way of *doing* things in the material sphere; and economics, appropriately, has become, ever so safely, in all craven cowardice, an *axiomatic* science at one pole, and a '*praxiology*' (as Lange (1945) put it perceptiently a long time ago) at another. Even the ever-sceptical Karl Popper (1972) could hardly make headway against this crown jewel of capitalist ideology: how can one, in all reason, falsify axioms?[17]

Mainstream economics has thrived on this absurd (but snugly self-validating) set of premises, with the thoughtful (if naive) amongst its ilk occasionally venturing out in brief, if usually unsuccessful, empirical forays into 'reality', supposedly to 'test' the axioms. But, of course, that's dissembling, in regal style; to borrow a leaf from bourgeois philosophy itself, no amount of empirical evidence[18] alone (supposedly) can 'prove' that a proposition is 'universal' – the time and space constraints of the observer being far too finite for any such inference. On the other hand, if evidence was (more plausibly) preponderantly against its axioms, economics could switch gears and argue that its universal laws were merely 'statistical laws' that didn't always hold, and so on.[19] So, in fact, economics simply legislates, magisterially, how the world *should* be, and then presumes (turning its back squarely on reality forever) that that is how it *really* is; the world, meanwhile, plods on, innocent of any of the sins of 'theory'. I have never met a successful businessman who knew a single theorem in economics (I know a lot of unsuccessful ones who do know a lot, by the way!); similarly, I can't think of a single major business school anywhere that could last a day if they took the theorems of economics seriously.[20] Being practically-minded, they investigate the world as it appears to them, rather than through any absurd filter of a priori premises. And appearances, however evanescent they may be, are just a step closer to reality than tendentiously 'inspired' introspections! At any rate, I know of no practical science that enjoys this extraordinary status of near total irrelevance in the realm of applications! To state the moral: *the entire enterprise of neoclassical economics is rigged to show that laissez-faire produces optimal outcomes*, but for the disruptive operation of the odd externality (a belated correction) here and there.[21] The fact that economics has had to stand reality on its head to 'demonstrate' this thesis only shows the extent to which zealotry can go to defend a material interest.

But how does one seriously tackle a *science of assumptions*? Not empirically, because 'evidence' is always a contextual affair, neither abstract, nor general; rather, one needs only, I argue, a coherent set of *counter*-assumptions. That is, indeed, all it would take to deny and ignore mainstream economics. Set up premises directly *contra* the premises of economics and we have, presto!, a different economic system (if as imaginary as the one dear to neoclassical dreams)! A counter-economics is no more (or it is no less?) 'real' than the economics of our professors, of course, but is as legitimate as theirs for being based on the same airy nothingness (and we can then safely cite no less an authority than Nobel Laureate Friedman to the effect that the 'realism' of our fundamental assumptions is quite irrelevant to their scientific value!).

So, for sake of argument, I could legislate a new set of premises,[22] where social groups (not individuals) are the prime economic 'agents', deemed fundamentally altruistic, systematically avoiding self-interest in favour of group interest, thinking that less is better, and so on. Lo and behold, we would then erect a new economic theory with a new set of 'laws'[23] (instead of indifference curves, of course, we might now craft sinuously hooped curves of social affection, behaving quite perversely!). But why then does this new, and entirely possible, 'economics', not have a ready patron? Because such postulated traits simply do not answer to the behavioural needs of capitalism. Period.[24] And, to assume what needs to be proved is, of course, an old artifice in the fine art of dissembling. At any rate, contrary to the pretensions of both mainstream and Marxians, the truth is that there are potentially as many 'economics' as there are culturally-derived value systems in human society.

Classical Marxism, converted by academic opportunists into a vulgar antipode of neoclassical 'economics', fares little better; the 'assumptions' needed to make Volume One analyses (specially value theory) 'work' are more than equally as heroic as neoclassical ones, and deserve to be just as securely martyred.[25] Worse, in many respects, Marxian economics internalises many of the philosophical premises of mainstream economics (attesting to their shared *materialism*, where the *primacy* of economic motivations in the general sphere of social conduct is readily granted[26]), to its lasting discredit. The question might then well be raised: what is it that Marxists say and do, qua economists, that neoclassicals don't?[27] I argue that there is a radical difference in their *ontological* assumptions about capitalism,[28] though the gulf is often exaggerated, and is much narrower, in actual *academic* practice, than frequently assumed; the very fact that non-Marxians like Robinson or Kalecki[29] can accept so many of the macro statements of a Marxian 'economics' sustains the fact that liberal theory (such as the so-called 'Cambridge School') can appropriate much of Marxist 'economics' safely without prejudice to its interests. And the fact that an arch-conservative like Schumpeter (see 1976), directly or indirectly, supported so many of Marxian views on capitalist growth is another indication that the two domains are perhaps not that far apart. *Indeed, the premises that Smith and Marx shared in common – faith in science, belief in 'progress', and a shared metaphysic of materialism vis-à-vis human motivations – quite outweigh their otherwise significant differences.* It is worth noting, in this context, that *all materialist visions of emancipation are, inherently, self-immolating*; only moral critiques carry the immanent promise of transcendence. In this important regard, viewed from a non-Eurocentred perspective, capitalism and socialism are only the two (equally ugly) faces of Janus.

All paradigms carry three inescapable attributes: a set of '*assumptions*' constituting the infrastructure; a corpus of '*theory*', or a more or less cohering set of propositions based on those assumptions; and a definite '*policy*' imperative (apparently) flowing from the theory. Of course, it would be naive to imagine the scientific process as a sequence moving in that (logically) schematic, if satisfactory, order, from initial assumptions to final policy; the truth is exactly the obverse: *it is policy that guides the selective choice of assumptions, with 'theory' a mere rationalisation of the former.*[30] Easy to see why Marxists have never had the heart to seize upon the vacuity of the fundamental neoclassical assumptions about economic behaviour; because Marx's assumptions, about an idealised 'capitalism', in Volume One of *Capital*, are equally untenable.

Let me state the matter now succinctly. *There is no such thing as an 'economics' (construed as a set of deductive propositions from arbitrary 'assumptions')*, whether it is neoclassical, Marxian, or Martian for that matter, stripped aside from the containment of its many social veils. There is a material dimension to social life, to be sure, but it is one completely encapsulated in a cultural matrix, where the 'economic' moment arises as an *interdependent resultant*, so to speak, rather than as a prime mover.[31] There is a social economy; but there is no 'economics'. The truths of the economic life (*being concrete and contextual*, in the main) have to be gleaned, quite regardless of the paradigm involved, by direct, patient, careful observation – by *induction*, so to speak – not by abstract 'theorising'[32] (*sober reflection suggests there is no other way in any form of knowledge-gathering activity, natural or social: even realism, at its best, is not the gift of an empyrean inspiration, soaring above us all, and falling upon a few, like manna from heaven, but a brilliant derivation from the exoteric, empirically-sullied, facts of the social life*). In this regard, unlike the fields of botany and zoology, regrettably, the voyage of the *Beagle* in economics has not even begun.

But even were it to begin now, it would be too late, for some other important reasons. Unfortunately for emergent economic theorists, it is only a spontaneously-evolved capitalist economy, competitively subject to an unfettered 'market', operating 'behind our backs', so to speak, that allows for specific economic outcomes to be 'theorised' and speculated about – unlike, say, the more self-conscious systems such as medieval European feudalism and/or state socialism, where the key economic parameters are 'set' quite transparently by human agents, acting more or less publicly and 'voluntarily'. In this day and age of state and corporate direction, and near-global macro 'management', the spontaneous urgings of a 'blind', self-propelling, economy (if indeed such an entity ever existed) are considerably held in check; and, as such, today's capitalisms are getting more and more like those other modes of production where the key agents and players are identifiable, and broad trajectories of most key variables are wholly the premeditated assignations of controlling agencies with determinate strategies. Unintended consequences still operate, of course, as they must; but a far better guide to the macro dynamics would flow from a *political* analysis of the state and its major corporate allies, as opposed to any, old-fashioned, 'economic theory'.[33] *Corporate empires, today, are run simply like other empires*; theories of administration, management, and war games are, appropriately, far closer to the ground (particularly in the penumbra of 'prediction' so dear to the Friedmanite) than the antiquated mechanics of an 'economic' theory self-consciously embedded in the archaic fable(s) of simple competition.

4   Realism

The economic science of capitalism is not absurd because it is *irrealist* (any more than, say, the near-abstract Volume One analysis of Marx, which gratuitously disregards entire chunks of capitalist ontology[34]); rather, it is simply *irrelevant* for being a fantasy world of an ideal, rational capitalism where all motions are mutually equilibrating,[35] in a Newtonian coordination of the elements. Gerard Debreu won a Nobel prize for his work on the speculative robotics of general equilibrium;[36] by that token, anyone who can devise an ideal model of the nature of, say, a Martian topsoil hypothesized as ideal for the growing of Martian rutabagas should equally qualify for a similar award; economic theorising always scores high marks where reality and relevance are not important![37] Any realist questioning, in fact, leaves the science completely befuddled, and ever so bemused. It is true that the vulgar (but conscientious) practitioners, closer to the ground in a manner of speaking, keep looking (morosely) for empirical confirmation of their theoretical absurdities[78] (such as wages equalling labour's marginal product), but the great ideologues, e.g. Walras in the past or Debreu in the present, leave such coarse terrain completely alone. *In all ideologies[39] (Marxism included), the naive empiricist is seen as the indelicate boor who fails to leave the workings of idealist fantasy alone.* Let them eat their empirical confirmations, is the prevalent attitude! And yet, we cannot speak of a 'science' that can exist (and thrive!) in sovereign defiance of empirical application and testing! *Asserting the fact that the empirical domain is only one dimension of reality, and perhaps not the critically 'generative' one, is far from implying that it is either irrelevant or unimportant.* A critique of empiricism is highly plausible, even necessary; but a nihilist critique of simple empirics is absurd. At their worst, both neoclassicism and vulgar Marxism have shared this enduring taint of leaping lightly over the simple world of 'appearances',[40] to avoid decisive refutation.

The dodges employed by neoclassicism to defend against simple empirical refutation are Homeric in scope. The laws of demand, for example, allow for quantity demanded to rise, fall, or remain stationary, as price changes, because there are normal and perverse customers much as there are normal and perverse 'goods'. *This means, of course, that almost anything is possible*[41] (although neoclassicism cannot face up to this fact, without, in effect, losing face!, realism should teach us that, at the level of individual behaviour, which is the chosen domain of the neoclassical, *it is emphatically true that 'anything goes'*: only aggregates display clear patterns – the individual, on the contrary, is *'free'*. In effect, not a single proposition of neoclassicism can be established on an individualistic methodological basis, i.e. in its chosen domain)! And yet Samuelson (1966, p. 61) could contentedly claim that the law of demand is the most verified 'law' ever 'discovered' in economics (naturally, since it allows for all possibilities!). Truth is that economics is incapable of *discovering* anything, since its genius lies in facile fabrications, such as the marginal productivity 'theory' of distribution where the market allocates just desserts to all factors according to their 'productivity'.[42] The greatest empirical defeasance of realism, in capitalist economics, consists in its viewing production and consumption as individual rather than social activities, such that externalities and interdependencies are, at first blush, assumed away. Of course, the added fact that consumption may itself depend upon the nature of production makes the equations even more indeterminate.[43]

Can realism, of the Bhaskarian kind,[44] be brought in as a useful critique of the misplaced ontological assumptions of neoclassicism?[45] I think the answer is in the affirmative, for it easily cuts the ground from under the latter's dissimulating methodological fiction of an *individualist* ontology residing paradoxically within the *social* order of capital. More generally, to merely state (the fact) that an institution such as the 'army' is not simply the plural of 'soldier' is sufficient to implode the pretensions of that high, if misguided, rule of scientific method (at another remove, the so-called 'paradox of thrift' is where Keynes comes close to understanding the radical limitations of 'methodological individualism'). More importantly, critical realism goes well beyond the schoolboy stage of correcting epistemic errors (of the neoclassical world view), to the more fascinating task of discovering the *generative mechanisms* that produce the phenomenon of neoclassicism itself. In fact, herein the signal, a priori, philosophical superiority – in terms of depth – of critical realism: that its protocols demand that we not merely criticize the irrealism of a model, but also *explain* why the putatively unreal and the erroneous arise, and persist, as social forms despite their repeated violation(s) of reality. As such, for instance, a realist Marxism can, (and must) explain the 'errors' of neoclassicism as much as why the erroneous thinking still endures (be it as 'false consciousness', 'ruling class tool', 'fetishism', or whatever); neoclassicism, however, is unable to offer any such symmetrical explanation as to *why* Marxism exists as a counter-ideology (though it may well deny the validity of Marxian theorems on a different plane). Neoclassicism, therefore, simply lacks the social analysis (*for not being a serious social science at any stage of its monotonous evolution!*) to describe such a phenomenon. In this way, and on this scale, even vulgar Marxism is, warts and all, irrefutably superior, as an *explanatory* system (neoclassicism chooses not to explain, being content only to *prescribe* acceptable capitalist behaviour, in keeping with its status of a political *ideology of control*) to any version of mainstream economics (despite the fact that it is worse than useless in teaching us how, for instance, to operate a bank, even under socialism!).

But Bhaskarian realism actually goes one better. As I read it, the greatest realist discovery to date is the ontological hiatus between society and the individual or, speaking of economics, the 'gap' between the macro and the micro, reflected in their mutual antagonism and incompatibility. *I argue that it is an ontological truth extant in both nature and society that the domain of the macro is always subject to apparent regularities – 'laws' and 'controls' and so forth – while the micro sphere is always 'free', erratic, and capable of unpredictable movements* (even in physics, the debate between the relativists and the quantum theorists revolves around the not always appreciated distinction between the respective *logos* of the part and the whole). In this sense, no macro and micro theory, Marxist or neoclassicist, can ever be brought into sync; *it is a property of reality that the twain can never meet*. Of course, why this should be so is as unclear as why matter should be possessed of gravity; it just is. At any rate, the consequences of this realist discovery are profound for all the sciences and will definitely affect their internal development once the idea is generally disseminated and absorbed. And only one important derivative of this insight is the fact (I pose the matter enigmatically here, but I have devoted a forthcoming book to the subject) that what we call social change is both cause and consequence of precisely this hiatus between the two dimensions.[46]

It is generally assumed (indeed, an article of faith in Anglo-American economic traditions) that philosophy and methodology, being 'soft core' forms of knowledge (as Joan Robinson expressed the idea once: methodology is a 'bastard' science!), can proffer no *substantive* truths (whether in economics or in any other discipline), only formal propositions. But the foregoing point gives the lie to that sentiment directly; the discovery of the conflict and incompatibility between the macro and the micro domains is a substantive ontological discovery immanent in critical realism, of obvious importance to the sciences generally. I treat this as Bhaskar's greatest contribution to philosophy, although he seems not always aware of the importance of his own discovery.

On the other hand, it is also clear that critical realism, by itself, cannot offer a parallel economics; it can only correct where correction is due, and by and large this rectification will be visited upon Marxian political economy, which has always been in serious need of a non-positivist philosophy of science to check its expansive and effusive proclivities, particularly when it comes to airy speculations about the nature of the communist utopia. The fact that society is an *open*, not a closed, system is enough, for instance, to require amendments of all inexorable Marxian 'laws of motion'; there are no such things, *only tendencies and counter-tendencies* (as brilliantly described by Marx in his great, but misunderstood, chapter on the falling rate of profit, possibly Marx's most sophisticatedly '*realist*' analysis of all!) *with the outcome left wide open*, subject only to conjunctural, situational, determinisms (in the plural). Class struggle, for instance, is real enough; but its outcome, on Marxist lines, at any rate, is no historically-given certainty. Nor can the so-called 'economic' be the determining element in the putative 'last instance': there is simply no such last instance except perhaps on the day that the globe blows up. In the same vein, (material) bases cannot 'determine' so-called (ideological) superstructures, as in hoary Marxian dicta; *rather, there are many sites of social practices, each with its own 'base', and its own rationalising justifications*. Religious practice, for instance, is as real as economic or political practice, and generates its own set of illusions. Similarly, the fabled distinction between absolute and relative autonomy, that has dominated discussions of the state in Marxian political theory, is simply inutile; there is nothing, no stationary *centre*, to be autonomous from![47]

Clearly, then, critical realism 'opens up' Marxism and surgically excises its laggard deficiencies; and it does so by offering a more sophisticated social theory than Marx (though building upon the latter's intuitions).[48] We can now confidently situate the great Marxian revolution in the history of ideas: *Marx was, simply, the first realist on the royal realist road to science*, vested with all the raw genius of a precursor. It is quite unnecessary to dwell on the implications of critical realism for neoclassicism, given that it spells nothing short of sudden death for the latter's somewhat neolithic philosophical posturings (wavering, clumsily, and quite carelessly – for an ideology in power suffers from no need for justification – between a traditionalist, hard-bitten positivism, and a 'new wave' of postmodernist hermeneutics, à la McCloskey) – *if it is taken seriously* (but, of course, it won't be: I had one of the most preeminent economists, and philosophers, of our time, assure me, quite contentedly, that he couldn't fathom it at all).[49]

5   Against Eurocentrism

It is clear then that critical realism[50] can sharpen the tools of science, and serve as a critique of all schools of economics that specialise in airy 'model' building. For models, if totally accurate in what they depict, are superfluous; and if they are not, they are quite useless! *Their real social functions, in the social sciences, are as ideological constructs to help recruit and consolidate scientific communities (i.e. they are 'policy' tools)*. But the real unasked question is whether, and why, 'we' need 'science' (critical realism included) and 'economics' at all? The *subject* (i.e. the 'doers') of the scientific enterprise is often left quite anonymous; though it is clear, materially speaking, that this terrain is populated by the governing techno-scientific elites that serve as His Corporate Majesty's interpreters, soothsayers, and sycophants. What is taken for granted in almost all of scientific discourse is the *legitimacy* of the academy and the scientific process, as though the university, and the effete elites it nurtures, are charitably endowed with only a public-spirited scientific curiosity about the world and nothing else.[51] Nothing, of course, could be further from the truth; *the scientific establishment is as corrupt, and in much the same ways, as the general state of corruption in a capitalist society* (sharing the egregious ills of socialism, similarly, when located therein).

The modern university presupposes an organised scientific establishment, itself serving as a loyal instrument of state. Indeed, *science is simply another name for the systematic record keeping and surveying requirement of a predatory system built upon unlimited greed wedded to virtually limitless power*.[52] The corporation and the state are the trustees of this carefully controlled scientific process, whose object is a varying mix of profiteering and control over subject populations (workers, women, minorities, tribals, etc.).[53] The largely co-opted intellectual class that dominates this process is arguably both parasitic and undemocratic, posing as great a threat to the liberty and freedom of the vast populace as imperialist armies regularly do to weak and/or small states of the Third World.

Who is it, then, that is in need of the science of 'economics'? Whom will critical realism serve, once understood, and digested? Is it at all likely that scientific understanding will be appropriated by ordinary people who stand outside the process (though serving regularly as 'insiders' in the form of victims,[54] experimental subjects, and so forth)? Hardly. The scientific urge, in the modern era, is a *corporatist* one; ordinary, hapless people are its subject population, usually denied their rights, rituals and practices, in the name of science and the higher wisdom of the masters of the polity. *Stated succinctly, science is become now simply the master tool of corporate enslavement* (see Lyotard, 1984), no less in socialism as in capitalism; getting better at it, or even more scientific at it, is still no guarantee that the resulting process/ products will either extend, or even preserve, the domain of freedom for humbler people.

It is this disconsolate fact, in this period of world mastery of capital, that dictates an attitude of extreme caution with regard to scientific paradigms, *en général*. Given the infamous history of the twentieth century, in the area of the *abuse* of science (a history all but suppressed, forgotten, and apparently unknown even to many radicals) it would be entirely safe to venture that the less science we have, the better off we possibly might be; the less economics, the better off, and so on. Very much in this vein, critical realism is no amiable friend of the people, and not just for being ever so wilfully inaccessible – I personally know top notch scholars, both in and out of economics, who quite *literally* don't understand a word of it – but because it looks upon the world with unfailingly corporatist eyes. It is arguably superior to the established ideologies of the already rich and powerful in its insights, but it probably craves that very same power; and what if such power were to come its way? Millions had to suffer unthinkable horrors so we may now know that Marxism is a flawed guide to political practice; how many victims will critical realism claim, when it gets its hour under the sun? The question is worth pondering, lest we forget ...

In this spirit of populism – and I take the personal position *that freedom is a far higher order value than science*[55] – I reject and distrust critical realism as much as the economics and philosophies it opposes and lays bare. I know, from the acuity of experience, that critical realism is no palliative when toothache strikes; it can neither feed, house, clothe, nor warm, nor nurture, those whom it touches. It is, in the European vein, just another bright idea. Frankly, I think that we of the non-European cast (as much as women and minorities living *within* European domains), have had enough of such hollow stimulations. It is high time we turned away from these perilous snares to discover some of our own bright ideas (slowly coming to light today in myriad fields: in agriculture, in nutrition, in healing in cooperative coexistence, etc.; not bright perhaps, I think, so much as *warm* – their purpose being not to exude the cold, harsh glare of intellectual illumination but the far gentler, more ambient glow, of human warmth?); I rather suspect that their time, not that of critical realism or economics, is nigh.

My Western realist comrades will have to forgive me; but this is a statement of an enlightened apostasy. Supposedly scientific mantras ('free market', 'communism', etc.) have, in our own times, and often with our own unthinking participation, destroyed countless lives and threatened the very survival of this fragile planet. What we need now is not newer mantras, or better methodologies, but far simpler *logics of resistance* to the plans of the rich and the powerful. **Contra Bhaskar, scientific knowledge is neither a necessary nor a sufficient condition for human emancipation.**[56] The latter stems from a moral, spiritual, and personal resolve to struggle against iniquity, injustice and oppression. Ordinary people such as rubber-tappers in Brazil, workers in Poland, and peasant women in India, amongst innumerable others, have heroically shown the way (repeatedly) to resist the depredations of capital and the state without consulting the manuals of science, or visiting the in-salons of the hip intelligentsia; *it is they that stand between us, today, and the realm of Flash Gordon.* For science, today, is the regrettably co-opted province of an emergent, engulfing, *technofascism* based on the unscrupled harnessing of the icy hoards of instrumental reason. Since the time of the capitalist Enlightenment, Western science has been a cruelly misanthropic, misogynist, and warlike force that has fostered only the terrifyingly oppressive climate of Big Brother and Organised Intolerance – *an adjunct of imperialism, an* *accessory to racism and genocide, an accomplice of Stalinism and fascism, and a dire threat to workers, women, minorities, 'other' cultures, other species, and the wretched of the earth, generally.*[57] Philosophical realism, as a form of counter-rationalism, can and will, I am afraid, offer only a loyal, effete, opposition to that grim, colourless, and despotic world; what we need, however, in stark contrast, most desperately, and urgently, is an *exit*, an affective escape from its noxious exactions.[58] It is time – indeed it may already be too late! – to bid a fervidly passionate farewell to all the regime(s) of corporate (and materialist) reason devolving from the great European Enlightenment. Let critical realism, brimming over with its blinding intelligence, *interpret* the world, by all means; we wish to remain busy, henceforth, in the much more modest task of trying to *save* it.[59]

Notes

1 The clearest statement of this triumphalism may be found in Fukuyama, 1989.
2 Associated with the economist A.A. Alchian, who likens economic competition to a Darwinian survival-of-the-species game of natural selection, in which the amorally defined 'fittest' agents survive. See Alchian and Allen, 1964. Of course, Marx and Engels had, more than a century ago, savagely ridiculed the crude naturalism of such statements.
3 For a disclaimer see Joseph et al., 1990. Also, for the first *non-Eurocentric* account of the incredible, but forgotten, contributions of non-European mathematics, by the same author, see Joseph, 1992. Astonishingly, even educated Europeans remain convinced that the theory of evolution, the law of gravity, the description of the circulation of blood, or even Pythagoras's theorem – to state but a few major ideas – are all *European* discoveries; the truth, for those who care to seek it, is quite otherwise.
4 For a ringing critique of perhaps the most egregious piece of such rewriting – in this case, of African history – see Davidson, 1987 and Bernal, 1987.
5 See Marx, 1969, for an extended discourse on this subject.
6 For this claim, see Bhaskar, 1989a, ch. 1.
7 For a fiery denunciation of this phenomenon, see Feyerabend, 1978.
8 See Mirowski, 1988, for an exaggerated statement of this idea.
9 Usually David Hume is seen as the originator of this orientation with his passionate injunction to 'commit unto the flames' that which could not be quantified.
10 Malthus, for instance, employed his spurious mathematical progressions (purporting to represent ratios of population growth and food supply increments) with great effect, the maths being viewed generally as the

clincher in an otherwise wholly specious argument. Even today, economics employs quite unnecessarily complex mathematical tools to keep the laity (and fellow social scientists) in humble wonderment.

11 For the humanist critique of scientism, Feyerabend, 1978; for a more tendentious perspective see Hayek, 1942–43.
12 For a fuller statement of this argument see Kanth, 1986; also chs 7–11 in Kanth, 1992.
13 See Arrow, 1987, for a full specification of the (capitalist) 'rationality' postulate.
14 It is the critical importance of these premises to the coherence of the neoclassical paradigm that leads Friedman to propose a spurious 'methodology' of ignoring the realism of premises in economic argument.
15 Senior, Mill, Cairnes, Robbins, and the Austrians, all shared this fundamental conviction, in varying degrees. For the very best single source on the history of methodology in economics, see the work of Blaug, 1992, despite the fact that, true to his personal conservatism, the (potential) contributions of radical critiques (specially Bhaskarian realism) remain quite unspecified.
16 The a priori, axiomatic, nature of these pronouncements is obvious and continuous from Ricardo, through Cairnes, 1965 and Robbins, 1935. For latter-day apologetics in this vein, defending the metaphysics of the 'rationality' postulate, see Boland, 1981.
17 The Lakatosian methodology of 'scientific research programmes' would have little difficulty in disposing of neoclassicism as a degenerate science; of course, that is missing the point. Neoclassicism always was a *political* research programme.
18 A famous *Methodenstreit* between Carl Meger and Gustav Schmoller debated the deductivist versus inductivist problem as early as the 1880s (see Hutchison, 1973); closer to our times, similar issues were 'debated' between Terence Hutchison (1956; also 1973) and Fritz Machlup (1978, pp. 143–44), and yet again between Lester and Machlup in 1946.
19 For clarification, see Blaug, 1992, ch. 6.
20 As is well understood by the profession, any form of empirical research in the macro economy has to abandon all pretence of neoclassicism; there economists have to function as classical (or even Marxian!) economists paying all due attention to *non-rationalist* and *non-individualist* social agents.
21 Many have long recognised this all too obvious truth; in times of yore, Letwin, 1964: more recently, the amazingly candid reflections of Blaug, 1992. For a detailed study on the Ricardian roots of this orientation see Kanth, 1986. Of course, macro economics, in *practice*, is almost, by definition, *contra* the conceits of neoclassicism.

22 I am being only partly satirical here; truth is that entire social economies, tribal and pre-capitalist forms generally, have been based precisely on such considerations (fitting easily within a postulated 'Gandhian' economics, e.g.) until they were ruthlessly swept away first by capitalist colonialist depredations, and later, by equally virulent socialist crusades. Today, of course, the antihuman monstrosity of capitalist ideology is visited upon the entire planet.

23 It is not often recognised the extent to which economists' discussions of 'social welfare' are based on prior adherence to the postulate of *methodological individualism*, consciously or unconsciously, explicitly or implicitly. As such the whole bag of Paretian postulates are vitiated by an arguably false ontological assumption (this applies as much to the work of Kenneth Arrow as John Rawls). See Hennipman, 1976, who continues to view Paretian ideological jugglery, akin to much of the economics mainstream, as a positive, 'analytical' tool.

24 The reasons for the gaping emptiness of the black hole of neoclassicism are all political and historical; briefly, capitalist economics entered the world *defensively*, suffering the scorn of conservative criticism first and radical socialist critiques later. Now that the socialist bloc has collapsed, and with it, the apparent extinction of all its enemies, perhaps economics will slowly shed its ideological wraps and begin the quite novel task of emulating a true science, which is to begin with *real facts*, not arbitrary premises.

25 The best single source for an understanding of the Marxian system remains the old classic of Paul Sweezy, 1970.

26 Thus, for the simple Marxist, religion can be explained in economic terms, but economics cannot – legitimately – be explained in religious terms.

27 If we include so-called 'radicals' alongside the Marxists, their record, at least in the US academy, of providing a serious alternative to mainstream science (apart from mainstream *politics*) is quite pathetic. See Bronfenbrenner, 1970, and Lindbeck, 1971, for an early, and largely accurate, survey of issues. Quite aptly, therefore, Mark Blaug characterizes the whole group as simple-minded 'voluntarists' (see Blaug, 1990, ch. 3).

28 It is in this area that Bhaskarian realism comes into its own, irrefutably showing the individualist epistemic – the so-called *methodological individualism* – of capitalist economics as being fatally flawed in an *ontological* sense. See Bhaskar, 1989b.

29 The presumptions of this school are neatly summarised in Hollis and Nell, 1975.

30 I have shown this in the case of Ricardo (Kanth, 1986), but it can, I think, be demonstrated for any and all paradigms.

31 The great error of both capitalist and Marxist theorising is to extract the 'economy' from its cultural base and then treat it as the determining foundation of the latter. The truth is ineluctable: the economy is always embedded in a cradle of values (no more or less so, be it capitalism, or, for that matter, even socialism).
32 The so-called Carnegie-Mellon school, in economics, aside from most business schools, takes this approach, although the scientific scope of their research agenda remains as 'bounded' as their vaunted doctrine of 'bounded' rationality. See Simon, 1957.
33 Indeed, this much is apparent even in standard oligopoly theory where the existence of self-conscious strategies invites not new modes of economic theorising but the application of political and military codes of gamesmanship in a Machiavellian world of power struggles.
34 One important caveat is due: the fact that this paper, basically, offers an *external* critique of science does not, by any means, preclude it from also holding existing pretenders to Eurocentred science to the latter's own *internal* canons of acceptable scientific practice. There is no 'contradiction' between the two types of critique; rather, they are complementary.
35 For rejection of the notion of equilibrium, Robinson, 1962, at her acerbic best, is unsurpassable. For the empirical irrelevance of neoclassicism, except as a guide to a *praxiology*, see Lange, 1945 and Hollis and Nell, 1975.
36 Frank Hahn (1985, pp. 19–20) blithely assures us that general equilibrium theory is of 'great practical significance'; and yet he could still yield that the theory 'makes no formal or causal claims at all' (1984, pp. 47–48)!! In point of fact, the notion of 'general equilibrium' is purely and simply an ideological construct: it has *no* practical or theoretical significance at all.
37 As a nineteenth century observer of the Ricardians remarked, the strength of the economists lay directly proportional to their distance from the facts!
38 On the generally negative findings in this area, see Fisher, in Oswald, 1991. For similar discoveries vis-à-vis the 'rationality' postulate see the summation of evidence in Frey and Eichenberger, 1989; significantly, empirical counter-evidence is, in mainstream economics *newspeak*, invidiously titled 'anomalies'!
39 See Latsis, 1972 and (ed.) 1976, for a flat rejection of the 'immunising stratagems' of neoclassicism, the clever ruses indicating the latter's status only as a 'degenerating' research programme.
40 Marx was fond of saying that if appearance and reality coincided there would be no need for science; however, less subtle Marxists have taken this to mean that appearances are not a part of 'reality'. Perhaps Bhaskar

(1989a) offers the best clarification here with his stratification of reality into the real, the actual and the empirical dimensions.

41 As Brown and Deaton (1972, p. 1168) argue, 'theory', in this sphere, was little more than a 'fable'. Importantly, the positivism of economics does not allow for the entirely plausible ontological possibility, in economics behaviour, that 'anything goes'; hence the clinging to a determinist theory in face of the merry dance of chaos that is reality.

42 On the vagueness of this schemata, see Thurow, 1975.

43 The strategy of neoclassicism in dealing with its counterfactualities is instructive. First it models the untruths (say, e.g., perfect competition) as canonical edifices, then it drags in the truth (the *contra* empirical evidence) as infelicitous 'anomalies', or 'externalities', to be worked into the models by way of exception! In effect, the so-called 'anomalies' are simply egregiously lapidary refutations of the 'models'!

44 I speak of Bhaskar's 'scientific', 'transcendent' or, as I will refer to it henceforth, '*critical*' realism quite exclusively in this paper; of course, there are many other forms of realism as well, with the economics establishment hosting its own resident realist in the form of Uskali Maki. For a Bhaskar-inspired piece on economics, see paper by Lawson, in Backhouse, 1994.

45 For the relevance of Bhaskar to economics, see Kanth, 1992.

46 This has profound, and ultimately negative, implications for the Marxian theory of revolutionary change. For a full explication, see Kanth, forthcoming, 1997.

47 Many of these propositions will, of course, be denied as being *really* 'Marxian' by defenders of the faith. I shall refrain from quoting chapter and verse.

48 Bhaskar is incomparable in this area as well; in fact, arguably, his chapter 'Societies' in Bhaskar, 1989b, is possibly the best single treatment of the subject in modern times, beginning, so to speak, where Marx leaves off.

49 Of course, intellectual critiques, even at their best, can hardly dent the neoclassicist monolith (as the Sraffians discovered to their naive dismay decades ago). The neoclassical has always lived quite securely, and opulently, in contempt of ordinary canons of common sense. The realists must understand that stating the truth does not, by itself, bring down the citadel of untruth.

50 More, perhaps, than other writers, I treat the framework of transcendental realism as almost exclusively instituted by Bhaskar, thereby neglecting many of his precursors (including Marx). While this posture may or may not be correct, it is certainly undeniable that realism reaches its greatest philosophical sophistication in his writings. With Marx, the speculation comes as a heady aperitif; with Bhaskar, it's the last, gratifying sip of cognac.

51 Scientists have many (carefully cultivated, and largely self-serving) virtues; self-criticism is not, unfortunately, one of them.
52 On the whole problems of intellectuals vis-à-vis the state, see the excellent critique in Chomsky, 1986.
53 On these issues, see Watts, 1983 and Illich, 1971.
54 For some specifics, see Bodley, 1982.
55 See Kanth, 1994, 'Postscript', for more on this theme.
56 This is directly *contra* Bhaskar's assertion (1989a, ch. 1), echoed also in Lawson's work (1994), of the indispensability of science to emancipation. At any rate, matters here are quite simple; by Bhaskar's own admission, *realism is simply an under-labourer for science – therein, the inherent, almost terminal, limits of both philosophy and philosophising.*
57 For some passionate notes on this subject, see Shiva, 1989.
58 See Feyerabend, 1987, for a lyrically impassioned appeal to flee the realm of corporate reason before it's too late.
59 For it is only in his *XIth Thesis on Feuerbach* that Marx is arguable, and supernally, superior to any, and all, varieties of scientific realism.

Part II
'DEVELOPMENT' STUDIES:
RETROSPECT AND PROSPECT

3 Theory and Policy in 'Development' Studies: An Overview of the Mythology of 'Progress'

1

It was 1917 that defined the decisive watershed in the history of the twentieth century, marking a fission, eventually leading to a series of consequent fissures, that was to leave a devastating impact both on the self-confidence of European capitalist civilisation and on its outreach in captive colonies and neo-colonies in far-flung continents. Much as the great French Revolution of 1789,[1] and its accompanying philosophical 'enlightenment', which divided Europe fundamentally, and irreversibly, from almost all of its prehistory, the Bolshevik Revolution altered the map of world capitalism, throwing up an important, if only an initial, barricade against its predatory expansionism, and providing an early spark of hope of national liberation for the host of non-European peoples chafing under the yoke of European imperialism. The emergent socialist republic of the Soviet Union, though weak and impoverished in itself, was to provide, nonetheless, for the next 70 years, political, diplomatic and military support for both national liberation struggles and struggles for socialist transformation, within the context of what was eventually to be termed the '*Third*' World, or, more apologetically, the '*developing*' countries.[2]

However, fortuitous circumstances aided the Soviet resolve; the near-collapse of the capitalist order in the Great Depression of the late '20s and early '30s (at a time when even Stalinist misery was producing impressive economic strides in the USSR), and the consequent imperialist war of the late-capitalist-comers, Japan, Italy and Germany, against the traditional supremacy of Anglo-American capitalism, weakened the centre of world capitalism decisively, given the near destruction of 'civilised' Europe in the holocaust of imperialist struggles. While the 'West' (with the critical exception of the USA, protected as it was by two rather sizable, and conveniently placed, oceans) lay critically – almost mortally – wounded, the USSR was to emerge as a new industrial giant pushed to economic extremes by the terror unleashed by the forces of the Third Reich. It was the confluence of these two processes that ensured that at least formal decolonisation would, henceforth, be firmly on the agenda of European powers. The final push towards this objective, of course, came from liberation struggles 'internal' to the colonies, whether nationalist or (nominally) 'socialist', across Asia and Africa; and, with the breaking free of the torpid Chinese giant from European, American and Japanese colonialism, the process was to become irreversibly encoded into history. A distinctive 'Third World' had been carved out, through the machinations of cold war politics and the heroic struggles of oppressed non-European peoples – and with the steadfast support of the USSR, the newly-created fringe republics of Eastern Europe, and newly-emergent Maoist China.

Regardless of how Third World nations themselves viewed the matter (an issue treated only as a regrettable infelicity), the *macro* logic of the world economy, locked now in life-and-death struggle between a resurgent (but restructured) Western capitalism (with the forced admission of defeated Japan into its ranks), and militarily powerful Eastern bloc socialism, dictated that the 'Third World' would now be destined to be the pawn in a deadly East-West struggle for the hearts, minds, factories and paddy fields of the ex-colonies.[3] The future of both capitalism and socialism appeared to rest on the uncertain backs of the restless, anarchic, and effulgent masses in Asia and Africa, still staggering unsteadily after the long, deep, dark and dismal slumber of colonial rule. Their 'development' – in directions suitable to either capitalist or socialist agendas – was too important a matter to be left to the nations themselves, or to the class struggles therein. Whilst the USSR quietly went about building, and bolstering, anti-imperialist forces in these regions, Western governments and agencies – far richer than the Soviets and almost infinitely more sophisticated in their array of techniques – went about toppling governments and imposing pro-capitalist (or, more simply, pro-Western) dictatorships, wherever possible, through means fair, foul and unspeakable.[4] But such clandestine and covert activities required more positive backstopping; accordingly, Western *economic* policy – a potent adjunct of what might be termed 'NATO' foreign policy – was now directed, with the assistance of a dozen newly created 'international' agencies, to assuring the conditions of capitalist reproduction in the Third World. The USSR had not merely provided the political and military provocation for decolonisation; it had also, by dint of example of its own internal transformation, provided the nucleus of the idea of 'planned' or 'guided' development (in both theory and practice) that would be seized upon eagerly by development mongers seeking, anxiously, to plan (hastily), for capitalism in the periphery.[5]

The availability of vast amounts of funds, dispersed through various 'banks', 'foundations' and 'institutes', created the basis, as intended, for a healthy and vigorous new academic 'discipline' titled, neutrally, as 'development' studies, *the crux of whose efforts – internalising the policy slant to perfection – was the creation and stabilisation of capitalist social institutions* (see Kanth, 1991) *in the near-exotic conditions of a non-European cultural milieu.* All of mainstream development theory, whether conservatively laissez-faire, or social democratically interventionist, grappled with this central problematic in the early years of the inception of the 'field' of development studies (during the first and second *'Development Decades'* as the United Nations was to christen them), as indeed all the way down to this day, despite the sorry collapse, recently, of the so-called Soviet 'threat' (although it is obviously still premature to pass final judgment on a situation essentially in flux, as the ex-Eastern bloc countries still struggle for a distinct socioeconomic identity) which had originally spurred the, not quite dispassionate, and apparently seamless, 'inquiry'. Development theory (and theorists) were profoundly influenced by the emergent politics of this world-historical conjuncture; indeed it could not be otherwise: for social theory – inevitably – is only a masquerade for *policy*.

2   Mainstream Initiatives

Given the policy context just outlined, one begins to appreciate the enormous significance of the early paper by Arthur Lewis (1954), which defined the implicit problematic of the times explicitly even if it left the matter – at a practical level – somewhat indeterminate. Employing a formal model of *'dualism'*, loosely approximating the Marxian departmental schemata in *Capital*, and the similar analyses practically employed by early Stalinist planners – a major influence on the later 'Keynesian' interventionists as well – Lewis went on to sketch the fundamental importance of capital formation to the scheme of things (hardly a novel idea, given the heritage of classical economics, but quite exotic given the usual dominance of the unreal dream world of neoclassical economics) in the context of 'growth'. The paper is so commonplace in its observations that one might be quite incredulous as to its lasting influence until one realises that, underneath the inescapably tautological pseudo-reasoning, endemic to mainstream economic science, lies an important affirmation of the true goals and objectives of the development crusade. Indeed, in this regard, the paper makes only two rather simple, but politically critical, points: (a) that the initiation of capitalist economic growth requires the existence of a capitalist/entrepreneurial class; and (b) that subsequent capitalist evolution requires that income distribution be skewed in favour of this same 'saving' class.

In effect, Lewis had defined the 'problem' of the Third World to a nicety: to 'invent' an industrial bourgeoisie and ensure its continued hegemony over state power. However, there was the obvious catch; how is one to 'produce' a capitalist class where, under presumption, it doesn't exist? The traditional route of social revolution was blocked off by cold war strategy (Gerschenkron, 1962, for instance, had actually advanced the thesis that, even in the case of civilised Europe, 'late' industrialisation had always been 'explosive' in its trajectory); a revolution was too dangerous to risk since its outcome was insecure – peasants and workers might just as easily seize power, in a revolutionary situation, as the bourgeoisie, even when the latter came equipped with foreign assistance. Lewis offered two possibilities: a capitalist class could be 'imported' (the classic *neo-colonial* solution, in what was to be called, not always satirically, '*industrialisation by invitation*'[6]) from abroad, or some form of 'state capitalism', pursued along the lines of India or Egypt, creating capital – domestically – on 'public account'.[7] His sketch did, however, prove quite prophetic: for, the trajectory of peripheral capitalism has, historically, taken both of these different forms, from neo-colonial Hong Kong to state capitalist India. Nonetheless, given the fragility of autonomous capitalist development, it is probably fair to say that Lewis was far more successful in identifying the key problematic than in offering any ultimately satisfactory resolution.

Professor Rostow's work (1956; 1960) followed soon upon the heels of Lewis, with a slightly more avowedly anti-socialist stance;[8] Lewis's hesitancy and caution about the success of a capitalist development of the periphery was now corrected with a historicism (despite the corrective to this misuse of history available in Gerschenkron, 1962) that was necessarily quite spurious. As remarked, Lewis had put more emphasis on the 'problem' of capitalist infusion than on the means to its achievement. While adding nothing to this latter analysis, and significant only for its bleakness (a pessimism to be echoed also in Myint, 1954) in this regard, Rostow nonetheless secured something rather important for 'free world' ideology: the idea of the *inevitability* of such a transformation by reference to a mechanistic, bowdlerised, 'history' of economic change forced into a preset 'stages of economic growth' which assured – as if history were a grand drama enacted for a specific purpose! – the eventual approximation, for all, to the standard (and style) of living of the United States. The '*takeoff*' being only a question of time, Somalia would surely turn into Sweden – some day! Curiously, as an academic aside, Rostow had tried to turn the specific history of the English bourgeois industrial revolution (much like a many a careless Marxist) into a general scheme of world history, echoing Marx's well-known – if rather dubious – phrase, penned in 1867, to the effect that, 'The country that is more developed industrially only shows, to the less developed, the image of its own future'.[9]

At another remove, as early as 1952, whilst the colonies and ex-colonies were only barely finding their feet in the new world order created by the crisis of imperialism, and the rise of Soviet power, Ragnar Nurkse (1952) had defined a fairly comprehensive eco-political agenda for 'developing' countries, with primary responsibility for growth to be placed in the hands of Third World governments themselves. In so doing, Nurkse was to introduce into the idiom of development studies the enduring characteristic of Western development mongers, a 'dualism' of sorts, of preaching Smith at home and Keynes abroad. Given the world situation, the West could not afford to wait for tardy, privately-inspired, 'laissez-faire' capital accumulation; instead, the state was adjured to carry out the essential tasks of what Marx had termed *'primitive accumulation'*, in hothouse fashion, the key to success being the ability of state power (astonishingly, and in chilling revelation of its real agenda, no stricture was placed upon the 'form' of government: after all, when it came to non-European peoples, any form of despotism would do just as well!) to extract revenues from non-capitalist sectors so as to channel them into capitalist use, or 'public finance', as the euphemism went (Myint, 1954, was to make the same point: that the 'free play of economic forces' could not be expected to break the *vicious cycle* of poverty, or the *low level equilibrium trap*, in these regions: some form of organised direction and *'countervailing power'* was needed). Nurkse urged *'balanced growth'* (in this idea, as much as in the specificity of the need for 'state direction' Nurkse was following a path laid by Rosenstein-Rodan (1943)), an essentially indefinable notion – and vagueness has its uses – drawn both from Marxian departmental schemes and Keynesian adaptations of the same. Much was made about breaking the 'vicious cycle' of poverty: and yet this was to be done by *reducing* consumption further! Given Third World political structures, there could have been no doubt as to which of the social classes would be called to bear the burden of this 'belt-tightening', enforced by state power. At any rate, Nurkse, by suggesting that the burden of the funds should be raised through internal, domestic policies of legal seizure and confiscation by a strong, mobilised state, did offer a major policy alternative to the Lewis idea of massive capital transfers (which was more on the lines of a Marshall Plan, involving a considerable transfer of resources). The West was to find it quite congenial to advocate state tyranny for the *'backward peoples'* (the choice, if telling phrase, of Myint) while full of the pious platitudes of individual liberties and freedoms for denizens closer to home.

3   The Radical Reaction

The reaction to the various policies of imperialism came from various sources – indeed diverse sources – gathering strength in the '50s and '60s, as the world experienced an efflorescence of revolutionary activity in not merely the Third World, but the First and Second as well: it was the age of Fidel and Che and Mao, and the heroic peasants of Vietnam, who were to teach the premier imperialist nation a lesson it would never forget. Neo-Marxism, Third-Worldist, and New Left perspectives bloomed, quite indiscriminately, worldwide: from Havana to Paris, and from Prague to Peking. Not all these perspectives were necessarily socialist or working class, or even peasant-based, however; indeed a good bit of *Third-Worldism*, as with the Nehrus, Nassers and Nkrumahs, was simply a good, old-fashioned *economic nationalism* with incipient ruling classes in newly-emergent nations chafing at the tight economic straitjacket they faced in world markets under the firm control of imperialist world centres[10] (whilst the so-called '*nonaligned*' group of nations was always a potpourri of strange bedfellows, a great many amongst them, India and Egypt, for instance, concealed their eminently bourgeois aims under a pseudo 'socialist' rhetoric; this had the *triple advantage* of getting Soviet support, disarming the Left opposition domestically, and blackmailing the West for economic aid). A good example of this kind of dissatisfaction with the place of the Third World in the economic world order of capitalism is the work of Raul Prebisch (1950; reprinted 1962), an Argentinian who became director of the ECLA in Chile, issuing what came to be called the '*ECLA manifest*' in 1950.

Latin America, of course, was somewhat different from Asia and Africa, in the sense that direct colonial rule had been successfully overthrown, for the most part, a good century earlier, and also in the important sense that (native traditions notwithstanding) it represented a continuation of the original, settler European culture. However, the continent was quite clearly a *neo-colony*, primarily of the US, and secondarily of Britain, Spain and other European metropolitan centres. Prebisch's work must be seen only as a protest against the subordinate status of Latin America within Western capitalism. In essence, his analysis was extraordinarily superficial, locating the fundamental problem of '*peripheral capitalism*' (a notion important in itself) in the adverse *terms of trade*, between the continent and metropolitan countries, arising from various structural factors (indeed '*structuralism*' was the term applied to this perspective, although a loosely-defined 'institutionalism' might have been a better term) such as the former's excessive reliance on primary commodity exports, leading to a drain of resources that ensured that 'underdevelopment' was continually recreated in the periphery. The alternative was to be termed '*programmed industrialisation*', enabling domestic accumulation, not under laissez-faire capitalism or socialism, but rather within an uncertain mix of what might be termed, for want of a better phrase, Keynesian social-democracy.

More serious and profound – but with its provenance in Marxism – than this rather tame national bourgeois agenda was the work of Paul Baran (1957), standing antipodal to the now-popular Western academic Marxian tradition of seeing imperially-exported capitalism as good medicine for the colonial world (as, say, in Warren, 1980). Essentially Baran was repeating the Leninist thesis of the retrograde and reactionary nature of capital in its imperialist phase; boldly and categorically, with the example of India in mind, Baran forwarded the thesis (obviously unpopular with *Eurocentric* Marxists) that it was the captive markets of the Third World that fuelled England's otherwise unaccountable takeoff into sudden industrial supremacy, whilst colonial 'capture' of the '*economic surplus*' of colonies – simultaneously – led to their chronic regression. The proposition had splendid dialectical relish to it; contact between the First and Third Worlds, historically, accentuated development in the one and retardation in the other. And this was an idea destined to remain an abomination to both imperialist scholars and orthodox Western Marxists.

The challenge of Baran's thesis was soon to be supported by the work of easily the most recognisable, if notorious, name in development studies: Andre Gunder Frank (1966). Original scholarship, moral vision, and revolutionary fervour mark his work with a special, indelible character. With Latin American country studies as initial examples, Frank established the case for two major theses: one, that the periphery only develops when freed of metropolitan strangleholds; and two, that only a systematic *delinking*[11] with world capitalism could ensure the prospects for an autonomous escape from underdevelopment, or the condition of being colonised, either directly or indirectly. Reinforcing the Baran idea, Frank permanently enshrined the distinction between '*undevelopment*', a more 'natural' condition, from '*underdevelopment*', an *artificial* construction of colonialism, a distinction that is arguably fundamental to any serious study of the Third World. Indeed, it is with Frank that *EuroMarxism* suffers a first cut (hence the odium imposed on Frank by a generation of EuroMarxists), later on to be further lacerated by a host of Third World scholars (as in Banaji's (1972) valiant attempt to theorise a '*colonial*' mode of production free of EuroMarxist stereotypes) led by Samir Amin (1976; Amin actually preceded Frank in publication, albeit in French, and had to wait until the '70s for world recognition), a prolific theorist of world capitalism. Amin was to craft Frankian ideas – although developed independently – into a historical, non-ethnocentrist,[12] Marxian mould, developing important conceptual tools to understand the complex, *disarticulated* modalities of peripheral capitalism,[13] as opposed to the logic of First World *autocentrism*. A more potent challenge to the pretensions of mainstream theory and policy than the Frank-Amin school can hardly be visualised. And, for a while, it looked as if mainstream theorising, if not mainstream policies, overt and covert, would simply fall apart of its own sustained weightlessness. In point of historical fact, of course, it both did and did not – as we shall see;[14] at any rate, the Frank-Amin orientation did capture the vital thrust of the important countercurrents to the mainstream initiatives that took hold and dominated the literature, for a period.

The crisis of the '70s, for world capitalism, was deep and severe. The growing military equity between East and West, coupled with uncontrollable Third World challenges to Western capitalism and European cultural domination (*never had countervailing forces against the West been either so strong or as successful*: even the predacious World Bank, under the stewardship of Vietnam war architect, Robert MacNamara, was to admit, weakly, to a short-lived, but conciliatory, '*basic needs*' strategy, an idea first touted vigorously by the more '*Third-Worldist*' ILO in 1976) had shaken the confidence and might of the West profoundly. Economically staggering under stagflation, and the recessionary gloom of the '70s (auguries of the breakdown of postwar *Fordism*[15]), politically hounded by the increasingly organised and unified protests of poorer nations in the United Nations, and militarily checked by a strong Eastern bloc, even the ideological establishment, 'development' economists amongst them, started to betray chinks in its armoury. Established journals of corporate imperialism started to pay attention to '*dependency*' arguments, and the more apolitical members of the tribe of development studies began to suspect that they were indeed standing on shaky, if not actually shallow, ground; that, perhaps 'economics', as conventionally constituted, simply did not have all the 'answers' to the seemingly intractable development dilemma. Traces of this otherwise atypical melancholia were to be echoed in the 'state of the discipline' paper by A. Hirschman (1981) where he laments the passing of an age, in a sombre, self-critical, and retrospective mood: '... I cannot help feeling that the old liveliness is no longer there, that new ideas are ever harder to come by and that the field is not adequately reproducing itself'.

But history, as always (a fact not always appreciated by determinists, of both Left and Right), is full of surprises. The crisis of imperialism was resolved not by the amelioration of a transition to a true social democracy, as might have been expected at the time, but by a fierce and quite unexpected turn rightwards. The Thatcher-Reagan era marked a profound restructuring of capitalist institutions and ideology, with the inauguration of a new, rapaciously predatory stance towards both the Soviet Union and its Third World allies. With a post-Maoist China[16] implicitly giving support (or at least neutralised, for the most part), the instruments of an international, right-wing, capitalist crusade were very quickly forged. Direct US military interventions, the Grand Intimidation of the *Strategic Defence Initiative*, and increased covert and overt political and economic strikes by a coordinated Western alliance, against both socialism and Third World nationalism, were to alter the balance (of terror) yet again in favour of Western interests. This wholesome revival of right-wing market ideology was to rub off, creditably, on economics as well. The retrospective soon turned into a promising prospective; Deepak Lal's paper (1985), chock full of World Bank platitudes, and the shallow, if hoary, free trade rhetoric of *'getting prices right'*, expressed the mood of a newfound success succinctly.

More cautiously, as befits a brilliant, mature scholar, but no less supportive of the essential thrust of mainstream development strategies, was the retrospective by Amartya Sen (1983) defending the whole shabby enterprise (within which, of course, he was a significant entrepreneur) robustly. However, that much was only self-defence; more importantly, and interestingly, the paper calls, quietly, for an abandonment of older perspectives and a shift towards recognition of the sociopolitical 'rights' and priorities (expressed in terms of the *neologisms* of *'entitlements'* and *'capabilities'*) of peoples as better indices of 'development', away from traditional economic criteria focusing, usually, on per capita availability of goods and services. All this was about as original (except in the nether world of mainstream economics, where the blind shall always lead the blind) as apple-pie, being only a paraphrase, but unacknowledged, of ideas that radicals and Marxists had fought hard to be heard on and about, unsuccessfully, for decades, both in and out of academe. Despite the trite nature of these pronouncements, mainstream development theorists embraced these ideas warmly, correctly seeing in them new hope for a new lease on life for an otherwise discredited, failed profession.

A much more convincing retrospective was to come from the pen of Vandana Shiva[17] (1989), whose torrid, but refreshing, Third World *ecological feminism* told, easily and convincingly – indeed passionately! – of all that had been (wantonly) missing in the Western (and socialist) crusade, the horrors of which are still visible in the many scars on both the physical and cultural landscape of the world as a whole: in all its first, second and third segments. Hers is an eloquent plea for doing away with *factory fetishism*, ecological degradation, and racial and sexual oppression; and for putting *people* – not policies! – at last, at the centre of things. Today, the world over, feminist and ecological concerns stand at the centre of the gamut of varying moods extant in the current period, reflecting the obvious uncertainties of a new order, still in the making.

5

Looking at it now, in the late '90s, it is clear that the original cold war is now over, having been 'won' decisively in a military sense by the West, and in a much more important political sense by the East (the peoples of the Eastern bloc have won important new freedoms even if at a cost they have yet to realise; the *peoples* of the West, of course, have won nothing). The fractured European family is now united again, a fact of overriding political significance; the original barricade against Western expansion, the USSR, now lies prostrate (although not totally enfeebled) – and its many dependencies in the Third World stagger about, shaken and uncertain, naked to all their enemies. The *age of imperialism* is upon us now a second time; it is one world again; alas, a world renewedly under the European capitalist heel (as the recent Middle Eastern conflagration illustrated profoundly and prophetically): back to *pre-1917*, one might speculate, except on a higher technological plane – and so, the wheel of the twentieth century has turned full circle. Indeed, the self-confidence of the West has been restored to the point of major imperialist 'foundations' – e.g. Ford and Rockefeller – having quietly packed up their 'development' kitbags to go back to supporting their local philharmonics: the fate of the Third World, being now securely within Western purview, is of no further significance. One can only speculate on the nature of the resistance to come (if not already leading an embryonic existence) to this *'new world order'*, endorsing some of the objections already present in the work of Shiva, towards an affirmation of the fundamental principle, sagely ignored in all of development studies by most traditions, orthodox Marxist or mainstream: the right of peoples, clans, tribes, villages, et al., to *self-determination* – to say *no*, to the plans of *others* involving them. In some respects, therefore, we have regressed to beginnings, in the development psyche and circumstance; whilst, in others, we have traversed millennia, trespassing into visions of the future.

6   Against Progress: the Miasma of Development

A retrospective on the postwar crusade called 'development' and 'modernisation' – easy, accepted, euphemisms for the continuation of the 400 year-old game of plunder, pillage and enslavement, as practised by metropolitan Europe and its civilisational offshoots on the feckless peoples of Asia, Africa, and Latin America – is surely long overdue: to put it plainly, the development crusade was simply *colonialism* as usual, but in modern guise, with the trappings of science added on, to secure it an honorific, if quite spurious, legitimacy. While it is to Emperor Nero's credit that he merely fiddled while Rome burnt (perhaps in remorse?), the development crusaders stood around indulgently pouring gasoline on the flames as peasants and tribal societies, their cultures, and their livelihoods, were incinerated and dispatched into oblivion – *all in the name of the liberal-radical rhetoric of civilisation, progress and amelioration.*

Looking back now, after almost four decades of 'development' theory, ideology and practice, cutting all the way across the political spectrum, it is almost impossible to believe that almost all of the panaceas advocated by the anointed seers and savants rested on one indelible, if noxious, principle, so obvious as to be unnoticed: *that a set of experts, largely through self-selection,* had both the right and the capacity to plan, think, experiment, and hope, on behalf of others *upon whom these plans were, ultimately, to be foisted. All of development theory, Marxist or neoclassical, took this unstated principle as its point of departure, in splendid contempt of what ordinary people – that undistinguished mass of common humanity! – might think, feel or experience. Both capitalist modernisers and Marxist revolutionaries had prefabricated plans, requiring only the seizure of state power or the unwitting acquiescence of common peoples to allow these plans to be carried out, in experimental fashion, and with a sovereign disregard for the rather simple, democratic political precept that it is the* people, *for better or for worse, who need to exercise the right of choice over their destinies,* even if these choices do not maximise a net dividend as defined by political economists, right or left, *with their own specific political axes to grind. Astonishingly, 200 years after the great French Revolution, and 70 years after the Bolshevik Revolution, neither socialist nor capitalist ideologues would give even nominal credence to this inalienable right of peoples.*[18]

In is in the '90s, today, that the consequences of this Great Default are becoming apparent in the real histories of nations and political systems worldwide, even if the correct political lessons have still not been learnt by their leaderships. In the case of the self-dissolving socialisms of Eastern Europe, 70 years of paternalism, sometimes benign, often tyrannical, involving major economic and social restructuring and major projects of mass access to basic needs[19] – impressive in their own right, specially in relation to the disgraceful record in the advanced capitalist West in this regard – still did little to secure broad legitimacy, let alone any popularity, of such regimes, for the best part either endured with sullenness, or evaded, often, by the old stand-bys of silence, cunning and exile. It must be remembered that even the Gorbachevian Revolution, obviously to be applauded for the welcome relief (reprieve!) it finally brought to long-suffering populations, originally was an *expert initiative from above*, intended to secure only the greater ultimate glory of the (failed) 'system'. *Once again, people were being seen, by their governing classes, as but means to other ends*:[20] such as growth, development or progress. It is a major irony, compounding the preexisting tragedy of the Soviet regime, that perestroika was a trickle-down idea, and glasnost but a ruling elite ploy (that failed, as intended, but succeeded in a different way).

In the capitalist West, the apparent victor in the long-standing East-West encounter, a cynical political system based on voter apathy and a de facto plutocracy masquerades as 'democracy' and 'freedom', within carefully defined structural bounds of the parametrics of private property and 'free' markets, an ideology-cum-institutional setup now being exported vigorously through the concerted efforts of the multilateral institutions of imperialism: the World Bank; the IMF; and the OECD, etc.[21] The 'successes' of the so-called NICs have already been taken as ready evidence of the hoary old capitalist fantasy of 'getting prices right', and 'laissez-faire' (in spite of mass evidence to the contrary: of *'getting prices wrong'*,[22] as practised for decades in South Korea, and Taiwan, aside from the steady, massive doses of state direction), to say nothing of the rhetoric presenting these nations as the bastions of 'freedom' in Asia, despite the easy refutation (also, of the myth that capitalism and democracy are 'Siamese twins') in the tolerated – indeed encouraged – prevalence of dictatorial regimes, in this part of the world, even of the *'bloody Taylorist'*[23] variety. But, despite the rhetoric, resistance to capitalist encroachments on communitarian properties, sentiments and relations, is as real a trend in the *periphery* (as much as in the metropolitan *centres*, with their own growing 'green' initiatives), as is the resistance to Stalinism in Eastern Europe. In a smaller, but no less important way, the heroic Chipko tribes of India,[24] much like workers in Poland, bravely resisted 'modernisation' in favour of self-determination and community values, cocking a snook at the arrogance of power reflected in the self-assurance of Indian government planners and private developers alike, ready to ram 'progress' down the throats of people presumed confidently to be powerless, illiterate and unable to think for themselves.

Although by no means a mass movement, struggles such as those of the Himalayan Chipko women are a sign of the times as much as the restlessness in Eastern Europe, the effulgence of the 'Greens', and the brave defiance of the defenders of the forest in the Amazon,[25] a sign of the birth of a new consciousness that is *self-directed* and aimed at the preservation of community and self, and *the construction of non-alienating practices*, allowing for both to coexist non-antagonistically. This is a bottom-up, *trickle-up* consciousness that is gathering strength, in uncoordinated fashion, across north and south, east and west. And, virtually everywhere, it meets the resolve of the planners and their ruling class partners – securely locked together by the newest catechism of development ideology – to deny them their rights, their rituals, and their practices in the name (always) of a higher rationality: of the calculus of efficiency and the maximand of growth.

Indeed, it is in this *fetishism of productivity* – and the worship of economic growth (indeed, the standard economist, Marxist or neoclassicist, is the guardian high priest at the temple of *capital accumulation*) – that conventional Marxists join their class enemies, the neoclassicals, in passionate embrace of *economism*: the idea that increases in social productivity are 'necessary' *at any cost* – social, demographic, ecological, etc. – to anyone.[26] And it is this fetish that united the otherwise divided house of the *developmentalists*, the majority group amongst both state 'planners', virtually everywhere. Villages could be overrun, cultures destroyed, entire histories submerged and flooded, peoples relocated and uprooted, with complete impunity, in both socialist and capitalist variants of this rabid crusade. The idea that, in a human society, such *choices* involve recourse to values, rather than inexorable historical necessities, never once disturbed the tranquillity of these economic *determinists*, of both right and left, ready to act out the inevitable historical agenda on behalf, if not at the behest!, of their hapless wards. *That people, be they peasants, workers, the homeless, or women, have the right to make their own decisions – even if these be judged incorrect decisions by some outside agency – has never been acknowledged.*[27] But they do – and must – have that right: even if it were only to amount to a *right to be wrong*.

The central issue, therefore, of all development theory has always been – once again, so obvious as to be unmentioned – *political power*, and its exercise. The development crusaders have battened on this power (a power denied to the helpless *objects* of policy), however illegitimately attained – indeed economists have never questioned the legitimacy of power in any existential context, simply taking it as a highly instrumental 'given' – managing to inflict unbelievable human suffering in the process, making 'mistakes' that rarely return to visit the remote architects of policy.[28] There is a political moral here, and one that will be drawn – as indeed it is being drawn – by many more in the future: that the *subalternity*[29] of the masses, and the minority rule of the masters of the polity – the twin bases of despotism – are unlikely to be a tolerable or tolerated condition for much longer. For *self-determination* is an idea that is flouting traditional notions of representation and democracy; and it is a movement that will continue to trouble – and challenge – the smug elitism of both Marxists and the mainstream as they go about trying to change the world – even, as they have in the past, *against its will*.

7

The parallels between the old ways and the new, revealing the unbreached continuity between colonialism and *developmentalism*, are too compelling to ignore: here, an example of the murder of an entire social system – the society of Bengal – under the auspices of British colonialism, and its 'modernising' legions, leading, instructively, to the almost stereotypical creation of a 'Third' World by the First. Indeed, the plunder of Bengal is only a representative sample of the depredations of colonial despotism putting much of the so-called Third World in context.

In the mid-seventeenth century, a visitor from France, Bernier, was quite justifiably astonished at the prosperity of Bengal (before it was to be systematically laid waste by the British). He wrote, in all enthusiasm:

> It exports in abundance cottons and silks, spice, sugar, and butter. It produces amply for its own consumption of wheat, vegetables, grains, fowls, ducks and geese. It has immense herds of pigs and flocks of sheep and goats. Fish of every kind it has in profusion.

Indeed, Bernier was to compare the wealth of Bengal favourably to the prosperity of Egypt (itself yet to fall prey to European despoliation); similarly; in the mid-eighteenth century, Robert Clive, Imperial Viceroy of India, was to write home suggesting that Bengal's capital city of Murshidabad was as 'extensive, populous and rich as the City of London' – quite heady praise, coming from a renowned mercenary and an avid looter.

Within but a quarter of a century of these encomia, *rational* English savagery had reduced the province of Bengal to rubble: as a visiting, but shocked, English Member of Parliament was to write, in the 1780s:

> Many parts of these countries have been reduced to the appearance of a desert. The fields are no longer cultivated; extensive tracts are already over grown with thickets; the husbandman is plundered; the manufacturer oppressed; famine has been repeatedly endured, and depopulation has ensued.

And yet, in 1772, Warren Hastings, Governor of Bengal, in the face of this incredible human tragedy (*the Great Bengal Famine of 1769–70*) – so grim as to make the very name of Bengal synonymous with famine and disaster! – was to boastfully write home to the Directors of the East India Company:

> Notwithstanding the loss of at least one third of the inhabitants of the province, and consequent decrease of cultivation, the net collection for the year of 1771 exceeded even those of 1768 ... owing to it being violently kept up to its former standards.

8

If colonialism spelt wilful death and destruction in the past, the later course of so-called 'development', with the added acquiescence of domestic, but still neo-colonial, ruling orders, has built upon that very human base of desolation, dislocation, and marginalisation, producing the enrichment of a few, at the expense of the many. Let's take the case of the Punjab, a capitalist success story with its so-called 'green' revolution, standing (doubtfully) at the apex of this triumph. In quite typical capitalist accounting amnesia, it is always the 'benefits' of agrarian technologies that are touted (in purely *quantitative* terms, incidentally: area of land cultivated; productivity; volume of production, etc.) in this context; now to restore, pointedly, the forgotten side of the ledger – the *costs* of the supposed economic miracle.

Firstly, it is emphatically not the case that all agrarian indices have shown an upward trend, as is usually believed, suggesting, prima facie, that even the quantitative successes of the green revolution need be evaluated with great care (with all the opportunity costs scaled in appropriately). While, in general, rice and wheat production registered great advances, pulses and oilseeds (equally vital and necessary nutrients) actually showed a marked decline: a greater than 50 per cent decline in the case of pulses, from 370,000 to 150,000 metric tons between 1965–80; with oilseeds declining from 214,000 to 176,000 metric tons.

Secondly, perhaps more importantly, the introduction of wheat and rice monocultures has destroyed the natural genetic diversity of traditional patterns of cultivation, with consequences, if not already manifest, that are yet to be reaped; indeed, more than 40 new insect pests, and a dozen or so new diseases in rice monocultures, already identified, have indicated the nature of the blight to follow. Thirdly, soils have been seriously degraded by toxicity, salinity, and micronutrient deficiencies, while flooding connected with the Bhakra Dam has waterlogged over 2.5 lakh hectares of arable land. Even more critically, an astonishing 65 per cent of some 12,000 villages was to be *submerged*, with over three million people floundering in acute distress and dislocation, and over 1,500 people *killed* (quite predictably, an even bigger dam, with World Bank blessings, was projected for construction over the Narmada river, further south, posing even greater dangers to human, plant, and animal life), all to make way for the economic 'miracle' to come.

Lastly, the entire agronomical structure of the green revolution enhanced peasant dependency on mega-corporate capital, exacerbated water scarcities, and created the obvious accompaniment of that perennially deep and wide socioeconomic polarisation that unmistakably marks a mature capitalist society. Perhaps it is small wonder that the entire region is now prey to grimly murderous social conflicts almost unthinkable even in the near past. Economists must wonder at the nature of the colossal destruction – of nature and social relations – underlying their notions of technical and physical productivity. Indeed what the *GNP* conceals, in its accounting, may be far more critical to the survival of society than what it computes.

9

While the relations of capitalism are now forcibly internalised by the elite orders in all parts of the globe, there is no question that the capitalist drive, in its inception, *was philosophically first systematically rationalised in the context of European society* – and it is still in European civilisation (including its American offshoots) that this orientation is most successfully embedded, against all other forms of pre-capitalist social outlooks. So Russel Means, Native American philosopher and activist, is not off the mark when he has this to say about the putatively '*European*' approach to life itself.

Europeans may see [Marxist materialism] as revolutionary but American Indians see it simply as still more of that same old European conflict between being and gaining. Being is a spiritual proposition. Gaining is a material act. Traditionally, American Indians have always attempted to be the best people they could. Part of that spiritual process was and is to give away wealth, to discard wealth in order *not to gain*. Material gain is an indicator of false status among traditional people while it is 'proof that the system works' to Europeans ... Most important here is the fact that Europeans feel no sense of loss in all this. After all, their philosophers have despiritualised reality so there is no satisfaction (for them) to be gained in simply observing the wonder of a mountain or a lake or a people *in being*. Satisfaction is measured in terms of gaining material – so the mountain becomes gravel and the lake becomes coolant for a factory ... I do not believe that capitalism is really responsible for the situation in which [American Indians] have been declared a national sacrifice. No, it is the European tradition. European culture itself is responsible. Marxism is just the latest continuation of this tradition, not a solution to it. There is another way. There is the traditional Lakota way and the ways of the other American Indian peoples. It is the way that knows that humans do not have the right to degrade Mother Earth, that there are forces beyond anything the European mind has conceived, that humans must be in harmony with all relations or the relations will eventually eliminate the disharmony. All European tradition, Marxism included, has conspired to defy the natural order of things. Mother Earth has been abused, the powers have been abused, and this cannot go on forever. No theory can alter that simple fact. Mother Earth will retaliate, the whole environment will retaliate, and the abusers will be eliminated. Things come full circle. Back to where it started. That's revolution.

In conventional, Eurocentric, rationalist, discourse (of the liberal and orthodox Marxian kind, divided only, one might think, by a *common ideology*!) this kind of talk is dismissed as mere hankering for a lost utopia, nostalgic, sentimental, and quite hopeless (in the same way as Gandhi was debunked by the secular intelligentsia, in East and West, as a well-intentioned dreamer, despite his astonishing *practical* achievements) such that the universal cravings of self-provisioning and self-determination – *the proven critical barricades against commodity production* – are routinely disparaged as but quaint forms of a misguided 'romanticism'. Indeed, to be romantic, by definition, is to want to turn the clock back; on the other hand, when you're dealing with a time bomb (called predatory capitalist expansion, inimical to all life forms, natural and social), maybe turning the clock back is not such a bad idea. As at least one Indian peasant family said to me, more or less, on a recent visit to the subcontinent: they did not, contrary to the soothsayers of modernism, wish to be saved, developed, ameliorated, or uplifted; but they did earnestly wish for one supreme blessing – *to be left alone!*

It is high time economists, dizzy with the heady elixir of state power, took heed of these simple sentiments reflecting the primal demand for a genuine 'laissez-faire', ridding the ordinary, long-suffering populace of the corporate extortions of state and capital. Freedom, and independence, autonomy, and self-direction, are much higher order values than 'development', 'progress', and 'modernisation'. All these latter, dissimulating slogans of *modernism* spell only the enlargement of servitude, and of a corrosive dependency on either capital, or the state, crippling human initiatives, and reducing radically the bounds within which the convivial life (however simple and unadorned) is lived. The critical, desperate, need today, east or west, north or south, is to stave off a ruinous corporatisation of the human universe, led by Western prefects, and aped by their servile allies throughout the world, that threatens to summarily choke off the perennial founts of *cultural freedom*: liberty; diversity; and self-expression. If we fail in this, then the twenty-first century *will* be an Orwellian, *technofascist*, nightmare, defining – for victor and victim – the very nadir of human devolution.

There is no such thing as *underdevelopment*, except within the regressive paradigm of Eurocapitalism (and 'socialism'); there is, however, a more unambiguous category that defines a domain: *the ex-colonial world*, which does share certain critical commonalities despite the uniqueness of each of the myriad cultural commonalities within it. *Use values are simply immeasurable by the funereal standards of exchange value; the clash, in the epoch of modernism, is precisely between these two radically disparate modes of social existence.* Use values, for aeons, have been the cradle in which the human spirit has been nurtured, the source of all the civilities of life; in a few fell centuries, the buy-cheap-and-sell-dear conquistadores have threatened the very existence of such autonomous constructions; it is time that the (warped, alien, and self-serving) materialist yardstick, manufactured and perfected in the West, was abandoned. In cultural terms, in the arts of life, in the ineffable dignity of being (rather than doing or having) it is the 'First' World that is denuded, barren, and overrun by the Teflon of possessive corporatism and its manifest of greed – it is their ascent to civilisation (not 'development') that the world awaits now, with bated breath. The misanthropic inventors of the concrete cemetery of Manhattan can hardly presume to teach the rest of the world how to live.

Notes

1   See Hobsbawm, 1962, for an important discussion of the (aptly termed) world-historical significance of the French Revolution.

2   Today, with the 'discovery' of the so-called newly industrialising countries, mainstream theory identifies a Fourth World within the Third: and, if one adds the special status occupied by the OPEC countries, then we have a Fifth, as well, and so on. The capacity to discriminate between peoples is, apparently, boundless.
3   A credible account of the policy thrust towards what was to be termed 'modernisation' is available in Hoogvelt, 1982.
4   From the deposition of Arbenz in Guatemala, to Mossadegh in Iran, Lumumba in the Congo, and Nkrumah in Ghana; from Allende in Chile to Manley in Jamaica; from the occupation and invasion of Panama, Grenada, Nicaragua et al., the Western record of suppressing and sabotaging popular regimes in the Third World (whilst propping up reactionary dictatorships) is a sorry one indeed, occupying a choice place in the annals of shame.
5   Much of the inspiration for the much-acclaimed Harrod and Domar models of growth were the informed consequence of the Soviet planning experiment.
6   For a critical discussion of this strategy with respect to the region of the Caribbean – the original focus of Arthur Lewis – see chapter entitled 'Dependency Theory in Action', in Blomstrom and Hettne, 1984.
7   For this thesis of deliberately nurtured state capitalism, see Bagchi, 1982.
8   For an exposé of the ideological stance contained in Rostow's work, see Baran and Hobsbawm, in Baran, 1969.
9   See Kanth, 1992, for an examination of the nature of Eurocentric extrapolations from history.
10 Quite opportunistically, EuroMarxists of the genre of Warren, 1980 and Brenner, 1977, conflate radical dependency theory with bourgeois dependency theory, dismissing both of them as expressions of a dispensable 'nationalism'.
11 For a full account of the sociopolitical meaning of delinking, see Amin, 1990a.
12 For Amin's recent work on this issue, see his *Eurocentrism*, 1988.
13 A very current and detailed analysis of the disarticulation of African economies is to be found in Amin, 1990.
14 For a purely academic perspective on the theory underlying development studies, quite unmediated by any political rationale, see Hunt, 1989.
15 For one account of the breakdown of the so-called 'Fordist' regime, see Lipietz, 1987a.
16 For more on the politics of post-Maoism in China, see Hinton, 1990.
17 For an account of the ecological and social ravages of the much-touted 'green revolution' in India, see Shiva, 1991.
18 In the case of capitalist ideology, past or present, with its insistence on the essential safety of elite rule (Mosca, Pareto in the past; Kornhauser,

Pye and Verba in the present) based on mass apathy, the question is not even posed: of course, in the case of Marxian political thinking, one might be misled into hoping for something better, but the very title of an early Lenin pamphlet, 'Better fewer, but better', puts the matter to rest quite effectively.

19 The discovery of the 'basic needs' approach to development matters, announced to the world in the mid-'70s by the ILO and the catechism of the United Nations for a short while after, before the great Reagan reversal, is illustrative of the lateness of bourgeois perceptions and their inherent political cannibalism: the idea was central to the Bolshevik Revolution – indeed to virtually all visions of socialism – and revived again in China by Mao, i.e. it was a socialist idea long before the development establishment co-opted it, briefly, to secure legitimacy for their international depredations. In similar vein, the UNDP, in the '90s, has recently discovered 'human development' as a selling vehicle (under the tutelage of Professor Mahbub-ul-Haq, lately a member of the murderous military regime in Pakistan); at this rate, somewhere in the twenty-first century, the World Bank will discover the existence of 'people' and announce it in full-colour glossies. After all, as a recent IMF journal banner (*Finance and Development*, September 1990) announced, it is time the poor were made 'more productive'.

20 For a perspective on this idea, see Molyneux, 1990; Friedgut and Siegelbaum, 1990.

21 For just a dip into the bottomless pit of capitalist machinations, see Branford and Kucinski, 1988; on the other hand, the speeches of Reaganite World Bank presidents since Clausen are models of clarity with respect to the export of capitalism.

22 For some detail on this issue, see Amsden, 1990.

23 A term used by Lipietz, 1987b.

24 See, for a full account, Bandhopadhyaya and Shiva, 1987.

25 The martyred heroism of Chico Mendes and his intrepid band is now part of folklore; for the story, in his own words, see Mendes, 1989; for a detailed account, see Hecht and Cockburn, 1989.

26 Whether in the construction of the Aswan Dam, destroying Nubian settlements and burying priceless treasures, or in the toxic poisoning of Lake Baikal (or, for that matter, Love Canal) and the cover-up at Chernobyl, or in the many depredations on tribal and village lands and rights in India, the record – capitalist or socialist – is a sorry one. Let no-one apologize for these Himalayan blunders that will stand as a bloody testament to the worship of growth.

27 A lone, but fearless, contemporary voice (still a voice in the wilderness, for all practical purposes), speaking to this, as been the tireless effort of Paul Feyerabend – mediated through invective and satire – to call attention

to the covert tyranny of science and reason; see 1979 and 1987. One must also acknowledge, in this regard, the gentler musings of Gandhi, and the wisdom therein.

28 'Errors' made by elite planners rarely come back to haunt the original schemers – the designers of the Ford Pinto, or the planners of Gosplan, misallocating food supplies, could not have been the immediate sufferers of their gross negligence. For an attempt at construction of a different vision of a cooperative society of producers with real accountability, see the imaginative paper by Ernest Mandel, 1986, which remains interesting despite its utopianism, or perhaps because of it.

29 Perhaps the pithiest definition of subalternity, as a social condition, comes from the pen of Rudolph Bahro, erstwhile political prisoner in East Germany and now organiser of the Greens in Germany; see paper penned in his earlier phase of radical Marxism, 1989.

Part III
ARGUMENTS IN POLITICAL ECONOMY: OLD AND NEW

4 Economic Theory and Arms Expenditures: A Resumé of Issues*

Is economic theory, as currently constituted, capable of adjudicating the merits of particular kinds of spending in terms of their distributive or aggregate impact on the 'economy'? It will be seen, with the case of arms spending as an example, that variability in the choice of 'assumptions' underlying economic analysis renders answers nebulous and inconclusive, leaving the field wide open to purely speculative analytics. Economics is not just a functional 'box of tools' as reassuredly imagined in some forms of discourse: it is simply an engine that will go anywhere depending on the tracks one sets for it. We get out of it, in other words, only what we put in (though probably in an ever-diminishing ratio). In this essay, a serious attempt is made to evaluate the impact of arms spending 'theoretically', in terms of the various paradigms, though the effort ends only in reinforcing the scepticism about economic analysis just outlined. To this day, barring some minority schools, economics has made little effort to study the real workings of people's function and activity, in the material sphere, stripped of select 'assumptions' drawn from the alienated (and alienating) domain of the European capitalist Enlightenment, with a non-personal, estranged 'civil society' marked off from an aloof, and authoritarian, 'state'. As such, real economics knowledge exists not in schools of economics (who live blithely within their own netherworlds) but in the wizened, contextually loaded, little heads of local businessmen fully alive to cultural, and other, parochial nuances that simply may not be generalised. Perhaps Galbraith said it best when he suggested that (academic) economists give advice, to all and sundry, not because of any special inside knowledge they possess, but simply because they are so often invited to.

The Background of Theory

Classical economics was characterized by two specific features: a macro awareness, not merely of the 'economy' as a whole, but also of the institutional linkages that bound the economy to politics, society to the individual, etc.; and, a *policy* interest, i.e. economics, or rather 'political economy', was conceived as a *policy science* – the science of *legislation* – that sought understanding for the sake of transformation.[1] Science was considered purposive, fraught with 'normative' aims. Spawned in a dynamic time, it internalised this concern with its deep and heartfelt involvement in the problem of growth and accumulation. While maximisation of output was a premier concern, it was always located in a dynamic context with the key variables viewed in motion. Neoclassical theory, popularly dated with Jevons, Menger, Walras, et al., was actually conceived within the womb of classical theory, with Senior, among others, marking an important vehicle anticipating the slant of the new economics. The contrast with its ancestor could not be more clearly drawn. Macro emphases shifted to *micro* analysis, dynamics to statics, with the scope of economics narrowing to exclude so-called 'exogenous' factors. There was a turn from normative to putatively 'positive' concerns: policy was to be left to professional policy makers, institutional factors being either taken as given, or simply excluded from analysis. At another level, the concern changed from growth to *allocation*, the latter seen as deriving principally from the micro decisions of microactors.

In the early decades of the twentieth century, the pace and form of economic and political changes, no less fundamental than those of classical times, warranted a return to classical preoccupations, given the massive depression of the '30s, the whole was beginning to look more vulnerable than the parts – and, consequently, the macro perspective returned to favour. The linkages between social and economic issues became acutely visible and clear; and the idea of a *political economy* returned, however, shamefacedly, from out of exile and banishment. Extant policy was discovered unadaptive to circumstance; so economics took up its former (rightful?) place of adviser to governors, and counsellor to the opulent. Growth and distribution appeared, now, marginally more important than 'rational' allocation. The system could afford some measure of irrationality, but not, apparently, a lack of *employment* and income. Keynesian economics, accordingly, restored, in great part, the policy dimension to economics.

Subsequently, the supposedly 'exogenously'-given policy entity – *war* – largely took care of the growth problem. The issue of equilibrium in a stationary state, as much as optimal allocation, reappeared as both justified and justifiable and neoclassical theory rose as a phoenix from the flames to subdue and swallow the Keynesian restoration of classical purposes. An incipient return to laissez-faire economics, in a positive framework, loomed apparent, as the age of affluence progressed. But the exogenous devils did not mark time for too long, returning new perils in the form of stagflation and unemployment. And, for the second time this century, the equilibrium micro-allocationists, in their new, if dissembling, *'we are all Keynesian now'* guise, have appeared, though not at all cowed by the resurgence of the seemingly perpetual conundrums of assuring steady growth and politically acceptable distribution, internationally. However, despite the recent collapse of the 'socialist' challenge, thus far, a new theoretical orthodoxy, as distinct from merely a hard core policy bent for privatisation, at any cost, has not yet arisen: so we live, perhaps, in rather auspicious times.

As a thumbnail sketch of economic philosophies, the foregoing account is seriously incomplete for not mentioning perspectives that have consistently opposed, rightly or wrongly, these mainstream drifts. From the 'Ricardian socialists', to the many-hued radicals, and Marxists, of yesterday and today, there has always been a steady countercurrent of economic thought that has argued for commitments that take us beyond, but including, classical concerns. In these perspectives – and it is a wide spectrum – economic analysis is not merely an aid to analysis, but rather an instrument of social transformation. In such heterodoxies, even qua analysis, economics was rated deficient unless the institutional frame was explicitly invited in as an explanatory datum. Briefly, the characteristics of a structured system – despite internal contradictions – defined the parts; the macro logic governing micro actions, and the parts meaningless without the whole. This larger coherence, easily missed by more myopic analysis, defined the internal rationality, and irrationality, of economic systems.

Obviously then, there is, always, a choice of perspectives. And, each angle of exposure illuminates different things, for different purposes. As social data all things are perhaps worth looking at for their own sake, of course, micro factors being no less real than macro factors; and neither can be excluded from analysis in any frame, though the order of causality and priority is a different question altogether. And the choice made here reflects, if it is not actually predetermined by, one's latent or manifest intent. The position taken in this paper is more eclectic than the conventional mainstream/radical wisdom would allow, but at least it is made clear; before seeing how the part impinges on the whole, it must first perhaps be explained how we think the whole (politics, social relations, etc.) structures the parts. The impact of a sub-sector – the arms industry/defence spending – on the system (the capitalist economy) is thereby contingent on how we conceive the whole, i.e. our notions as to the *political economy of capitalism*, except that this has not always been the economists' method – with exceptions – in the main, since about 1848.

The Foreground of Capitalism

To remind ourselves of the ultimate, and real context: a system of predominantly private ownership of the means of production where production is usually carried out in anticipation of profits, with the market as the principal, but not the only, intermediary between supply and demand. This much most – if not all – schools can agree on. But secular tendencies? Permanent contradictions of material interests? Micro rationality versus macro irrationality? Here, the differences begin. In classical economics, as appropriate to the times, pessimism and optimism were intertwined. Accumulation, though more or less regular, was far from being problem-free; there was the Malthusian population bogey, the Ricardian fiction of 'stationary' states and diminishing returns, and everyone's falling share/rate of profits. With Say's Law, despite Malthus's tendentious but highly relevant protests, the Ricardians denied deficient demand as a problem, while in turn recognizing, just as tendentiously, problems of *distributive* shares. Left alone, however, with laissez-faire and profits in command, on the optimistic side – Malthus apart – the economy was considered almost ideally self-managing.

For neoclassicist theory, with no fixed factors except its own fixations, exogenous population growth, and a smooth (and at least), twice differentiable production function; with diminishing marginal products and reversible decisions; with perfect competition, maximising behaviour, and Say's Law – accumulation was, or could be, crisis-free, so long as the market was undisturbed by non-atomistic agencies. And, as with Pigou (see 1933), an assumed 'wage-price flexibility' would assure full employment. With Keynes, the unaided internal harmony suddenly vanished, as with Malthus in an earlier era; instead, contradictions and paradoxes appear. Declining propensities to consume, cumulative propensities to save, and institutional rigidities, announced the problem of effective demand raised earlier by Malthus (and others). Sluggish, and probably unsocial, investment behaviour called for state intervention to restore full employment, with undue 'animal spirits' requiring fiscal and monetary clamps. Fine-tuning was admitted, therefore, as both economic, and political, necessity. Non-mainstream approaches pointed out a series of inbuilt problems, not always consistent with each other. At least from Marx onwards, the capitalist growth process, reflecting its internal constitution, was seen as involved, whether hopelessly or manageably, in *'contradictions'*, of which insufficient demand was only one factor. The processes was *'crisis'* ridden; and in the Marxian scheme, crises were believed to be of two, related, kinds. One set of problems was caused by, and expressed in, a *falling rate of profit*; and another set was associated with problems of *'underconsumption'*, i.e. the declining ratio of the rate of growth of consumption to the rate of growth of means of production. Both provoking these phenomena, and caused by them, was of course the *class struggle*: in both the economic and the political senses. Non-Marxist, and *neo-Marxist*, critics of orthodoxy located other factors making for instability: Schumpeter, with irregular bursts of innovating activity making for cyclical, but explosive, growth; Steindl, with the growth of *monopoly* eventually retarding the accumulation process; Galbraith, with a bureaucratised economy and state dominating the market; Strachey, with his model of oligopolistic instability, and regressive income distribution; and Baran and Sweezy, with the problem of the disposition of an ever-rising economic '*surplus*' in wasteful and 'irrational', forms, etc.

The Nature of the State: the Demand Side

The question of the role of the state is an important one, in relation to capitalist growth and stability – with specific relevance to armaments expenditures – and the various schools necessarily have different determinations (political economies) of this issue as well. For the classicals, the state was an *unproductive* consumer; even though, as in Smith, defence, or security, was considered more important than opulence. The state had both political – being constituted to '*defend the rich from the poor*' – and economic, i.e. *infrastructural*, functions. In neoclassicism, this agenda is only marginally altered, 'infrastructural' functions being permitted, but the 'political' function shrouded in a necessary beneficence. At any rate, 'politics' was treated as not within the necessary scope of economics. In Keynesian economics, the shift was more radical; state intervention carried positive employment and output effects; public investment was granted a 'productivity', hitherto denied in mainstream economics, equivalent to private investment. Deficit financing, far from being a tax on a fixed fund of saving, was seen as ultimately enlarging the investable surplus. As the *simpliste* equations ran, 'I' determined 'S', and not vice versa.

In radical and Marxian views this simple, if deceptive, clarity is absent; and there is scope for much disagreement over the precise economic role, and impact, of the state, despite a consensus, not far apart from Smith's views, on its primary political functions. Very schematically, the alternatives: in some versions, state expenditures are an offset to underconsumption, i.e. to aggregate demand, and hence to instability. In others, state expenditures are an offset to a declining rate of profit, and hence a stimulant to accumulation. And then again, and only slightly differently, state expenditures may also serve as a means of 'absorption' of the economic 'surplus'. Basically, however, the question at issue is whether state expenditures are '*productive*', or '*unproductive*', i.e. whether they are essential, or not, to the expansion of accumulation. Another view, though not always stated clearly, might consider the resolution of the question as contingent upon whether state *taxes*, direct or indirect, fall primarily on profits or wages, so as to better evaluate the *class incidence* of the budgetary process. And here, the Smithian-Marxian distinction between 'productive and unproductive' labour becomes an object of focus.

In classical and neoclassical theory, the state is an economic minus, or at best an 'indirectly' productive agent to the extent it aids an 'infrastructural' development. In Keynesian economics, its role is to offset deficient aggregate demand, the issue of 'productivity' being either nonsense or irrelevant. In Marxian literature, aside from its political role, which is more critical (and depending on how the budgetary class conflict issues involved are resolved) state expenditures are capable of being: a) positive; b) negative; or c) both. And, in the neoclassical-Keynesian synthetics of modern times, perhaps surprisingly, exactly the same reservations/options apply, as displayed particularly in the context of arms expenditures.

The Arms Industry Approach: The 'Supply' Side

The relevance of this sector for the economy in terms of stability and growth cannot be determined unless one specifies which of the models of capitalist growth – and its internal constitution – one subscribes to. Data on its impact on output, employment, competition, industrial structure, distribution and growth, even where available, alter in significance within different framework. And, even within a given scheme, all manner of contradictions are possible. While this paper does not argue for any one approach, it does insist that the analysis of the arms industry cannot be outside the framework of military spending, any more than the latter can be discussed outside the political economy of capitalism. Some implicit support for this position may perhaps be found in the discussion that follows.

One cannot view the arms industry[2] as a mere appendage to, or a privileged enclave of, industrial production at large, even in purely quantitative terms. Summary statistics, such as they are, seem to indicate an increasing overlap between military contractors and civilian manufacturing concerns (involved in the military business). In 1974, for instance, 65 of the top 100 firms were co-producers in both sectors; in 1982, six of the top 25 corporations were military contractors. The direct and indirect implications of this military penetration of the economy are necessarily, thereby, considerable. The degree of concentration is quite high in the market for military goods: in 1958 over 70 per cent of contracts went to the top 199 (55 per cent to the top 25) firms. In 1961, the 100 largest military contractors shared 74 per cent of the value of awards, as compared with only a 35 per cent share of output for manufacturing concerns in the top civilian 100. In 1965, 27 corporations, with over a billion dollars in assets, captured 25 per cent of all contracts; in 1978, the top five cornered 22.5 per cent of all contracts. However, the higher concentration in the military industry is probably counteracted by the degree of *subcontracting* with something slightly under 50 per cent farmed out to other, smaller firms. The difference in concentration ratios is unlikely to be the critical difference between civilian and manufacturing industries, anyway; for, ultimately, the structure of the corporate economy is only likely to be duplicated in this sector as much as any other.

The growing militarisation of the economy is probably more significant than the issue of concentration. For three straight decades, since the second world war, *the Pentagon has been the largest single source of demand, with the military budget never dipping below 5 per cent of the GNP* (these ratios do seem to be in decline in the '90s). Critical capital-goods industries are particularly dependent on government contracts, with Pentagon purchases averaging 16.0 per cent of all durable manufactured goods between 1960–73. Sample data between 1975–83 showed strictly arms procurement a steadily rising component of overall defence outlays from 17.3 per cent to 25.7 per cent. Within the same period, the Pentagon funded 38.1 per cent of all research and development (R & D) expenditures, public and private. About 25–35 per cent of *all* scientists and engineers were on Department of Defense (DOD) contracts between 1950–78, with the percentage rising to over 60 per cent in fields like aeronautics. Close to two million jobs depended directly on military contracted production. The Reaganite buildup in the '80s promised even more of this, with the defence budget growing at about 9 per cent annually between 1981–87 extending over 7.5 per cent of the GNP in that last year. Should it appear that expenditures on armaments are a thing apart, the rate of growth of arms expenditures was about 16 per cent in the same period (growing twice as fast as the military budget), exceeding, as the *Economic Report of the President* (1982) had it, the 14 per cent rate of increase in the three peak years of the Vietnam buildup.

It is obvious that military expenditures and armaments spending are not the same thing, being quantitatively apart (in 1983 direct arms expenditures were about 25 per cent of total defence outlays down from a high of 29.5 per cent in 1969). Arms exports as a per cent of GNP displayed a steadily rising trend between 1967–76 rising from 2.9 per cent to 6.8 per cent. Commercial sales also increased, rising from 22 per cent in 1971 to 30 per cent of total sales in 1975. But to separate the two conceptually, in both the economic and political sense, on the basis of arithmetic, will not do. For one thing, the two kinds of expenditures are correlated, and are perhaps even complementary (a correlation also existed between armaments spending and GNP between 1969–83). The macro logic of defence spending and arms expenditures, however, stems from the same premises. There are quantitative purposes, however, for which the distinction is worth retaining, such as, for instance, the direct employment effects; but more of this later.

Convergence?

The structures of the arms industry, the military-industrial firm, and the civilian-industrial firm, are growing similar in many respects. Here, the 'convergence' hypothesis of Galbraith (1967) provides a closer fit than the Weidenbaum thesis. For Weidenbaum (1968), to illustrate one perspective, it is government that is increasingly assuming the role of the private 'entrepreneur', while the military contractors are steadily acquiring the characteristics of a governmental bureaucracy, thus blurring the distinction between public and private activities (a matter considered deleterious to private enterprise by conservatives). For Galbraith, on the other hand, large corporations, military and otherwise, are being co-opted into the governmental machinery itself within a sort of *state capitalism* (or 'Pentagon' capitalism, as Melman (1970) calls it). For one such as Weidenbaum, the reasons for this phenomenon lie in the ever more minute Pentagon control exercised over the contractor, from dictating choice of product and the source of capital funds, to regulating the internal operation of the firm such as wage levels etc., all resulting in deleterious effects on risk-bearing and entrepreneurship. For Galbraith, it is the growing complexity of technology and bureaucratization of corporate 'planning' that fuel this integrative tendency between state and civilian-inspired production firms. While Galbraith's position is the more 'sociological' of the two, being more holistic, one can easily take a different view. One can argue that the 'difference' between the industrial corporation and the military supplier lies in factors other than the nature of the final customer. To be sure, the state as sole, or even the principal, customer leads to conspicuous, and only too well publicised, forms of waste and irrationality in production and organizations. But the state as *final patron*, if not the final customer, is no less true of more civilian-industrial corporations. It must be remembered that Chrysler (predominantly a civilian-industrial firm: in 1981, military sales contracts were only 13 per cent of total sales), no less than Lockheed (predominantly a military-industrial concern: in 1981 military contracts were 51.3 per cent of total sales), received generous federal largesse in times of acute financial distress. The fraternity between the large corporation and the state, to exaggerate but little, must be considered an institutional fact, at least within the context of US monopoly capitalism.

Another difference, again one to be treated cautiously, pertains to profit rates; and the contrasting is usually thought to reflect adversely on the civilian firm. One study (Weidenbaum, 1968) estimates the average return on investment at close to 18 per cent for the defence contractor, while only about 11 per cent for civilian industry. However, the issue is more complex than that. Profits as a percentage of invested capital were similar in large-scale corporations, defence and non-defence, about 12.4 and 12.1 per cent respectively (in 1959); for smaller size companies, defence business profits were much higher (25.9 per cent) than either civilian or defence industries as a whole. Profits, as per cent of sales, were larger (after taxes) in the defence sector than civilian manufacturing. In 1981, E-Systems Inc., a defence contractor, showed a total return to investors of 102.88 per cent; but not far behind was a civilian concern – Dean Foods – with 96.93 per cent. Two comments are relevant here. More important than the difference in profit rates (for there are many ways to calculate profits) is probably the risk-free guaranteed nature of profits in military industry; for it is by no means clear that profit margins of oligopolies such as General Motors are necessarily lower than defence contractors. But the chances of the occasional super-windfall (Northrop once made over 500 per cent!) are possibly greater, given the nature of the defence contracting process. With profit margins guaranteed, as much as the virtual certainty of product obsolescence during the production period, cost overruns (averaging almost 300 per cent over original estimates) might be expected to follow quite 'naturally'. The resulting inefficiencies and waste are only too conspicuous; but, to the extent that non-defence corporations exhibit oligopolistic and monopolistic features on a similar scale, the difference in this regard is only one of degree – not of kind.

But a more significant difference, at the level of macro implications, between the arms industry and civilian industry, pertains not so much to organisation, profit margins, cost efficiency, or technology, as to the nature of output itself. Armaments are neither consumer goods (if they are 'goods' at all) in the conventional sense,[3] nor investment goods; as Melman (1971) writes, one can neither live in, wear, or ride a missile or bomb – neither can we employ it to produce further goods and services. Melman argues that the growth of this sector can be treated as *'parasitic'* growth, whose full economic cost is the *double measure* of resources actually used up and the productive use-value foregone (opportunity cost). On this basis, he reckons that the $1,100 billion military outlay between the years 1945–70 actually cost the nation something closer to $2,200 billion, or an amount equivalent to the *total value of the reproducible wealth of the nation*, excluding land. And this, quite apart from other collateral effects, both moral and material: from inflation to *militarism* as a way of cultural expression. Aside from the moral effects, the interesting fact is that Melman raises a substantive issue that has been all but forgotten since Smith and Marx: the distinction between *productive and unproductive* expenditures, an issue germane, if not always determinate, to the question of growth and accumulation.

Arms as 'Output': Nature, Impact

For Smith, the process of accumulation was intimately related to this important distinction:

> There is one sort of labour which adds to the value of the subject upon which it is bestowed; there is another way which has no such effect. The former, as it produces a value may be called productive; the latter, unproductive labour (Smith, 1970, pp. 429–30).

Expenditures on domestic retainers, public retainers (state), and armies, retard accumulation, in this scheme, by withdrawing potentially productive workers from the accumulation process. For Smith, the labour that adds to value by producing material (and necessary) goods was productive labour. With Marx, there is a modification of the notion; the 'materiality' criterion is dropped, so services, too, may be brought under the 'productive' category. Productive labour, quite simply, is that which produces 'surplus' value:

> That labour alone is productive, who produces surplus value for the capitalist (Marx, 1961, p. 509).

Also labour could be necessary, without being productive, such as labour engaged in the sphere of circulation, for instance. So, productive labour is labour engaged with capital (not 'revenue'), and producing a useful commodity. The diagram makes clear:[4]

	Labour producing use value	Labour producing use value
Labour producing surplus value	Production workers in industry, services	–
Labour not producing surplus value	Unproductive workers, state employees, etc.	Circulation workers

Now, to add to Marx's departmental schema. As is well known, by making the distinction between department I, producer goods, department II, consumer goods, and department III, luxury goods (arms included), and setting the requirements of macro balance (with uniform rates of profit and wages) it may be shown, *with suitable assumptions*, that the output of department III *does not enter into the reproduction scheme* (something true for neo-Ricardian, Sraffian models also). Thus, department III, apparently, only functions as a means of 'absorption' of surplus capital. Is this then the 'function' of armaments in capitalism? Certainly, this comes close to Melman's view. But whether this production constitutes a 'drag' on economic growth is quite another question. And how would capitalism be affected if such an 'absorption' industry were not available?

However, the matter cannot rest there. Since production in the arms industry is carried out under the stewardship of private capital, no less than in civilian production, the labour involved in such production is not necessarily 'unproductive' (i.e. it does produce surplus value), as per Marx's own definition. The following diagram serves as illustration:

	Departments I and II	Department III
Labour producing surplus value	Productive labour	Productive labour
Labour not producing surplus value	Unproductive labour	Unproductive labour

There is an apparent contradiction; for, while the labour is *productive* (implying that surplus value is produced) in department III, the output does not re-enter the cycle of production as input, i.e. as *accumulation*. So '*necessary*' output is distinguished by separating departments I and II from department III, while productive labour produces surplus value *regardless of where it is applied*. So, while profit rates are affected by the output of department III, overall growth remains unaffected. Is this then the effect of armaments? But aren't profit rates linked to growth? *Does the theory of exploitation then, differ from a theory of growth?*[5]

The fact that the principal buyer is the state introduces a further element of complexity (and confusion) into an assessment of the economic impact of this sector. If state expenditures are financed out of wages, then government purchases would truly make possible a net increase in investable surplus for the economy as a whole. However, should state purchases be financed exclusively out of profits, as was the classical assumption (especially with Ricardo), with the premise of an irreducible wage, then the excess profits of the arms sector are merely a '*deduction*' from profits elsewhere. If, as might more likely be the case, the state draws revenues from both wages and profits, the issue gets substantially more fuzzy, with the net effect a function of the relative weight of each tendency. Also, the specific mode of public deficit financing, whether taxation or borrowing (and, with the category of 'borrowing', between 'debt'-financing and 'money'-financing) will carry differing implications, not merely for the investable surplus but also for inflation, interest rates, consumption, etc. The argument that state purchases detract from surplus value brings radical/Marxist thinking close to neoclassical speculations as to the size of the budget imposing an impediment to capitalist growth. Thus, for Mattick (1969), as much as for Friedman, the state, in this form, becomes the vehicle for the destruction of the market economy.

To review Marxian analysis of the arms economy further. For Kidron, the 'permanent arms economy' is the expedient to stave off the crisis of *overproduction*, with the arms industry draining surplus capital and expending it unproductively:

> In so far as capital is taxed to sustain expenditure on arms ... it is deprived of further investment; in so far as expenditure on arms is expenditure on a fast-wasting end-product it constitutes a net-addition to the market for 'end' goods ... one obvious result is high employment, and ... rates of growth amongst the highest ever ... their production has no effect on profit rates overall (Kidron, 1968, p. 49).

The arms industry is a stabilising force, for Kidron; and, the high employment (but is high employment – full employment – consistent with 'capitalist' objectives in the first place?) it generates is conducive to economic growth. But profit rates are unaffected because, he argues, department III does not enter into a determination of the overall profit rate (which is actually the neo-Ricardian/Sraffian *obverse* of the 'Marxian' thesis of departmental schemes and productive/unproductive labour). For Kidron, armaments production affects growth positively, and profits not at all; and it is a permanent 'offset to the tendency of the rate of profit to fall'. But how, then, does arms production (department III) sustain growth if it is irrelevant to the reproduction of the system?; only because of the high employment it generates!

For Mandel (1970), on the other hand, arms expenditures fuel technological innovation, thus rasing capital intensity not merely in department III, but, through spin-offs, across the economy, thus affecting profit rates and employment adversely. While conceived as a means to offset the negative effects of accumulation on the 'organic composition' of capital – and hence the falling rate of profits – the arms sector actually enhances this eventually, because capital intensity in department III is unlikely to be less than in the others. However, by prompting inflation and increased taxation out of wages (arms production is financed out of the profits of department II and wages), this sector is seen as arresting this very decline. So the effect is, in fact, contradictory. Mandel provides two conditions necessary for the arms sector to offset the declining rate of profit: a) department III needs to be less capital-intensive than departments I and II; and b) if department III makes possible a permanent increase in surplus value. Neither of these conditions is possible, he maintains. But there is possibly an error in b): for arms, thanks to state purchases, are capable of being sold at prices higher than their 'values', making for *super-profits*, which could raise the rate of profit overall. The issue overlooks, of course, the question of how the state *finances* its purchases. Contrary to Kidron, Mandel argues, consistently within the general Marxian schema, that the production of surplus value in department III *does* affect the overall profit rate. As he puts it:

> When they produce dum-dum bullets, opium or pornographic novels, workers create new value, since these commodities possess a use value ... which enables them to realise their exchange value (Mandel, 1970, p. 191).

And, in another work:

> The social rate of profit thus depends on the total mass of unpaid labour – surplus labour – set in motion by the production of commodities by social capital, irrespective of the sector in which this occurs (Mandel, 1978, p. 292).

And, importantly, Mandel notes that not all 'capitals' are pleased with the arms economy to the extent that some of them have to foot part of the bill (Mandel identifies the *'losers'* as department III capitalists). Thus the arms economy accentuates internal contradictions – tensions – within the dominant constellation of industrial interests. However, in Mandel's overall scheme, the question does arise as to how Marxian value theory and/or departmental schemes, *with the special assumptions they carry,* suffice to explain an area of monopoly and state directive. Baran and Sweezy, in their famous *Monopoly Capital,* in fact, break with orthodox Marxists on precisely these grounds. In any case, there is some confusion in the fact that, despite being unable to solve either the 'realisation' crisis, or the 'falling rate of profit' crisis, the sector is still seen as having contributed to 'accelerated accumulation'.

For Baran and Sweezy (1968), the arms economy is situated in the province of the 'absorption' of the ever-increasing surplus created by monopoly capital; but the effort is ultimately a failure because of several related reasons. First, high employment in this sector is ruled out by the fact of high technology and capital intensity; expansion is also difficult given the obstacles posed by the emergence of bottlenecks in the supply of highly skilled manpower. Further, the super-profits generated in this industry are seen as leaving unaffected the overall levels of investment in the non-military sectors. And, finally, the spin-offs from arms technology into civilian industry tend to aggravate unemployment. Obviously, there is much here that is similar to liberal-Left Keynesian ideas on the subject. However, a careful reading of *Monopoly Capital* conveys the impression that arms production both soaks up the surplus *and* recreates it, so the net effect is unknown. A permanent solution to a permanent problem?! At any rate, the 'absorption of surplus' idea is an important one, common as it is to Kidron, Mandel and Baran–Sweezy. But on the question of the impact of arms production on growth and profit rates, their arguments are fuzzy, inconsistent, and even contradictory.

The critical question, in Marxian and neo-Marxian analysis of the arms sector, is the role it plays vis-à-vis the 'realisation' crisis, and its ability to arrest the falling rate of profit; in the first, the employment and demand stimulating aspects need to be reviewed; and, in the second, the effects of the expansion of the arms industry on technology, *capital intensity*, and profits. For Kidron, the arms economy almost succeeds in both stabilisation and growth; for Mandel, it is growth accentuated by *instability*. For Sweezy, it is a welcome, albeit temporary, drain of the 'surplus'. A caveat; thus far, we have looked at the arms industry through the experience of the United States, i.e. with *private production* (for the most part), and *public consumption*, as the rule. It would be a different analysis, largely, in the case of the state as the *direct producer*, especially if production were to be financed through sales receipts, and not through public funds in the routine tax-, money-, debt-financing triad. In such a case, the state would be functioning, in Marxist analysis, as a '*collective capitalist*', both extracting and realising surplus value, thus directly aiding both accumulation and profits. While not impossible, this situation is unlikely to be welcomed by private capitals, even if the budgetary incidence situation proved more favourable to them in this context.

The radicals, then, seem to ask the right questions, even if their answers are less than satisfactory and, in addition, quite inconclusive. Actually, the strength of the radical analysis is not so much that economic problems are conceived holistically, as that they are not conceived as 'economic' problems, pure and simple. It is in the political analysis, then, that this approach yields more fruitful hypotheses. And, perhaps more so than any other province, the arms sector is deserving of this type of consideration.

Arms and Militarism: Politics, History

Why does the arms sector receive such generous state attention? The reasons, at least for capitalism, are *both* historical and structural-functional. The historical factors have been examined in large volumes; and, on this score at least, the radical theories have provided powerful explanatory schema that conventional theory cannot convincingly set aside. Beginning with the dynastic wars of late feudalism, and through the era of classic colonialism that followed, the arms industry was, both in size and employment, as significant as any major civilian enterprise. In Britain, for instance, naval productions and armaments were among the earliest large-scale undertakings, whether by private or public custodians. The correlation of such expenditures with the national debt (in fact even the very *inception* of the instrument of the national debt was related to the need to finance war expenditures) and deficit financing, is also an institutional fact of the late eighteenth and early nineteenth centuries.

The quest for securing and protecting markets, clearly underlying the age of modern imperialism, and the need for capital exports, given the rising surplus domestically (especially in the case of England), made for the expanded production of armaments in the early twentieth century, in spite of the legacy of Ricardian and post-Ricardian (neoclassicist) distrust of state expenditures generally. That 'security' was more important than 'opulence', as Smith had maintained, seemed obvious to policy makers – especially when one was the condition for the other, as in the case of assuring security for one's own colonial or neo-colonial markets. To put it briefly, to the extent that capitalism is a system dependent internationally on the expansion of markets, the 'imperialist', or simply 'policing', aspect follows quite naturally; and there need be little controversy over this. High theory apart, the average reader of newspapers – far shrewder in these matters than the dull economist – might surmise as much.

Putting aside the issue of imperialism, there are other factors deriving from the political economy of capitalism that make for the renewed expansion of, or at least the continued support for, this industry. Here, Reich's (1978) paper provides a useful, if conventional, 'Marxian-Keynesian' analysis. In his rendering, firstly, it is insufficient aggregate demand dating from the '50s – after the conclusion of second world war hostilities – that called for a *special stimulus*: hence growth rates, in the US, might have been lower but for arms, military, and defence expenditures. Secondly, the arms economy was chosen as the appropriate instrument because of the high preference enjoyed by the sector in a capitalist economy: it is highly profitable and, hence, attractive to corporations; also, defence 'needs' being anybody's guess, production can be indefinitely expanded; finally, similar spending on large-scale social expenditures would only undermine profitability, with the state competing with private capital, and weakening traditional work 'incentives', while also leading to a widespread questioning of the enshrined legitimacy of the private economy and profit-oriented production.

With Galbraith (1969), on the other hand, the 'military' industrial complex' takes on a new life and purpose of its own, for such is the logic of '*bureaucracy*'. His explanation revolves around the following factors. First, it is the self-serving nature of the bureaucracy itself – called into being by the technological complexity of modern society – ever seeking to expand its own power and influence. Second, the community bogey, kept alive by cold war rhetoric (along this logic, some other bogey would now need rapid invention: perhaps the 'Islamic threat'?), allowed for an unprecedented delegation of power to the military interest, along with a high concentration of skilled personnel serving it. Third, the secrecy shrouding the 'defence' effort helped to keep all matters tightly within the purview of the private and public bureaucracy, with outside opinion simply uninformed about (and excluded from) the logic of these issues. Fourth, the rise of an all-purpose hegemony of fear-psychology silenced all but a few honest (and doubting) critics. And finally, the lack of prominence of other factors in the national life, such as race, poverty, inflation, etc., *at the time of the creation of the complex*, enabled it to sail on unhampered by any considerations of the social opportunity costs of such expenditures. Thus arms spending is a self-justifying policy promoted by a self-serving Pentagon-state-corporate apparatus. And this is a point that may usefully be tagged on to the Reich analysis.

Melman (1970), for his part, is equally sociologically-oriented, approaching the military-industrial complex by means of C. Wright Mill's famous theory of the *power elite*. For Mill, the elite was built around a tripartite system of ruling strata, based on economic, military, and political structures. For Melman, it is the new '*state-managerial*' elite, located within the military machine itself, that dominates the system. By contrast, in radical, particularly *Marxian* theory, the capitalist ruling class (representing, usually, industrial capital as the *hegemonic* capital) ultimately constrains all other elites within the system, through the state apparatus, which is only '*relatively*' autonomous. For Melman and Galbraith, therefore, despite many useful insights (such as the 'ascendancy' of the military in the age of the cold war), the MIC[6] is divorced from both the larger historical, and structural, causality. The implication follows that such 'aberrations', possibly only temporary, can be set right without altering any of the institutional premises of capitalism. The empirical truth of this, of course remains to be established; theoretically, however, the schema is weaker, especially if it is applied to the earlier phases in the history of capitalist arms production – and a 'theory' that is empirically so specific is possibly not a very useful 'theory' at all. On the other hand, the Reich perspective stands to gain a much-needed perspective with the inclusion of such factors within its own causal schema.

The MIC is an unnecessarily elaborate designation, whose rhetorical value surpasses its explanatory power. To the extent that military production is industrial production, such a 'complex', large or small, possibly exists wherever a military capability of the indigenous kind exists. Needless to add, the sheer size of the US economy gives the term a specially awesome respectability. However, from what one knows of the history of capitalism and the imperialism specific to it, no structural transformation of the economy has resulted from this process nearly as significant as the turn of the century emergence of monopoly (or *oligopoly*, in more fastidious usage) as the dominant form of industrial organisation. The logic of capitalist growth has not been modified by the emergence of this organisational construct (i.e. the MIC); and, if at all, it has probably only reinforced it, with all its conventional contradictions. So the MIC will simply not do as an explanatory variable; rather, *it is the fact to be explained*.

The Arms Industry: 'Reformed'?

Those, like Melman (1970), who view with alarm the structure of the arms industry (by examining concentration ratios, monopolistic structures, etc.)

are making the error of viewing these developments as though they were unique to this sector, instead of being, as they are, the constitutive trend of *all* industry since the inception of this century. The rise of monopoly, and corporate planning (within, of course, an *overall planlessness*), predates the defence industry, obviously. The arms industry, as the major sector within overall industry (providing, now, close to *50 per cent of net capital formation worldwide!*), merely took on the stamp of the preexisting dominant structures of the economy as a whole, rather than contributing something new of its own. Or, to put it differently, it is unlikely that 'waste' can be reduced by simply legislating a 'competitive' structure in this industry ('cost efficiency' will probably only lead to increased profits in the sector, given the nature of the 'demand' side of the problem), if such an action were possible at all. While efficiency in the arms industry may be desired on marginal welfare grounds, and is a good stick to beat the military with, in terms of *political economy* the concern is at best misplaced.

For one thing the structure of the arms industry is more 'demand inspired' than otherwise; for another, even monopolies are capable of producing some efficiencies; and finally it is far from clear that the resources thus 'released' will ever actually be put to 'good' economic use. It is highly unlikely that the present rate of unemployment prevailing in the US is entirely due to the wasteful diversion of resources to arms production (for the 'transfer' effects of competitive efficiency assumes full employment, mobility of resources, no wage-price rigidities, and other such neoclassicist fantasies). More to the point is the *logic of the capitalist investment process, driven by profit not employment generation*, whether viewed through the lens of a Marx, Keynes or a Kalecki.

Even standard theorists have emphasized the 'impossibility' of a market system in the arms industry, not so much due to issues of political economy as due to purely economic factors. Peck and Scherer (1962) argue that a market system can 'never exist' because of:

a) the sheer scale of expenditures involved;

b) the 'unique' uncertainties due to risk of obsolescence, changes in strategic planning, and 'unforeseen' technical difficulties;

c) the 'problem' of determining the product characteristics demanded by the buyer; and

d) the problem of setting price in the context of the monopsony vesting in government.

Actually, their conclusions may be true, but for institutional factors quite apart from their putative 'reasons' which are far from convincing. The 'scale of expenditures' is a poor argument when measured against the resources of the giant corporations of today; and the natures of 'uncertainties' in different industries are each likely to be unique, such as, e.g., the oil industry. Similarly, the risk of a change in government policy affects every corporation that invests overseas (and even domestically); and 'product characteristics' demanded by the buyer is a problem that is 'solved' every day in the civilian market, being part and parcel of the entrepreneurial function itself. Finally, monopsony is not such an unusual market situation (it is curious, but instructive, that Peck and Scherer list as 'problems' precisely some of the tasks that those who glorify private enterprise would see as well within the normal capacity of the market system). Rather, the real reason is that this industry is considered too vital to national security to leave to the machinations of the profit motive, unreliable as it is, alone; and, as such, state regulation stands in little need of 'economic' explanations and/or justification.

The Arms Industry: 'Converted'?

The issue of 'conversion' capability is often raised (particularly now in the aftermath of Soviet collapse), the biblical yearning for beating swords into ploughshares being apparently, at least nominally, with us all. There are two issues here that need to be separated. To examine first, the economic feasibility, and second, the political feasibility: as Melman points out, conversion is different from '*reconversion*' such as happened after the war when corporations simply returned to the civilian market at the conclusion of the war effort. However, the new situation is one of a corporate expertise that has, from the start, been devoted to military production. Can such technology-intensive specialist industries find suitable civilian avenues of investment? And, besides, how will the sheer numbers released from military production be absorbed productively? Melman rates the task difficult as things stand, without a new Marshall Plan declaring war on poverty and raising the incomes of the bottom 20 per cent. For firms exclusively involved in arms production, as distinct from those which are offshoots of parent civilian corporations, he judges the 'conversion' capability well-nigh impossible. And the costs of conversion (in a full employment, optimal distribution of income context) he reckons would probably run even higher than average defence allocations annually ($100 billion at the time he was writing (1971) as against an annual average of about $80 billion since).

As with Melman, Messrs Leontief and Hoffenberg show some initial strain on the economy with a sudden cut in military expenditures (each $100 million cut in the DOD budget leading to about 2,000 workers idled in civilian employ, and over 6,000 in the uniformed forces), with the immediate change in employment negative. And, needless to add, industries heavily involved in military contracts, such as electronics, would be hit particularly severely. Also, to the extent that high technology has been an item of military patronage, the short term slow-down in innovation might affect the trade balance adversely (in context of the open economy) given existing deficits in balance of payments, competitive efficiency problems vis-à-vis the Japanese (auto, electronics, etc.), and so on. Such economic conjecturing, whether with the sophistication of input-output models à la Leontief, or merely on the basis of informed opinion, can be endlessly confusing, varying with the *choice of assumptions* (the bane of economics as a 'science', of course).

The political issue, however, is more finite in its logic. To put it simply, given the will and the right focus in expenditures, the '*conversion*', while not without complications and adjustments, is more than possible (just as much as the sudden collapse of the Soviet Union was, contrary to the conventional wisdom of the pundits, right or left). But, given the current correlations of forces, with the institutional and historical factors in mind, such a transition is improbable, at least within radical conjectures, without a fundamental and structural change in the logic of capitalism (and/or a rise in the strength of *anticapitalist forces* within capitalism). And, given historical trends in US defence budgets, this might seems a relatively safe venture in hypothesizing.

Arms Industry: Functions?

Regardless of how the arms industry originated, in a structural-functional sense, the enlightened policy maker can readily see the following functions potentially given in the military budget. First, and not necessarily in order of importance, it is a relatively immune avenue of expansion of bureaucratic power and influence (the expansion of military budgets being synchronous with the expansion of officialdom and its sphere of venality, graft, and corruption); second, as a form of Keynesianism ('*military Keynesianism*'), bolstering key demand in critical manufacturing industries, and placing a rising floor under the traditional business cycle when more conventional stabilizing expenditures are impermissible, as with the present ascendancy of the new mood of free-market ideology. Third, and this is only marginally separable from the second, by subsidising private investment and 'socialising' costs through outright gifts of production facilities, R & D grants, and the like. Fourth, by virtue of all of the foregoing, shoring up profitability when high interest rates, and/or low marginal efficiencies of investment, lead to a slump in anticipated profits. Fifth, the potential output and employment effects, both primary and secondary. Sixth, the clear payoff in the development of high technology necessary as international competition intensifies in major industries. Seventh, its function as a counterweight to 'progressive' income distribution implicit in social services expenditures. The fact that these, and other, functions may seem to be logically suggested (despite their internal contradictions) is not to imply that they are the *real* impulse for such expenditures; for, politically, and this would be a fact uppermost in radical analysis, the need for a defence (and offence) capability second to none follows (for the 'leader' of world capitalism) rather routinely from the nature of capitalist imperialism as we have known it in this century. The defence of opulence is only possible through enhanced policing of all sources of potential, and actual, supply and demand.

Arms and 'Surplus' Capital?

In one important respect, the history of capitalism presents analogies that one should not ignore. In the second half of the nineteenth century, one avenue of investment alone accounted for 40–50 per cent of total private capital formation: *railways*. By the first decade of the twentieth century, this area appeared saturated. Between the second and third decades of this century, the automobile utilised capacity – squandering resources, and polluting the environment, spectacularly – similarly, and, after the interruption of the war, resumed that role from the '40s on, alongside a robust sibling who matured rapidly with the years. And today, expenditures on armaments approach, and possibly even exceed, the proportion of net capital formation achieved by the railways years ago. The issue suggests itself readily: is surplus capital the real problem?

Of course, such a poser would link it with theories as old as Hobson's and Lenin's. But there is an immediate difference: railways were a necessary, infrastructural, *productive* investment. And the automobile, to the extent it replaced the railway as a mode of transportation is (together with the entire baggage of ancillary industries allied to it), though nominally a consumer durable, was perhaps similarly placed. In any case, its use value, within the logic of things as they are, is obvious. But armaments do not exhibit, readily, any such characteristics. In the case of both railways and the automobile, the state was not (at least with US facts in mind) the exclusive, or even semi-exclusive, customer. If arms are considered the current equivalent of railways and automobiles (and military production is the largest business in the US today), then one would have to grant that both productive and wasteful 'utilisation' of surplus capital are consistent with capitalist 'requirements'. Is this possible?

To pursue the idea: if *productive* utilisation of surplus only reproduces the problem of a growing surplus, as for instance Baran and Sweezy suggest, then the railways and the automobiles only renew the crisis in ever-expanding fashion. One might then speculate that, by fluke!, capitalism has now found a solution consistent with almost all its special requirements, with arms siphoning off surplus into '*dead-end*' stockpiles. As with Keynes, spectacular 'hole-filling', in a purely economic sense; and, better still, with a political fallout consistent with the norms of private enterprise. Upon this premise, one might hypothesize that the arms industry, or rather, arms production, will grow proportionately, give or take political irrationalities, with the growth of productive capacity, or even the GNP. Sample data – if reliable at all – between 1969–83 did show such a positive correlation between arms procurement and the GNP. Naturally, this is too simple to be true, except fortuitously; for, if arms are substituting for other traditional outlets now, other forms of substitution are possible in the future. Space exploration? Possibly, but perhaps with fewer capitalist virtues than arms.

In this context, one might consider Rosa Luxemburg's thesis (1968) that capitalism requires a *non-capitalist environment* in which to expand, so that with the closing of the frontier of the '*peasant*' economies, one way or other, the more conventional area for the export of capital is choked off. If so, then domestic arms accumulation is the internal *equivalent* of traditional arms export. This hypothesis might be tested by seeing the correlation between growth of armament expenditures and increasing worldwide 'protectionism'; if this holds good, together with a trend towards militant Third World regimes (far from the norm at the current time), then one might argue the case for a quasi-permanent arms economy not because of imperialism per se, but, paradoxically, because of the failure of more conventional forms of economic imperialism.

Empirical Tests?

There is much data on the opportunity costs of arms spending generally, and its sub-sectoral effects on other components of the GNP, but the feeling is inescapable that detailed empirical analyses of the industry, while highly informative in their own right, do little by way of answering the question of the impact on the economy at large – unless the dynamics of the functioning of the capitalist economy are satisfactorily explained in theory (i.e. in some satisfactory 'causal' sense). That is to say, the same data acquire different meaning in the context of different schools of thought. As a simple example, the *composition* of output is not a specially significant variable in neo-classical-Keynesian synthetics (except for the division between investment and consumption goods); as with Bentham, 'pushpin is as good as poetry'. But, in both classical economic theory, and in its Marxian variant, the issue of composition is critical to the accumulation process and stability, as just seen in the instance of the problem of 'state' expenditures. Besides, even if this were not a significant issue, *data are often incomparable, more often contradictory, and always volatile*: strong theoretical schemes cannot derive from data, in a simple fashion, while they certainly can lean on them, heavily or lightly, for support and substantiation. As in the Popperian scheme, it is as though data is better employed to contradict (received) theory than to construct it.

This is not to say sub-sectoral, and hence non-theoretical, questions cannot be usefully asked in an empirical context, such as the nature of the industrial structure, the nature of technologies employed, the rate of technological innovation, etc., which provide empirical information that is *specific*. However, the theory of the system cannot build on these 'microchips', for as has been emphasized, *the dynamics of the system are not internal to any one sector alone*, and least of all to the arms sector. So, to generalise current trends in empirical relations into 'theory' is probably foolhardy.

Economic Impact: Mainstream Perspectives

In more standard analysis, liberal-Keynesian or otherwise, the arguments are a lot simpler, eschewing institutional depth, and relying heavily on casual empirical tests. The 'theory' offered by Lester Thurow (1983), for instance, in a favourable introduction to a recent 'empirical' analysis, is astonishingly *simpliste* – to quote:

> All societies must set spending limits on current consumption, defense and non-defense ... If defense spending must go up, then private consumption must come down ... If we pay for defense by drawing the funds out of physical investment, civilian research, and development, or educating and training our labor force, we then will be undercutting the long run survivability of the very economy that we need to sustain defense spending ... Traditionally, 'spinoffs' have been suggested as compensating benefits to the costs of military expenditures ... But there is reason to believe that whatever the degree of 'spinoffs' in the past, they are fewer now ... Military hardware, as it increasingly moves into space, simply has requirements so specialised that there is little commercial applicability.

And the empirical study in question, in the same vein, confirms these ideas. The findings are as follows. One, industries selling to the Pentagon (and this must apply with particular force to the 'arms' industry) create fewer jobs per dollar than the average civilian industry (the three largest Pentagon contractors created fewer direct and indirect jobs than the median manufacturing industry: thereby a reduction in military spending creates more jobs overall in the economy). Two, the high reliance on highly skilled employees (four of the top five Pentagon contractors had a lower percentage of production workers than the average in manufacturing) creates scarcity in this elite stratum in the labour force, thus fuelling inflationary pressures – besides drawing away scarce talent from the civilian industry, far more vulnerable as it is to international competitive pressures. Three, the high degree of regional concentration (five states received 45 per cent of all awards; 10 states, 65 per cent of all awards), and the high degree of industrial concentration (10 industries accounting for 75 per cent of DOD purchases) in manufacturing, leads to the hypothesis that the national economy as a whole would not be hurt severely by reductions in defence spending.

Indeed, the same study maintains that, despite the fact that, in the '60s and '70s, close to 25–30 per cent of scientists and engineers worked for the DOD, with the Pentagon spending close to 40 per cent of all R & D funds, public or private, the spinoffs, if any, did little to enhance America's high technology industries which steadily lost ground to European and Japanese competition. The 'seeding' effect, apparently, had been less than an outstanding success, in technology. In fact, paradoxically, the very industries most heavily involved in defence contracting showed signs of losing ground in international competition, such as aircraft, electronics, and machine tools. And this, in spite of the US *spending more on R & D than France, West Germany, and Japan combined*. The costs of militarisation of R & D expenditures have, in this view, apparently outweighed the spin-off benefits. The study suggests that the constraint of *specific applications* posed by military research makes for less productive research than basic research carried out 'openly' in the private economy. Additionally, the irrelevance of cost vis-à-vis performance in the military makes for items which, despite ultra sophistication, are commercially simply inapplicable (the Anglo-French SST being a case in point). And finally, it is argued that since over 80 per cent of Pentagon contracts go to large manufacturers, the innovative aspects of small enterprises remain largely untapped.

The economic risks of expanded military spending are seen as reduced investment and growth in the face of higher budget deficits and rising interest rates, and restrictive monetary policies. The balance of trade is also seen as adversely affected with a higher scale of imports becoming necessary of strategic metals (chromium, titanium, etc.) and reduced competitiveness following upon the withdrawal of highly-skilled talent from civilian high-technology goods. The hypothesis then follows that a nation that spends a larger share of its GNP on weapons and soldiers will experience less investment and productivity growth than those that spend less (significantly, however, *inflation and unemployment were not found correlated with military spending*).

Another interesting finding, in the same study, is that civilian spending (by government), contrary to neoclassical and 'monetarist' views, did not correlate with poorer economic performance. Given the fact that most of such spending was on infrastructural items, such as education, transportation, sanitation, etc., this should not occasion surprise. The second explanation offered is that such spending directly bolsters private consumption, thereby boosting aggregate demand. So a 'switch' to a civilian-industrial complex, if politically conceivable, would not arrest capitalist growth (at least as far as the data in question goes) in the manner of theorising amongst some neoclassicists and Marxists. Finally, the study showed a positive correlation between military spending and consumption, but a negative one between military spending and investment. So the composition of aggregate demand is apparently affected differentially by the military budget. In terms of a political economy, shall we then say that the military budget is more of an offset to underconsumption than to surplus capital? *Only if one mistook correlations for causal relationships, and claimed just one set of data as sufficient to establish the relevant hypotheses.*

While one might accept most of these as provisional hypotheses – at least on the basis of the evidence submitted – the key problem that remains at the level of theory, an issue of political economy, is whether expenditures withdrawn from military applications would have been transferred 'automatically' to private investment. In fact this is not a novel argument, since Keynes himself posed the sluggishness of private investment activity at the core of his macro economics. To put it another way, if the arms economy is the 'solution', within capitalism, for the very problem of slow investment activity, then to see it as the causal agent accounting for the latter is a curious reversal of logic. Actually, however, the paradox can be resolved by recourse to a conventional piece of radical wisdom: *that attempted piecemeal 'solutions' to the contradictions of capitalism, and private enterprise, create even deeper problems. Armaments and military spending, then, are simply an irrational solution to an even more irrational system.*

Most of the foregoing applied to military spending, and one might want to separate the arms industry as not qualifying for the same status but, in point of fact, the fit is quite close. With the defence industry as a whole, the arms industry shares definite similarities. For one, it is equally, if not more, capital-intensive in its operations; the degree of industrial concentration is perhaps even greater than defence contractors at large; the reliance on highly skilled labour (fewer production workers than ordinary manufacturing industries) is just as high; the regional dispersion shows a similar skew; the reliance on Pentagon contracts is probably even greater; and the degree of technological intensity no less than other defence contractors in manufacturing. While empirically and analytically separable from the defence industry, therefore, the economic impact in the *macro* sense, *qualitatively*, is practically identical to the impact of the military budget (though quantitatively smaller, being only a component of the whole).

But even standard analysis is rent with contradictions, and rather different ideas prevail in the paper by Emile Benoit (1968), who argues that the civilian opportunity costs may be less than the cost of defence, as measured in terms of *market value*. That is to say, military production, far from competing with civilian production for scarce resources, actually indirectly or directly *contributes* to it. The factors Benoit mentions are several. First, and foremost, military production provides:

> The foundations for internal and international security and confidence without which civilian production would falter, and ultimately stop.

This, of course, is what I have termed pragmatic 'political economy', pure and simple. Second, Benoit argues, there are categories of defence spending that add to the productivity of resources later used in the civilian economy, providing goods and services for civilian use, and replacing goods and services that the civilian economy would otherwise have to provide for itself. The examples given are the education of soldiers, the imparting of specialist skills – radio repair, e.g. – of application in the civilian economy, and the provision of airfields and communications networks for concurrent, or later, use in non-defence activities. Additionally, he points out that R & D expenditures can, ultimately, serve the overall economy. So, cutting such defence activity would reduce output by more than the resources released from military use. And all this, of course, goes against the grain of liberal analysis, in the line of Thurow, De Grasse, etc. It is far from clear, however, why such activities could not be provided by a civilian economy for itself, and by itself, possibly even cheaper than via military conduits. But the first argument, concerning a world *'made safe'* for capitalism (if not for anyone else!) is, naturally, the more compelling one. And also these arguments are possibly not wholly transferable from military spending to arms expenditures, whose specialisation yields fewer benefits to civilian industry, specially when set off against the high costs involved.

Administration economists, not far apart from Benoit, needless to say, take a more sanguine view of the matter. Thus, the authors of the *Annual Report of the Council of Economic Advisers* (1982) say that concern over the economic impact of defence spending 'has probably been overstated'. They see the defence budget as economically bearable, barring a few odd strains here and there. They anticipate 'three results' which they deem important. One, the transfer of resources in durable industries to military production may increase relative prices in some of the affected industries. Two, the increased demand might, expectedly, lead to lengthened delivery time. And three, some 'temporary' crowding out of private investment might be expected to result. All these minor frictions are seen as providing a 'challenge' to Department of Defense administrators – but nothing that 'careful planning' could not manage and control. The economy is capable of accommodating the budget 'without experiencing an increase in the general inflation rate'; and that is the extent of the sage 'economic analysis'.

One point (a digression) is usefully raised by the Economic Advisers' *Report*, however: the question of *inflation via military procurement* which remains unsatisfactorily analysed by both mainstream and radical traditions. Standard theorists see inflation, in this connection, from the '*input*' side, i.e. inflationary pressures arising from increased demand for scarce resources (pushing up resource prices) fuelled by defence procurement. However, less often is the connection made on the *output* side: that is the fact that the outputs of military production, say armaments, 'disappear' from the market even though the purchasing power (from wages and profits which are spent in the civilian economy) enters the general market for goods and services. In a slack economy this, of course, should raise demand and output; in a tighter market situation, however, this *demand push* can have significant inflationary potential. From a radical perspective, it would appear that the 'cost' of solving the underconsumption problem is inflation (i.e. one of the cures for the 'realisation' issue), to the extent that the solution takes the form of armaments production. And this effect might be compounded if the armaments were financed through deficit financing taking the form of 'money' financing. But the *armaments-to-inflation* hypothesis needs a fuller specification of the mechanisms involved than seems available at present in existing theory.

Where there is a logical position open on any issue, inevitably there is the provocation for theory (or, 'theorising'). If Thurow (and De Grasse) and Benoit are positioned at the extremities, there is always the large, empty, inviting, middle (muddle?), and, accordingly, we find Roger Bolton (1966) arguing for the *duality* of military spending as both 'burden' and 'prop' – in different regards, the military budget is both stimulant and depressant. But which prevails, in the net? This is hard to specify, for again, mainstream theory is ambivalent. Are the counterforces of depressant and stimulant empirically capable of resolution either way? If so, then in one context it might be negative, in another positive: *the truth, in other words, is a contextual matter*. But theory is quite powerless to trace a clear direction. And where theory is impotent, tendentious arguments become powerful. 'Analysis' then only confirms stances arrived at quite independently of it.

Conclusion: Inconclusive Theory

I have reviewed, lightly, some of the issues raised in mainstream, and heterodox, writings on the question of military spending and arms production under capitalism, specially with respect to the problem of growth. Not only is there little consensus on the nature of the impact of this sector on such activities, there is even less agreement on the variables that supposedly enter into such an evaluation. All schools of economic thought can gain by a more careful specification of the relationships judged fundamental to a proper analysis, and placed in a form that is capable of being challenged (empirically) and refuted, for theoretical clarity is indispensable to any knowledgeable discussion. Indeed it may not be that existing theory is structurally deficient; rather that a *full specification* (without ambiguity and equivocation) of the implications of a schema (Keynesian, Marxian, etc.) has not yet been attempted, with any degree of care for internal consistency. Perhaps it is the *political overdetermination* of analysis, rather than want of scholarship, that is at fault; if so, the prognosis for theoretical improvement is bleak and economics will remain, as it is, *the fuzziest of all the sciences*.

To conclude: one 'finding' of this paper is that the differences *within* each theoretical tradition, mainstream or radical, over the question of the economic consequences of the arms economy are *homologous*, and there is scope for mutual agreement between otherwise opposing orientations. It is on the political function of military spending, then, that the schools are farthest apart. The strength of radical heterodoxy is that it provides a *political economy* where history, sociology, and economics fuse, without severe inconsistencies, into a powerful mode of explanation of factors both internal and exogenous to the arms economy. The self-imposed myopia of mainstream economics, on the other hand, with its sharp dichotomy between economic and non-economic factors, while useful as a heuristic device in some contexts, falters on macro issues such as this.

However, the larger truth is that *reality is a contextual affair*: grand theory, deriving from speculative assumptions, is simply inapplicable except on a random basis (i.e. by fluke). A mechanistic, deterministic view of reality – while powerfully self-fulfilling, in some respects – is quite inadequate; social 'systems' are open systems where invariant regularities simply do not obtain. Besides, human behavioural phenomena are culturally constrained; so there is no universal, technicist 'economics' that can predict anything safely and accurately. Economics needs to take cue from anthropology, or even ethnography, shunning the ridiculous physics envy that has dominated its rather impressive past. It is high time that the voyage of the *Beagle*, in economics, began in earnest, armed with the modest aim of *understanding* the bewildering diversity of economic life (rather than 'predicting' *events*, mechanically, within it).

Notes

* A version of this paper was read to the Seventh World Conference of the International Economic Association, Madrid, 5–9 September, 1983. As

such, the references to empirical data pertain to information available at the time.
1. See Kanth, 1986, for detail on this.
2. The data appearing in this section were drawn from a variety of contemporaneous sources, as of 1983.
3. Thurow, in De Grasse, Jr (1983), argues otherwise: 'From an economist's view, an MX missile is like a toaster ...' (p. 7). True: an MX could toast an awful lot of people!!
4. This, and the following diagrams, are taken from Gough, 1972.
5. As indicated, for instance, in Blake, 1958.
6. Henceforth, this will be the abbreviation for the 'military industrial complex'.

5 Sraffa, and All That: A Retrospective on Some Foibles of the Cambridge School

1

The attention of the Cambridge post-Keynesians (the few still remaining), in the mould of Lord Eatwell,[1] in recent years, has focused on an attempt to integrate a Sraffian theory of value and distribution at the micro instance with a Keynesian, albeit a modified Keynesian, theory of output and employment at the macro level – in the hope, as Eatwell writes, that such a marriage would prove a 'fruitful union'. As far as I know, this union has not yet been consummated, and even were it to be so, it would in all probability lead not so much to fusion as *confusion* (for, as will become apparent, both Sraffian micro and Keynesian macro rest on less than firm foundations), whose issue, if any, would only reproduce the weaknesses immanent in both lines of kinship. The putative post-Keynesian synthesis of Sraffa and Keynes is, I argue, a problematic matter at best, and a hopeless muddle otherwise.

Often, in this brand of syncretics, we see the unexpected recurrence of references to both Marx and the classical tradition, either with respect to theories of value, or vis-à-vis their ideas on accumulation (and I'll pretend not to notice who plays the role of *junior* partner in these enterprises), usually in the context of their being jointly juxtaposed against the neoclassicals. As indicated, the admixture of Sraffa and Keynes is heady enough; to add a dose of Marx to the compound makes of it an explosive matter producing, ultimately, quite a frothful, if mistaken, synthesis. A clarification is necessary, so we don't get a Sraffa-Keynes-Marx melange (and I think I got the order right, as intended in this discourse) to be propped up against neoclassicism in a united front – for the disparate elements simply do not blend the way it is suggested they do. And so, to start at the beginning with the micro foundations that are usually assumed to be securely established in Sraffa's[2] putatively *neo-Ricardian* analysis.

Is Sraffa a neo-Ricardian, as is commonly held, in matters of value and distribution? Fundamentally, Ricardo's distribution theory rests on diminishing returns in agriculture and Malthusian population theory, neither of which play any necessary part in Sraffa's analysis. Ricardo's net product does not contain wages, as Sraffa's obviously does. Ricardo's value theory is a labour embodied value theory, even if occasionally only 93 per cent or so, while Sraffa's is anything but. So where, one might ask, is the connection? Just one, of course; Sraffa 'solves' the problem of an *invariant standard* of value (which, while usually attributed to Ricardo, was nonetheless posed, as an issue, originally by Smith) albeit with altogether heroic assumptions (that quite approximate neoclassicism in their netherworldliness). And come to think of it, Sraffa's *surplus* is fairly identical to Smith's. Perhaps Sraffa is then – if anything – really a neo-Smithian? More so, certainly, it would seem, than he is a 'Ricardian' in any useful sense of the term.

Is Sraffa's value theory infallible? Let me juxtapose this in relation to Marx – for it is the latter's value theory that was supposedly demolished by Sraffa in the special context of *joint production* (to the mutual delight of both neoclassicists and post-Keynesians), as Steedman and Eatwell, and all of us well know; but less known perhaps is the fact that Sraffian analysis is itself quite vulnerable, in this regard also, on the following important scores, as has recently been shown. Briefly, in the same context of joint production:[3]

1   using Sraffian tables we can get negative prices using entirely plausible numbers;

2   realistic changes in the numerical models can produce violent instability;

3   reasonable alterations of parameters can also yield infinite rates of profit (since price manipulations are the key determinants of profits) if only a slight deviation from a uniform rate is allowed.

Quite evidently, then, the tables turned so skilfully against the labour theory, *using algebra alone*, à la Steedman, can now be turned back against the source, on the same terrain as that chosen by the neo-Ricardians. It doesn't pay to first bash the neoclassicals for converting a science into a technology, know-why into know-how, only to fall back, in the context of a critique of Marx, on the very same fountainhead of (a misconceived) mathematics. There are many serious, even critical, lacunae in Marx; muddled computations, on the other hand, are the very least of its sins.

And what about the neoclassicals-versus-Sraffa struggle, dubious as the battle may be? Again, the neo-Ricardians would maintain that the *reswitching* controversy brought down the neoclassical bastille (to the chagrin of the Sraffians, neoclassicism refused to lie down and expire, despite the formal correctness of their critique, an instructive primer on the persistence of paradigms) but a few clarifying comments place the matter in context. The very grounds on which the Cambridge School ridicules neoclassical theory, i.e. their use of counterfactual *assumptions*, are quite basic to the Sraffians as well – for example:

a) perfect competition – an idea rejected in post-Keynesian macro, but apparently quite kosher in Sraffian micro;

b) the notion of *equilibrium*: it recurs, in Eatwell's work, e.g. in the guise of a normal *long run level of output*, i.e. it is merely displaced from the micro to the macro domain, from short run to long run;

c) traditional supply and demand analysis, also rejected, in toto, by this school as neoclassical fantasy, is in fact explicit in Ricardo and Marx, and is *necessary and implicit* in the Sraffian system; the fallacy here is in not keeping the distinction clear between *prices of production* and *market prices*, by merely assuming their equality in 'equilibrium' – thereby defaulting on an analysis of the process by which market prices oscillate around the former.

The neoclassicals are not wrong: supply and demand (outside of state-determined price fixing) do determine market price (which is about as vacuous a statement as can be made: the *real* factors of interest are the forces that work through, and on, each blade of the Marshallian 'scissors'). Besides, neoclassical theory has another dimension never noted, or appreciated, by the Cambridge School and which remains quite unscathed by the Sraffian critique; neoclassical theory is also an *optimization* theory, a *praxiology* as Lange called it, to which post-Keynesians can add nothing, and from which they can take away even less. So, yes, the bastille may have been dented, but it is far from having been downed – although I rather suspect it was never attacked to let the prisoners out but only to re-establish a different command system over them!

2

The Cambridge School strips Keynes of practically all his ideas except *effective demand*; now Keynes, as is well known, admitted the Malthusian lineage of that concept with much affection, so let's rename this style of macro *post-Malthusian* macro, or more simply, *Malthusian* macro (to belatedly give credit where it's due). Neo-Smithian micro alongside a Malthusian macro!: somehow, it already sounds less potent, if more exotic.

But, to continue: not only is Keynes revised, in this discourse, he is told what to do, and say, post factum. I quote Eatwell:

> the crucial point is not whether Keynes actually did present a long run analysis or not; he ought to have presented such an analysis.

Now this, I submit, is gratuitous in the extreme. Keynes, owing to the grace of some higher power, was merely himself (an educated bourgeois, in his own self-perception, given to attending to practical and policy matters, and disinclined to fashion theory out of any other 'higher' impulse – traits that he shared, to a 't', with his noble predecessor, David Ricardo, equally given to 'policy-driven' theorising), and not a fashionable retroactive post-Keynesian. In short, Keynes satisfied himself with a neoclassical micro – 'Marshallian baggage', as Joan Robinson prosaically named it – and a highly *pragmatist* macro theory (which was only the ready-made rationalisation(s) for his policy initiatives, which were of far greater importance), trying to have his cake and eat it too, in time-honoured fashion: so that the so-called 'bastard Keynesians' – what an ugly phrase! – can hardly be blamed for quite simply, most of the time, reading Keynes *right*!, thereby repudiating the newfangled post-Keynesians in advance! If I may theorise: Keynes's is partly a theory, but mostly the *practice*, of achieving close to full employment with state stimulation of demand – a practical theory, in short, spawned by practical conditions (and a mighty short run theory at that). So Joan Robinson is quite right when she chides Garegnani for inappropriately imputing *long run* analysis to Keynes; to quote Robinson:[4]

> Keynes was interested only in short run problems – the long period was, for him, simply 'a subject for undergraduates'.

Yes, Keynes's theory was short run: to protect capitalism by means of state action, with a little help from *money illusion* – to permit as much employment as consistent with the liberties enjoyed by the Bloomsbury set (when Lytton Strachey, another member of that set, was asked why he was not out there fighting, in the first world war, to save civilisation, he is said to have replied, with the characteristic insouciance of the English upper crust: 'I *am* the civilisation they are fighting for.'). Short run theory, but informed with long run vision, for in the long run, we are all dead – or, indeed, worse; as seemed plausible at the time he was writing, there was a fate worse than death for his kind: 'we', just as easily, might have all ended up socialists!

To continue: the long run theory of output may well be a pet project of the Cambridge School, but it cannot be dragged out of Keynes. Indeed, the need to refer lineage back to Keynes (the modernist version of an ancient tribal form: ancestor worship!) seems so out of order when something so alien is being proposed, that I am not quite sure whether it is the bastard Keynesians or the post-Keynesians (neo-Ricardians) who bowdlerise the rather straightforward message of Keynes. The rub in this approach is a problem that was present in neoclassical theory from its inception, the effort to achieve what philosophers call complete *closure* – albeit within a logical model – in the face of a recalcitrant capitalist reality, which evolves always, apparently, just a little faster than theory. It was Keynes's unique pragmatism that disdained such efforts, and indeed 'modelled', so to speak, the very idea of *uncertainty*. To his epigones this won't do at all; in fact, Eatwell derides it as an 'imperfectionist' argument. Indeed he goes further, arguing that, compared to the idea of uncertainty, even the rational expectations models are superior, representing, in his words, a 'considerable advance'. Why so? Because once you admit uncertainty, then:

   the economy becomes bereft of any definite result.

We need to ponder this with great care, for it describes the attitude of many schools of economics: uncertainty cannot be admitted in theory *even if it accurately describes reality*, because it muddles our models up! No more ironic statement can be made concerning this engaging distance from reality of this tendency in post-Keynesian theory, and economics generally. Ontology is forced to live up to the demands of epistemology; we shall impose order on the world, even if there be none 'out there', otherwise our anthropocentric, ultra-'scientific', masculinist, egos would be seriously damaged. Sir Edmund Hilary (with the help of droves of nameless, doughty, Nepalese Sherpas, aside from the celebrated Mr Tenzing) 'conquered' Mount Everest because, apparently, 'it was there'; Mr Eatwell, *au contraire*, is persuaded to the drama of conquest even if it is *not* 'there'. After all, economists cannot just sit idly by.

To go further: this school insists upon the *separability* of value and distribution theory from the theory of output and employment; prices then are implicitly seen as unaffected by the scale of output. But this is to make implicit assumptions about returns to scale, *and* the nature of competition, prevailing. Now separability is all right as a heuristic device, so long as this separation is not conceived as an *ontology of the real*, as appears too often to be the case. Similar considerations apply to the notion of effective demand, which usually serves as a deus ex machina in the argument. Effective demand supposedly determines employment and output: but what determines effective demand itself? 'Distribution', perhaps? If so, what becomes of the vaunted separability of value and distribution theory from the theory of output and employment?

To sum up the foregoing, before treating one further issue; both neoclassical and Marxian theory, i.e. the historical alternatives to post-Keynesian theory (and I stress the term *historical*), clearly and unambiguously, specify their assumptions about the capitalist economy and the social order; one can agree or disagree with them (indeed, they may be right or wrong) but it is over an unequivocally specified environment. The neo-Ricardian/post-Keynesian theory lacks this specificity; the assumptions are ad hoc and/or unclear; and the definition of a real, not a modular, capitalism in its present constitution is not spelt out. The reference to institutional factors, usually parenthetical, is far from sufficient. To point to just one example, the *state* – references to which are plentiful, but vague; what does the state do? What can it do? What are its limits? Whose interests does it serve?, etc.; all such questions of a realist *political economy* are omitted altogether. Consider the neoclassical and Marxian alternatives on the other hand: be they right or wrong, at least they leave not much room for doubt as to where they stand on these matters.

3

Lastly, to address the key issue of *policy*: where does this 'analysis' lead to? Mostly implicit, but sometimes explicit, the references are, as far as the matter is determinate, to *three* policy issue areas: full employment, social control of investment, and 'reduction' of income inequalities. On the issue of full employment, it suffices to quote the incomparable Robinson again:

> Full employment is a right wing slogan ... if employment is an end in itself no questions can be asked about its content. What is work for? Only to keep workers out of mischief (*and to keep, one might add, capitalists in clover*); any product is as good as another (my emphasis in italics).

As for social control over investment, historically, both Adolf and Joseph showed us that diverting possibility well before Keynes. The question, in practice, is social control *by whom, and on behalf of whom, and to what end*? On this, these schoolmen have precious little to say. On the issue of income inequalities, all that needs be said is that if income inequalities were the only 'inequalities' of import under capitalism, perhaps the concerns of the critic would be considerably lightened. Issues of exploitation and wage slavery, imperialism, hierarchy and subalternism, anomie and alienation, patriarchy, racism, and ecological destruction, to mention but a few of the more delectable attributes of capitalist reality, do not even merit a mention in this reductionist, economistic, and hence quite sterile, discourse.

Stated baldly, the Sraffians are not *political economists* in the sense of, say, Adam Smith, or J.S. Mill, with interesting things to say about capitalist economy and society generally, but function only as a mirror image of neoclassicism, with their desiccated, and wholly deductivist, 'economics' (to say nothing of hidden political agendas). Even the economics of Labourite social democracy (trite as it is), one would think, requires a modicum of a broader social philosophy to support its uninspired platitudes. As it is, the platform of wage-led growth, within the auspices of a distribution-conscious, but securely, *capitalist* regime, is hardly distinguishable from any of the host of variants of traditional liberal Keynesianism. In fact, the lineage of this programme may, more accurately, be even further regressed to J.S. Mill, with his ideal of 'capitalism' in production and 'socialism' in distribution.

To conclude: however delusively, both neoclassical theory and Marxian theory offer you the promise of a utopia; the best of all possible worlds is either already here, or just around the corner – but the Cambridge School is bereft of any such *vision* (perhaps the promise of such a vision ended with the inimitable Mrs Robinson, the last stalwart of the 'real' Cambridge School) that has distinguished the great schools of political economy in the history of the discipline. But who knows? Perhaps that incidental infelicity may well be its strongest, if not quite its *only*, virtue!

Of course, the larger issue that remains effectively unstated, in all of this, is the intellectual bankruptcy of economics itself with its fatuous penchant for abstract model building always at a safe distance from 'vulgar' economic facts; as such, Mr Eatwell's demiurge, Mr Sraffa, was just as sublimely distant from reality as the neoclassicists his epigones were to revile forever after. It is high time (now that it has greedily appropriated the pure rent of a Nobel Prize per annum) that economics commenced the introductory task of getting its feet wet in the murky field that it has blindly pontificated about the generations: to learn, like a hiker in the woods, by observation, tabulation, reflection, and analysis – about the elementary facts of the economic life.

Notes

1 References to John Eatwell are taken from a digest of his ideas on the subject, submitted as a conference paper (to the Department of Economics, University of Utah, October 1986) entitled 'Notes on Effective Demand and Accumulation'.
2 The Sraffian bible is his clinically concise *Production of Commodities by Means of Commodities*, 1960.
3 A critical discussion of Sraffian-Steedmanite analysis may be found in Mandel and Freeman, 1984. Particularly noteworthy is the remarkable essay contained in it by Emmanuel Farjoun, entitled 'Production of Commodities by Means of What?', pp. 11–41.
4 References to Joan Robinson are taken from her pithy *Economic Philosophy*, 1966.

6 Why England Led the Way: Clues to a Critique of Eurocentrism

1

One of the more enduring – if not endearing! – myths of Western historiography (more specifically, *Anglo-American* historiography), shared oddly enough by conservative and classical (Euro)Marxist alike, is the notion that the triumph of the West was purely an *internal* matter, pertaining only to socioeconomic features local to Europe, rather than having anything to do with the immense saga of its predatory depredations, experienced quite viscerally as *colonialism* by its victims, in Asia, Africa and Latin America. The canonical version of the pioneering role of England in this process, lavishly dressed in Marxian trappings runs, broadly, as follows, in this, all but disbelieving, recreation.[1]

2

It is commonly accepted, or so the argument runs, that from the fourteenth century onwards there was a general decline in the viability of the pre-capitalist structures labelled as 'feudal' in Western Europe, if not also in the so-called 'Asiatic' regions of India and China, and perhaps also in certain parts of the Islamic empire.[2] Among the myriad indices of this slow, but eventually far-reaching, process were an increasing complexity in the social division of labour, the emergence of a small but prosperous class of merchants and craftsmen, a significant growth in urban centres, accompanied by an intensification of feudal pressures on a steadily differentiated peasantry, alongside the introduction of new and oppressive means of exaction of a 'surplus' revenue over and above traditional, and largely customary, feudal exactions.

Two portentous tendencies, consequences of the processes just outlined, appeared, thereby, on the canvas of European history; increasing peasant rebellions, and peasants' 'flight from the land', alongside spectacular mercantile accumulations of wealth, a combustible combination that threatened the very basis of the social relations extant in the period. Needless to say, in due course of time, Western Europe was able to shake off the mantle of a pre-capitalist past earlier than the rest of the world with truly earthshaking consequences. This *'primitive'*, or primal, accumulation, greatly facilitated by means as diverse as piracy, plunder, trade and slavery, cause and consequence of the drive for precious metals and subordinate overseas markets, was itself aided by the far from fortuitous maritime and navigational discoveries and inventions[3] of the time. The dissolution of feudalism took centuries to accomplish, as much the result of the growth of markets, trade and petty commodity production, with its corresponding reliance on the cash and credit nexus, as its own internal structural weaknesses pertaining to contradictions basic to its mode of production – the struggle of the producers against the relations of production and exploitation, as illustrated in the endemic revolts of the period, and, not unrelatedly, to the not inconsiderable growth of productive forces, industrial skills, science and technology, and in some cases, even population.

The mere accumulation of capital, be it money capital, commercial or merchant capital, or usurer's capital, was only a first condition for the emergence of bourgeois relations of production, and therefore a feature by no means incompatible with feudalism – indeed, quite the contrary;[4] the former process could only be completed by various other necessary conditions, namely the concentration of ownership, the dispossession of the real producers, the transformation of the means of production into capital, the creation of wage-labour, generalised commodity-production, and some degree of control over political power and economic policy. Early, incipient, capitalism, even mercantile, 'bourgeois' oligarchies, already existed in areas of Italy, the Low Countries, and Germanic principalities, by the sixteenth century, though growth was still restricted by the nature of feudal sanctions and controls. For industrial capital to emerge as the ruling interest, political struggles were necessary to challenge existing barriers to production. Significantly, the first challenge to the rule of immovable property and restrictive trade practices in Europe was to be posed by the seventeenth century revolution in England (to some extent anticipated by the Dutch struggles against the Spanish yoke), which proclaimed the emergent interests of manufacturers against both rentiers and speculators. To put it differently, the profit motive, geared to production rather than trade, had just been institutionalised as practical, political policy.[5]

By the turn of the eighteenth century, France, England, and Holland, were clearly flourishing mercantile empires, bidding for domination of trade and the plunder of wealth, as, when, and where possible, although limited domestic markets had brought about a general retardation in the accumulation of wealth in the face of opening possibilities of expansion of overseas commerce; competition between the three powers was, therefore, quite inevitable.[6] Holland, with its abundance of accumulated capital and advanced credit institutions, unfortunately lacked both a powerful military (naval) force, and a solid industrial base to compete effectively for the far-flung markets at issue. The French were certainly a matching industrial power, but France was, apparently, less willing than England to subordinate her foreign policy to purely economic ends, its autocratic political institutions and highly regimented 'national' industry standing in the way of posing an effective challenge to British aggression conducted almost solely with commercial gain in mind. The ensuring century of warfare left England, the victor, in control of almost the entire European colonial market, so that on the eve of the Industrial Revolution, Britain was the foremost maritime power with an industry free of guild and state interference, and a ruling class highly susceptible to commercial and industrial interests. Additionally, the colonies were to prove vital levers of acceleration of the processes of industrialisation.[7]

Of course the 'Industrial Revolution' is to be understood as the result of a highly variegated, multiplex, socioeconomic causation whose roots encompass the social history of Western Europe, as it was interconnected with its colonies to both east and west. The term 'socioeconomic causation' is employed as an inclusive one – the political and military aspects of the process being treated as specific impulses generated by a given social formation whose autonomy, though real, is limited, and, at any rate, whose legitimacy springs from the socioeconomic process[8] it accommodates. It would have been clear, then, to the eighteenth century student of history that, for better or for worse, large scale, privately driven, industrialisation, if at all, would necessarily occur in the European West rather than, say, the Asiatic world, so long as the structural roots of capitalism, and the degree to which they had taken hold in the soil of Europe, were understood. She would also have known that such a process, once begun, could hardly remain a localised phenomenon; the only unexpected aspect of the process being, to a competent historian, not the inevitability of the process of industrialisation (since even European oligarchies suffered from no lack of interest in that direction) but perhaps the *form* it took – that it would be experienced in the form of a *revolution*, even in a country of the undoubted prosperity of England. For England, indeed, was the first nation to experience industrialisation as a revolution.[9]

It is neither easy, nor perhaps even necessary, to make critical distinctions between 'domestic' and 'international' factors that accounted for England leading the way – the network of economic relations obviously cut across national political boundaries, and necessarily fused together in the period of colonial expansion. But, the very specificity of English social history from

1640 to the end of the eighteenth century demands an analysis of its particular features. Among the major developments of the period were the emergence of an increasing concentration of land ownership, the rise of enclosed farms employing wage labour, and the early maturing of capitalist relations in agriculture, in turn facilitated and complemented by revolutions in agricultural technique ('Townsend's Turnips', Jethro Tull's 'horse-hoeing' husbandry, Bakewell's improvements in stock breeding, etc.). Side by side went the large scale development of roads and canals, a widespread handicraft industry, and a ruthless break-up of the old village system

In short, far ahead of its European competitors, England, at the end of the eighteenth century, had created an expanding domestic market, an agricultural surplus, and a dispossessed proletariat within its boundaries, while being in a commandingly exploitative position, both commercially and militarily, overseas. Basically, the most crucial transition, that between two distinct modes of production, was taking place in England earlier than anywhere on the continent, and it was this new, admittedly incomplete, subordination of production to capital, and therefore a change in the class relationships of production, that marked the real watershed in the social history of England vis-à-vis Europe. Plunder without extra-economic sanctions[10] within production and exchange was beginning to gain ascendancy over the more mercantilist policy of 'exploitation through trade', together with a disaccumulation of mercantilist hoards in growing manufactory investment. After the Napoleonic wars, with most European powers except England devastated (only the region of Flanders seemed left with any industrial potential worth the name), England, freed from any immediate military threat, found itself free to engage in the profitable application of a century of technological advances, together with an unchallenged access to the markets of the world.

Pre-industrial England, as indicated, was already a market economy. The demand for food, fuel and clothing was not inconsiderable, and the associated industries pioneered many of the coming technological improvements. Trade had already facilitated urbanisation, and improvements in transport only aided the same, while commerce had provided the upper classes with steadily rising incomes. Abroad, a captive market existed; cotton lead the way in colonial profits – and also in capitalist industrialisation. In addition, the requirements of war-making gave a boost to production technology in heavy industry, e.g. shipbuilding and armaments, with huge state contracts paving the way. The mercantile fleet became carriers of world commerce, including especially lucrative booty like the slave trade. In all of this, of course, and rather vitally at that, the state was an eager and enthusiastic partner. *Politics, apparently, at all levels, was to be geared to profit-making.* Although agrarian capital still had a nominal hold on state power, powerful industrial interests found it not at all insensitive to their interests. The ruling aristocracy,[11] far from being a closed caste, admitted the parvenus most generously – Pitt's distribution of peerages, in return for financial assistance in the war, had already admitted the commercial bourgeois into their august ranks. Government contracts for munitions made for radical technologies in metallurgy, and stimulated the production of that basic metal for industry, *iron* – later to be the basis for exploding investments in that foremost of capital-intensive innovations: the railroad.

However, whether the agent in question was the government, the internal market, or technology, it must be recognised that, while in each of these cases, England seems to have been more fortunate than her contemporaries, these factors still do not explain her leap into industrialisation – indeed they themselves need to be explained, as they are by no means 'ultimate' indices, being, rather, resultants in the main, of more basic socioeconomic processes. For example, it needs to be explained why the state in England was more geared to the efficient pursuit of profit as against, say, the French state. To answer this, of course, one has to turn back to the structures of class interest, relations of production, and the nature of the productive forces in each case. *It may be argued, then, that it is the ascendant capitalist mode of production in the English social formation that determined the structure of economic needs, which in turn paved the way for industrialisation at that conjuncture in history, ahead of the rest of Europe and the world.* The revolutions in technology,[12] followed as a matter of course – both being led, and followed by, changes in the production relations of the time. England was the first country where the capitalist mode of production achieved decisive dominance vis-à-vis other structures; it was therefore only logical that the Industrial Revolution would be made in that context. It is not for nothing that Marx wrote, observing the English example, that the bourgeoisie cannot exist without constantly revolutionising the instruments of production.

Implicit in such an approach to the understanding of the nature of developments leading to the British advance is an obvious rejection of most popular notions that have sought to explain the same phenomenon in terms of suggestions of population growth,[13] England's insular position, the 'scientific temper' of its populace, the 'puritan individualism' of its commercial classes, etc. All these excellent advantages may have been real enough (although the case of population growth is probably the most doubtful 'cause' of them all; and, in any case, a redundancy of population in relation to means of employment may well promote stagnation and misery, and not growth), but they are, in themselves, rather *indices* of economic advancement than *causes* in any scientific sense (even a geographical quirk such as the insular position of England may well be better exploited by a superior mode of production).

Thus, if England had the 'mind, material equipment, and opportunity' for taking the lead, it was only so because of the far-reaching changes in social production relations (including the domain of politics) that had taken place over the preceding 200 years. It was an England where the business of politics was business, where an agrarian revolution had transformed the countryside, 'liberating' a fledgling proletariat, and introducing capitalist relations in agriculture; where an agricultural surplus was ready to support a non-agricultural population, and provide a base for accumulation; where incredible overseas commercial success, and military conquest, brought in wealth at rates of profit justifying continuing investment in the means of further production and, more so, justifying simple mechanical innovations to inflate output in a hurry; where the internal market, already strengthened by a spending, commercial class, was reinforced by improved and more economical means of transport (roads, canals); where a vast foreign market (except for the United States) lay unchallenged and monopolised by English exports (cotton again leading the way), with seemingly limitless possibilities; where, crucially, the separation between labour and property was tending toward a total divorce – leading to the growth of wage labour in accelerated fashion. The all-important conjunction was occurring, or had occurred: *the transformation of means of production into capital, and labour power into a commodity*, on a generalised basis. And this, indeed, was a first for England: industrial and technological innovation, on an expanding basis, was thereon to become the order of the day.

3

The foregoing, in radically encapsulated fashion, sums up the EuroMarxian case – some premises of which are also shared by liberal economic historians – for the primacy of England in the Industrial Revolution. Now to examine but a few of the glaring weaknesses, and elisions, in that finely-tuned analysis: firstly, the foregoing account converts concrete, real history (subject to the regress of unintended consequences and a whole slew of conjunctural determinations) into *necessity*, and from then on into a determinist, logical exercise which may now serve as a '*model*' of capitalist transition to be applied uncritically – indeed, oft-times with bad faith – to the prospects of capitalist transition in the 'Third' World (as in the work of Bill Warren, amongst Marxists, and Rostow amongst the mainstream). History can only be recorded and, within paradigmatic bounds, understood – not *modelled* (as though it were the product of a one-dimensional logic); for society is an *open* system where invariant regularities (as in 'models') simply do not obtain.

Secondly, the stress on factors *internal* to the mode of production (or, social formation, more correctly) in England omits any serious understanding of the contribution of the colonial world to the acceleration of economic growth in England. Indeed, it was *captive colonial markets* – achieved by dint of military and naval prowess – alongside stupendous colonial plunder, which fuelled the werewolf demand for English goods, necessitating expansion of the technical base of production in the unseemly haste that we usually glorify – quite foolishly – as the 'Industrial Revolution'. Indeed, the dismal decline of Britain after the loss of empire is thunderingly eloquent testimony to the decisive role of captive markets, and national resources, the world over, that perforce sustained the English miracle, based as it was on the wholesale appropriation of material values, quite unilaterally. Danish capitalism had to make do without a cataclysmic 'industrial revolution', one may note, because the world's markets and resources had not (fortunately for the non-Danish world) been forcibly yielded to the Danes (despite some ingenuity invested in this direction).

Thirdly, the autonomy of the political, and the military, moment is vulgarised, in such sketches, into an impossible economic determinism, where history is justified, as inevitable, post factum; e.g., as should be obvious to a schoolchild, had France prevailed militarily over Britain – as it very nearly did – the history of the Industrial Revolution (and its 'inevitability') *in England* would have taken a very different form. England did not prevail over France, on land or sea, by virtue of its being *a more advanced mode of production*, as is often implied in such discourse, military success being neither implied by, nor necessarily correlated with, economic power. The quirks of battle, in the case of the struggle between England and France, were hardly the gift of a higher 'mode of production', or a superior technology; England only proved herself (on the margin!) – like Europe generally – more 'efficient' in the gruesome business of systematic slaughter.

Fourthly, such analysis totally ignores the horrific obverse of English success: *the wanton destruction of the production forces of Asia and Africa*, as lay within England's ken, leading to their stasis and decline into 'Third World' status, as in the spectacular example of India, whose industrial base – *ahead of Japan in the eighteenth century* – was to be reduced to rubble, within the short space of a century, by British depredations (the destruction of the Indian textile industry to favour Lancashire was only the tip of the iceberg of the slash-and-burn economics policies of colonial rule).

Finally, it is the inescapable belief of this brand of thinking, that, despite the unscalable social misery engendered by the Industrial Revolution, *its benefits* (in productivity terms) *outweighed the costs* (a secular rendition of the idea of purification through purgatory) – a judgment at peace with normal bourgeois views on the question. Taken at face value, this is simply incredible – *that those who did not pay the costs can, nonetheless, tendentiously, evaluate the 'benefits', and the net balance between costs and benefits, in calm, dispassionate fashion*! Of course, the implicit – if puerile – faith, that 'socialism' would come and set right all industrial, and historical, wrongs made such a view more palatable to those (such as Marxists) who might otherwise have questioned such judgments; *but socialism has come and gone, at least temporarily, without any such historical redemption* having either been revealed or realised. Besides, Marx himself turned away, as is – or should be – well known, from such rationalisations of the grotesque deformities of capitalist industrialisation in the later period of his life, as he began to appreciate the full import of both capitalism and colonialism (as revealed in his correspondence with the Russian revolutionaries of his time). Whatever the sins of Marx and his epigones, clearly Marx himself was rarely a consistent 'Marxian'.

The implication is unmistakable: in its economistic form, Marxism has served as apologetics for the European enslavement of the world, in all its technological, economic, and even ideological, moments. Materialist dialectics, and scenarios, of 'objective' causation deftly excise – and, thereby, excuse! – the real flesh and blood humans, steeped with prejudice and passion, of their sins of omission and commission. Not only is historical responsibility evaded in such 'scientistic' analysis, but is even exonerated and justified, in the cause of an absurdly teleological view of 'progress'. As Marx was to write, in all insouciance, England was only fulfilling a 'mission' in India: it is highly doubtful whether he would have penned the same coolly prosaic and 'objective' lines had it been India that had, fortuitously, bled England – or better still, his native Germany – in the name of an implacable, historically sanctioned, 'missionary', destiny. If this form of tripe and onions has been the given legacy of Marxist fairy tales of liberation, it is easy to appreciate today the braggart delusions of a Fukuyama.

Stated simply, EuroMarxist discourse elevates British (European) achievement to the detriment of its generously contributing donors in the colonised world, additionally converting the English case into an entirely repeatable '*model*', indeed an exemplar, of the 'true' capitalist path. Further, it propounds and perpetuates the myth that capitalism is a '*progressive*' mode of production, *ex definitione*, that roots out retrograde forms of exploitation wherever, and whenever, it encounters them (thereby defending ongoing imperialism in none too subtle a fashion).

Lastly, it glosses over the unprepossessing fact that sexism, racism, slavery, piracy, plunder, and rabid environmental destruction, were the grim cornerstones on which European, capitalist, success was (and still is) built. Stated succinctly, it buries the spirit of Marx – and the inherent generosity of that highly problematic oeuvre – in the name of a reductionist, economistic Marxism that apologises for the wholesale destruction of civilisations, and peoples, in favour of the putative enhancement of the 'forces of production' (to the greater glory of the chimera of 'socialism').

Notes

1. For a textual confirmation, see the works of Hobsbawm, 1968 and Dobb, 1963
2. The precise dating of the process seems open to question – but in any case, the process was sufficiently long drawn out to permit an efficient ignorance of its beginnings.
3. 'Primitive accumulation', at least for Marx, clearly indicated the historical process of the *dispossession* of real producers from their means of production, along with the simultaneous confiscation of the latter as capital by their new possessors. Less discriminating writers have treated any form of accumulation of wealth as 'primitive accumulation' – which is untenable unless it can be shown that such wealth facilitated the process indicated above.
4. The accumulation of quantitative capital, far from automatically inaugurating the capitalist mode of production, served often to reinforce pre-capitalist relations; in that sense, the image of feudal society as a 'natural' economy may be quite misleading and also quite incorrect. Merchant capital thrived also in the Byzantine, Mogul, and Ming empires without significantly accelerating 'bourgeois' relations of production.
5. This is not to deny that the 'profit motive' also existed, say in France, and in other countries at that time; the desire for wealth, and its expansion, is one thing – but is quite another thing when entire national policy is subsumed by it: for the latter to happen requires a socioeconomic setting which apparently had not yet matured outside of the country in question.
6. Germany, divided and backward, was not yet a contender for world domination; it would more than make up for its laggard past in the twentieth century.
7. If quantity of wealth itself has any significance, it is putatively recorded that between the battles of Plassey and Waterloo, some £6,500,000,000–£1,000,000,000 worth of treasure was transferred from India to Britain. But numbers always understate the human and social consequences of the ravages in question.
8. History, as Godelier put it, is not a concept that explains but is to be explained. The phrase 'socioeconomic' causation does not deny reciprocity between social structures but posits that even reciprocating structures need to be referred back to the system of ultimate constraints located, or having some reference to, the mode of production – this 'bias' of course is basic to historical materialism and demands close scrutiny in the necessary effort to rethink Marxism.
9. The emphasis, of course, is on the word 'first'; something similar was experienced by the hapless populace of the Soviet Union.

10 The mercantilist aspiration was not totally antithetical to feudal interests, nor did it stop short of 'feudal' means of achieving them.
11 As Hobsbawm has it, they were a 'post-revolutionary' elite, unaristocratic and commercial-minded, with indeed few feudal virtues.
12 England by no means led the way in the sciences – the continent being far better equipped in that regard – prior to the Industrial Revolution. The early technological innovations only utilised scientific developments as were available to Western Europe for over 100 years. Subsequent technologies were 'called forth' by the demands of the capitalist market.
13 Many species of bourgeois thought (North and Thomas, for instance) ascribe the Industrial Revolution, if not capitalism itself, to population growth (particularly in the case of England): data is scanty enough, but if true for England, then it would apply to all of Europe, just as much, without producing the consequent in question. Historical evidence suggests, on a more general level, that correlations are certainly possible between growth of population and economic development (or even a decline in economic growth), but causation can hardly be invested, in general, in population as an independent variable; if anything, the relationship is *interdependent*, with the nature of the social relations and productive forces, or the ecosystem at large, exerting perhaps the primary pressure on population changes, in both size and composition.

Part IV
CLASSICAL ECONOMICS: MYTH AND REALITY

7 The Ricardian Rigmarole: From Policy to Paradigm

1

The crisis of 'modernism', with which we are all overlaid, be it amongst the Bantu in farthest Africa, or amongst native bookkeepers closer to home, is reflected, at one remove, in the estrangement of social thought from its social moorings, such that the latter is soon forgotten as the necessary predicate for the former. Representing this travesty triumphantly is the typical neoclassical, *micro analytical* perspective, in which postulated 'individuals', amputated from real social mechanisms, act out their hypothetically pre-specified scenarios blissfully free of all social conditioning (except, oddly enough, greed and avarice!). So long as this house of cards is recognised only as a dream world, all is well, so to speak. However, the purpose of self-conscious ideology is to provide a *substitute* for practice, while insinuating itself between viewer and reality so as to distort the latter permanently. In the crushingly capitalist civilisation of the twentieth century, this task has been all but achieved, in vast measure, in neoclassical thinking, with its lifelessly alienated, amoral theorems having chopped up the continuity of social life and social history into compartments sought to be hermetically sealed and shielded from one another.

In this netherworld of consequents but no causes, the economic is divorced from the political, science from morality, and theory from practice. We may then comfortably believe that economics is the study of wealth, and politics the study of power; both disciplines being as separable as wine and cheese (though 'admittedly', the oftentimes go rather well together!); or that the 'economy' and the 'state' occupy different spaces such that we can conceive of 'laissez-faire' as a perfectly feasible 'policy' that may be 'debated' at will, and restored/removed at pleasure. Theory, in similar disembowelment, may then be divorced from history, life from our construction of it. The tension that is so generated between the (individualist) ontology of society and its (subjectivist) epistemics is happily resolved by denying the reality of ontology[1] altogether, and implying that the latter may simply be dissolved into epistemics, in Weberian fashion (or neo-Weberians like Rorty) where we may construct the world as we care, for the latter is but so much play-doh in our supple hands of creation.

In such fashion, bourgeois ideology has recreated the world, rewritten history, and hardened the arteries of orthodox wisdom about everything; compared to this 'rational' totalitarianism of mind-set, ideology, and its associated politics of temperance and conservatism (in one word, *quietude*) the sadly uninspired propaganda of erstwhile Eastern bloc 'socialism' was but a low species of home-brewed, kindergarten, sop. One must not forget, however, that all the vaunted sophistication of Western social science has served only to buttress the poaching grounds of capitalism (and capitalists) both domestically and abroad: i.e. to maintain privilege, support prerogative, and bolster profits. The economist has, of course, performed a high-profile role in this endeavour being high priest, chief counsel, and grand inquisitor, all at the same time, for both the culture and rhetoric of capitalism. My 1986 book, to which this is but a postface, looked at the machinations of only one great forerunner of this ilk (while recognising the theoretical *differences* between neoclassical and classical traditions in economics, one must not lose sight of the essential sociopolitical *continuity* of class outlook contained within both), who set high standards for the profession in terms of partisanship, understanding, with the limpid vision of the farsighted bourgeois (much like Keynes), that 'theory' begins only where policy ends, such that the former is only a restatement of the latter: David Ricardo.

2

The history of economics, as another branch of pseudo-science, has faithfully reflected the class struggles of yore. Evaluations of Ricardo either follow the Marxian pattern of awarding high praise (despite glaring weaknesses, elisions, and evasions), but only as a gifted forerunner of the true master (see e.g. Rubin, 1979), or take the form of a cautious conservatism (see Schumpeter, 1954a) where Ricardo's 'analysis' is rejected (for its *correct* capture of capitalist ontology: the existence of *potentially* antagonistic classes defined with respect to ownership of means of production), while his policy goals are sought to be quietly assimilated into routine bourgeois economic practice without untoward fanfare. In both these disparate views, it is the zeal of class struggle that impairs clear (or clearer) vision as to *Ricardo's own historically set problematic*; and so, for over a century the real Ricardo has been veiled over by an implicit conspiracy of ideology, either defending him from errors uncommitted, or deriding him for the same. Both interpretations, incidentally, insult the memory of a great champion of the industrial bourgeoisie, at a time when the incoming system had need for champions of the selfless kind (unlike the 'hired prizefighters' of today, the toadies and the timeservers, the small-time jobbers, who do it for filthy, and far from sufficient, lucre: to paraphrase the poet, paid-for melodies may be sweet, but those unpaid are sweeter). Ricardo did for the bourgeoisie what Lenin only *tried* to do for the working class in Russia (and then, too, only for a while): invest them with state power. And he did it with the same single-mindedness that would brook no opposition, suffer no denials, and admit no refutations. The story of Ricardo, like Lenin, is about *policy*, and partisanship, and social engineering, not *theory*; the latter only followed, as the word does the deed in Goethe's famous aphorism (i.e. as the latter's 'phonetic shadow'). Neither orthodox Marxians nor mainstream economists are willing, apparently, to sustain this damning charge: 'theory', in their dissembling discourse, is moved to be 'independent' of its origins[2] – a thesis that none of them is either ready, or able, to 'prove', except by the familiar, if craven, ploy of strident assertion.

3

In the beginning, was the *deed*; whether as conflict and contention over policy, or politics, or class struggle, or combat over distributive shares, or the battle for mastery over state power: call it what you will. In the beginning, for the Ricardian awakening, was not, as fairytales would have it, received economic theory in general, nor even – that favourite with the philistines – the specific ideas of Adam Smith. Ricardo was not some starstruck watcher of the skies, conducting serious studies in abstract economics until he fell afoul of the *Wealth of Nations*, one day (whilst taking the salts at Bath, as legend will have it), being spurred to greater heights thereby.[3] No: (and how such puerile notions survive is beyond me) born of prosperous Jewish merchants and brokers, emigrated from Holland, but of Portuguese descent, David was to break with his family over a contemplated (but eventually consummated) marriage, though still managing to make an independent success of his labours at the Stock Exchange, (that grey and grim tutor of real economics!) acquiring financial independence at the ripe old age of 26. A life of toil being so cruelly denied, young David dabbled in many diversions, from chemistry to geology – even, at one point, in the ephemera of economics: but these desultory enjoyments of a dilettante are not to be taken very seriously. David was still on his way to becoming a major financial oligarch, of a select class of 'loan contractors' called for by Pitt's adventurous financial policies: his induction into the haute bourgeoisie, no mean task given his background and relatively young years, was to be complete by about 1813.

Thenceforth, it was the modalities of English social history that were to provide all the remaining grist to this gifted financier; the Napoleonic wars, French commercial policies, the Bank of England's responses, the trade situation, labour and agrarian unrest, and so on. In keeping with his financial pursuits, he had written a note on the Bullion Question, in 1809, related to the over-issue of notes by the Bank, which established him as a cautious 'Bullionist' – in consonance with his excellent, if somewhat conservative, bourgeois credentials. However, it was Waterloo that brought him to the fore of policy formation in what was obviously to be a new era of English supremacy, given the French debacle, an era whose significance and prospects, Ricardo appreciated as no-one else. Thereafter, his parasitic financial past notwithstanding, he was to identify himself with – and lead – policies favouring *industrial capital* with which, in the kind of intellectual recklessness that the profession has made its own ever since, the interests of the 'nation' were, somewhat wildly, identified. Protected from any personal financial worries, Ricardo was free to play the part of 'statesman', for the capitalist class as a whole (much like Keynes, with whom he shares many features).

The Ricardian 'problematic' was historically set by the given circumstances, by the parameters of the completion of the English bourgeois revolution, initiated heroically in the mid-seventeenth century. Never had captainship of industrial capital been vested in a more tactical intellect, alive never so much to 'larger' philosophical issues as to immediate sociopolitical necessities. On target, since his cannonade on the Corn Laws was fired off in 1815, he was never to stray off track with his chosen mission, cut off from seeing its all-total success only by his shockingly untimely demise of 1823.

4

1.

The Ricardian period,[4] which I situate between Waterloo and the French Revolution of 1848, and regardless of choice of index employed, was one of growth and structural change, conflict and crisis, wars and revolutions – or at least one that lived in the shadows of all of these; in short, a turbulent one, following upon the aftermath of two great political and social revolutions, the American and the French; two great foreign wars, the French revolutionary and the Napoleonic; and two great socioeconomic upheavals, the agrarian and the industrial metamorphoses, that irrevocably altered the historical destinies of the region, and then, by extension, the rest of the world. The calendar of social unrest, an able barometer of change, was never so crowded as between 1798 and 1848; the Naval Mutiny (1797) and the Irish Rebellion (1798); the Combination Act (1799) and the suspension of Habeas Corpus (1817); the Luddite (1816) and the rural revolts (1830); the Chartist revolts (1826–30) – to mention only the more famous events. Such was the mood at home – defiance provoking repression and vice versa; abroad, the successive destabilising influences of the episodic French revolutions from 1789 through 1830 to 1848.

State power, on the eve of this tumultuous epoch, was nestled in the hands of the agrarian (and commercial) interest – the Commons *manned* (quite literally) by the squirearchy, the upper house by the landed nobility – an alliance between commercial farmers, merchant capitalists, and their aristocratic overlords. The Industrial Revolution, together with the captive colonies and neo-colonies (*which made so much of the former so very possible*), and even the Napoleonic Wars, brought prosperity to these interests, which flourished, at least economically, as never before; however, even as the age peaked, the penumbra of new challenges became perceptible in the form, firstly, of the rise to high resentment and pique, if not prominence, of the manufacturing middle and not-so-middle classes, drawn from various strata, with their own interests and ideology; and, secondly, in the lumbering ascent to self-consciousness of the labouring poor, both rural and urban. Not until 1832 would accommodation be forced upon the landed oligarchy by the first of these entities in the form of significant, if formal, political representation in Parliament; and not until 1867 would the new power amalgam cede the same favour, similarly, to the second of the new social forces. The Ricardian period, and this accounts for much of its effulgence, was overlaid principally by the first of the struggles – although significantly cognizant of the stirrings of the second.

5

1815 was a year of moment in the evolution of English capitalism; with Napoleon having been granted his final sabbatical at Waterloo, the long-run battle between England and France for world mastery had just been decisively settled – but not yet settled was the feud between corn and cotton domestically,[5] the Napoleonic 'threat' having ensured a forced modicum of social peace between manufacturers and landlords until the resolution of Waterloo. After 1815 the floodgates of struggle between the two great social orders were to be flung wide open; and it was this great tussle that occupied Ricardo and his 'political economy', to the point of complete absorption, for the rest of his short life.

Looking at matters from the viewpoint of industrial capital, as Ricardo was healthily wont to do, duly enlightened as to its own interests, the long-run prospects for its own advancement (such that England, in its secure hands, could become the 'workshop' and foundry of the world) were blighted by at least three major obstacles:

a) the Poor Laws, as amended in 1795, for having impaired capitalist work 'incentives' and stemming the normal outflow of semi-starved 'hands' to 'man' those dark, satanic mills;

b) the Corn Laws, for impeding the import of cheaper, foreign-grown corn, thereby raising wages and preventing the emergence of a stable, foreign market for domestically-produced manufactured goods; and

c) the Reform question: it was, of course, largely, a 'Parliament of Landlords' that blocked the 'reform' of policy in directions more favourably to industrial interests (important manufacturing cities such as Manchester, Birmingham and Sheffield, for instance, had no representation, under the existing suffrage, in either House).

A cursory examination of Ricardo's interests, struggles and interventions (considered important enough by him to warrant purchasing a seat in the Commons[6]), reveals both the splendid class logic of his political endeavours and the special words of his impressive championship. In Parliament, he championed the case for 'reform' of the franchise (in favour, essentially, of middle class representation); in his major tract, *Principles* (1817), he made out (or, so he imagined) an almost foolproof 'theoretical' case against the Corn Laws and the landed interest. And he was not alone; the Ricardian mission was invested in a dazzling array of institutional commissions: from elite clubs to learned societies and mass circulation news media. Reforming Tories and progressive Whigs were courted avidly by the Ricardians as much as vice versa; Lord Essex and Lord Gladstone (no less) elected Ricardo to the Brooks Club in 1818; Althorp, Chadwick, Hume and Gladstone, in turn, were admitted to the Political Economy Club in 1821. On the public front, the Ricardian propagandists, Marcet and Martineau, were to enshrine the doctrine in popular literature, in the genre of bazaar tripe that could be expected to go over well with the masses. The ideology was compellingly hegemonic: there was science for the literati, petitions for the activists, formulae for the mobs – and, of course, 'laissez-faire' for all. And, atop this far-flung apparatus stood the Political Economy Club, the shadow government of economic policy, wherein the torchbearers of the governing class received economic counsel, under the presiding genius of Ricardo, patron saint of the bourgeoisie, the first amongst equals. And, for all, haute monde or hoi polloi, the rubric on the banner stood: let them read Ricardo!

6

For simple-minded historians, the Ricardian period was the age of laissez-faire; and so it was, in a manner, but not quite in the simple everyday sense of it. But laissez-faire did attach itself to Ricardo (and the Ricardians) much as *All Power to the Soviets!* is connected, inescapably, with Lenin (and the Bolsheviks); and there are other similarities to this not infelicitous analogy as well. Both were powerful slogans of mass appeal calculated to win maximal support from the 'people' – those tired playpieces of putty, forever doomed to be acted upon from without by the exactions of charisma and leadership; both captured the imagination of an age, and a people, quite thoroughly; and both, ultimately, sad to say, were altogether misleading in their nominal claims.

Laissez-faire was not the facile doctrine of 'nonintervention', as touted endlessly by the seemingly imperishable textbook traditions in economics (and other allied disciplines), to be counterposed to its alleged Keynesian opposite, either favourably or unfavourably, depending on the partisan interest involved; it was, quite remarkably, far more complex in its welter of intimations. Recall that the Corn Laws and the Poor Laws were viewed by the Ricardian ilk as impediments to capital accumulation; now both these laws could be presented to the public as examples of a perverse *'protectionism'* extended by a paternalist, landlord state: that is to say the Poor Laws 'protected' rents and the order that lived off them. Being enacted laws, both were examples of 'state intervention'; if one screamed laissez-faire as the touchstone of liberty and freedom, one delegitimised both the landlord state and its policies – Corn Laws, Poor Laws, etc. – simultaneously. The loftiness of the principle of laissez-faire quite matched, one might say, the lowliness of its wretched, self-serving, disingenuous instrumentality. Indeed, matters went a step further; so long as the state was in the possession of 'hostile' forces (i.e. 'landlords' in the case in question), to create a mass movement in favour of 'nonintervention' was a revolutionary move as it disarmed, for delegitimising, the enemy quite effectively: at least in terms of political justification for state actions. The Ricardian manifest did that effectively, but let no-one doubt the real meaning of that specious slogan: in the context of capitalism, as with the recent Reagan–Thatcher wave of reaction, laissez-faire has always implied state support for *capital* at the expense of other social orders.

In the context of the time, therefore, laissez-faire was the demand for *'protection' of profits* as against rents and wages; it was the demand for redistribution of income in favour of the captains of industry; it was the demand for restructuring the political order in favour, explicitly, of capitalist governance. Laissez-faire was, therefore, like Lenin's slogan, a call for *dictatorship*, but of a different order: of industry over agriculture, of cotton over corn, of industrial capital over all orders, and of capital accumulation above all other social priorities. It was this material underpinning to its otherwise philosophical abstractness, that gave content to the real, Ricardian, movement for 'laissez-faire' and, practically, gave muscle and teeth to the tightly constructed Ricardian vice (see Kanth, 1986).

7

What, then, of Ricardian 'theory', that died a natural death in mid-nineteenth century England, only to be revived again, in bowdlerised form, by the 'neo-Ricardians' under Sraffian guise? Quite appropriately, as benefits a policy science, theory was guided by the prior dictates of policy. To understand Ricardian pedantics in theory, one must first refer to the great advocacy that enveloped the entire paradigm. And Ricardian objectives, happily unlike his 'theories', were quite simple to comprehend; indeed, the great body of his theory was designed to demonstrate the following principal propositions, which, if established, would redound to the detriment of the Corn Laws and their architects, the landlords:

a) that the relative prices of corn and cotton were moving in ways antagonistic to the industrial interest;

b) that the rate of profit was falling, first in agriculture (the Corn Laws, allegedly, were forcing recourse to the poorer, less fertile soils), and then, by inference, in industry and the economy in general; and

c) that the stationary state[7] (that radically proximate day of doom), ever impending – like death and taxes – wherein all accumulation is at a standstill, was not to be foiled without an abolition of the Corn Laws.

The *Essay* of 1815, Ricardo's opening sally in the battle between corn and cotton, had hoped to demonstrate all these propositions, but with a simple 'farm model' of the economy, wherein the economy was treated as one giant farm with claims on output shared between landlord, tenant farmer, and hired wage labourer. This so-called 'corn model'[8] was constructed on two principal axial assumptions (aside from various auxiliary sub-assumptions) resting on two alleged 'laws': the 'law' of population, à la Malthus; and the 'law' of diminishing returns in agriculture, also à la Malthus (it is ironic that the 'Ricardian' model rested on essentially *Malthusian* supports; it is tragic, however, that Ricardo's overweening debt to Malthus's ever-incisive probings has never received its full due in the literature of economics[9]), West, Torrens, et al. The law of population gives a perfectly elastic supply of labour at a constant real wage (to employ the rather terse language of neoclassicism), while the 'law' of falling returns produces a declining net product at the margin of cultivation (be it extensive or intensive). Of course, viewed diagrammatically, the interaction between the two laws produced the wished-for 'stationary state'; that is to say, net produce per worker falls, with accumulation, while real wages stay constant, thereby delegating the advantages of superior lands to landlords in the form of rising rents, whilst doling out falling profits per worker to the ever-threatened, ever-squeezed capitalist farmer.

Never mind that both the axial hypotheses of the Malthusian law of population and the law of falling returns were either patently counterfactual (the doubling of population every 25 years or so was, even at the time, a wild exaggeration) or illogical (confusing fecundity with fertility, to name only one problem), or simply misapplied (diminishing returns is a proposition from comparative *statics*, misapplied by Ricardo in a *dynamic* context of accumulation); note, however, that they were supremely 'useful' assumptions calculated to produce the intended results. Indeed, mainstream neoclassical economics has specialised in borrowing this trick of *assuming what needs to be proved*, so as to proffer spuriously successful theorems in many areas. However, Ricardian 'blunders' did not stop at that; after all, purely empirically speaking, to wish away fixed capital, technical progress, and sectors other than the farm sector, was to wish away large chunks of reality altogether. Amongst these many problems was the issue of value theory that had been neatly excised, at least explicitly, from the calculations in the *Essay* of 1815.

It was the brilliant probings of Malthus, with his own landlord-based axe to grind (Malthus was not entirely reactionary in relation to the radical bourgeois stance of Ricardo: the former merely wanted cautious capitalist progress with an alliance between landlords and capitalist that would overlook their differences vis-à-vis the working class), that took the stuffing out of the hastily concocted 'farm' model; a lesser man might have admitted defeat, but Ricardo was made of sterner stuff. In two years, Ricardo came up with the Mark II version of the *Essay*: the *Principles* of 1817, where he obliged the world with a three-sector model (certainly, a step towards 'realism'), though retaining the arguments of the *Essay* intact. This time it is a *labour-standard* of value that is dragged in to yield the required condition of falling rates of profit, while costs measured in labour-time rise over substandard soils (to heap odium on landlords and the Corn Laws, it was imperative to *connect falling rates of profit to straitened conditions in agriculture*); however, Ricardo was to run into the parlous shoals of Malthusian critique yet again. The simple labour theory could only work with the assumption of equal capital compositions across sectors – whence the search for the holy grail of the *'invariable measure of value'* (invariant to changes in distribution). Again, it took the acuity of Malthus to demonstrate that such a perfect measure is simply impossible to be possessed of, given the fact of variations in capital structures, at which point Ricardo was to slide unhappily – a major regression! – into the shabby *empirics* of suggesting that in 'reality' (a domain his models had studiously abjured) such variation could not amount to more than 6–7 per cent! Needless to say, Ricardo was to turn away from his *invariable* standard to a much toned down *'medium'* standard, leading matters – somewhat suggestive of the hoary Duke of Marlborough verse – all the way back to early, indeterminate, beginnings.

Ricardian theory[10] – obviously! – was never to stand up to the promise of Ricardian policy; but few, at the time (other than those of the calibre of Malthus) could swear to that. And Ricardo was to sweep the hustings quite totally, as his agenda was to triumph, item by item, in the years to come: in 1832, the landed oligarchs were to be humbled into granting franchise to the 'middle classes', and a few propertied strata amongst workers (thereby excluding the vast majority amongst the latter); in 1834, the New Poor Law expunged the *'right to life'* provisions of the Speenhamland Poor Laws, outlawing relief outside the workhouse and making it, generally, *'less eligible'*, to use a savoury Benthamite description, thus consecrating the new socioeconomic status of the working class within capitalism quite definitely; and finally, in 1846, the Corn Laws were to be duly repealed. Ricardo had won, but posthumously – and, at a price.

A model tied solely to a policy consideration might soar high in esteem when the policy concerned is deeply embedded in the public consciousness; but, equally, when such a policy is consummated, is its demise already underwritten. And so it was with Ricardo; after repeal of the Corn Laws, the raison d'être of the Ricardian 'model' vanished: the model was, quite literally, useless. For, according to Ricardo himself, but for the Laws, profits would be endlessly buoyant and capital accumulation smooth and, largely, uneventful. What use then, a Ricardo, after 1846? His was not a neutral 'engine of analysis' that might be shunted usefully on to other tracks; the engine ran on one track alone and was promptly derailed when the track itself ceased to exist, for simply leading nowhere. Although imitative of the general construction of science in some respects, this, surely, was a *pseudo-science*, spawned by advocacy and nurtured by patronage and power.

8

After Kuhn (1962), a pseudo-*'sociology of knowledge'* approach has gained ground in mainstream discussions within the area of what has come to be termed 'paradigm shift' in the sciences. In point of fact, of course, the 'sociology' is completely subjectivist, individualist and rationalist, suggesting that there is, in the social sciences, clearly demarcable 'progress' *between paradigms*, measurable analytically, although, for diverse 'sociological' (this being, in fact, a matter of *social psychology* rather than sociology) reasons, various individual scientists either withhold or warrant their support, depending on circumstances, for the emergent *nouvelle critique*. This is a tidy little hermeneutic[11] tale – but one that offers only a descriptive, and inaccurate, video-tape of the rites of passage in ideational systems, without any analytical supports purporting to explain the transitions involved. The failure is one of deftly divaricating science from its real social basis, of stripping politics from class society and presenting scientific models as though they bore total autonomy from social struggles. This, of course, represents an *idealist* deviation from reality; in fine complement, there is a *materialist* variant of this position as well, with one such as Althusser, where science is similarly sanitised, freed from the murky, distempered world of praxis.

At any rate, the reality of class struggles in class society upsets this soporific fairytale quite dramatically. Indeed, I vouchsafe that there is no *single* grand tradition of economic theorising: only different schools preoccupied with different issues studied from different (class) points of view. *The rise and fall is not, primarily, one of theory, but rather one of issues, modes of production, and classes*: e.g. Malthusian ideas 'failed' in the struggle with Ricardo not because they were 'wrong' (indeed, it was Malthus's acutely perceptive critique of Ricardo that pushed the latter to yet further complex heights of theory construction), but because landlords failed as a class to win victory over manufacturers; Malthus was simply outclassed, denied a hearing, and drummed out of town. So, the Kuhnian model is dead wrong if applied uncritically to the social sciences: *schools are not replaced by others by virtue of superior explanatory frameworks, but by altered material conditions.* Fundamentally, then, analytical 'progress', accordingly, may only be measured unequivocally within schools, but not *between* them, since both objects of analysis and perceiving subjects are likely to be different. A careful reading of the real Ricardian agenda, in this context, places an interpretation on the issues of political economy as a science, and the ultimate eclipse of Ricardo, for instance, that differs not only from a 'Kuhnian' reconstruction, but also from a *conventional* Marxian analysis. Let us consider, by way of illustration, the following arguments drawn from my study of Ricardo.

Contrary to traditional 'Marxist' accounts, I have argued that Ricardian economics was not 'dumped' for its radical overtones (as in the Dobb, 1973, and Meek, 1967, readings) by class conscious neoclassicals, but because it became practically *irrelevant* after the success of the Ricardian cause (the Ricardian 'model', bereft of the Corn Laws, is no model at all; as Ricardo himself makes clear, the abrogation of the Laws, coupled with free importation, makes for uninterrupted accumulation, with no necessary conflict of interest between different classes; the rate of profit is, henceforth, perpetually buoyant), i.e. the model became politically obsolete and expired, one might say, quite 'naturally'. To believe that Ricardian theory was set aside for ideological reasons by scheming economists is to subscribe involuntarily to both *idealism* and *voluntarism*, where social ideologies are the product of 'conspiracies' that can succeed regardless of material conditions; rather, ideology itself, I venture, is the product of material conditions and cannot, at least for very long, outlast changes therein. Ricardian theory was not the inspired conspiracy of some loosely organised, ad hoc, social platform; it expressed concretely the struggle of industrial capitalism against the last vestiges of the political economy of the landlords – therein its historically limited *relevance*.

To dispose of another enduring myth, Ricardo was *not* more 'scientific', in some rarefied sense, than the so-called 'apologists' that followed, as Marx upon occasion hinted. His rigour, while admirable (to those who fetishize mere technique!), was ultimately *spurious*, and the mere adoption of the labour theory – standard – of value should not be grounds enough to constitute the difference between scientists and apologists (Marxian enthusiasm for the theory of surplus value notwithstanding), there being far more to classical political economy than, merely, a theory of value.

It is, similarly, *not true* that political economy is a 'science' only so long as the class struggle is *latent*, as Marx apparently thought, in what might well have been a throwaway remark: the 'neutrality' of science and even its 'correctness' was as doubtful in the case of Ricardo as later, when the class struggle is allegedly thought to have become more manifest. Indeed, the fact that the Luddites were active even before Ricardo set off on his theoretical quests gives the lie to the idea of the *latency* of the class struggle in early nineteenth century England. Of course, the Ricardian period was of tremendous significance in the social history of England, being the *decisive* stage in the struggle to establish the supremacy of industrial capital, and Ricardian economics – egregiously more so than Smithian economics, despite the obviously practical, anti-mercantilist nature of the latter[12] – was directly involved in the transformation of England in an industrial capitalist direction, constituting, in fact, the principal intellectual vanguard of that class.[13] To see a Ricardo as suffering from any class innocence, in this regard, therefore, is patent nonsense.

9

It is quite revealing, to turn to another dimension, to see how the different mainstream traditions in economics, all the way from their Smithian inception, investigate essentially different objects of analysis as given by evolving capitalist reality: Ricardo-distribution, Jevons-allocation, Keynes-employment, and so on, but all from a *common* class point of view: of the custodians of capitalist society. So neoclassical economic theory – at best –

is neither *more* apologetic, nor even *less* 'correct' than Ricardo's speculations: *they all bring a similar intent, but applied to a distinctly different problem.* Being axiomatic systems, in the main, their 'truth' is contained in their fundamental premises, which reflect, as they must, the vantage point of the ruling class. As Marx once wrote, the ruling ideology is the ideology of the ruling class; and the 'science' of economics fits well within that general cast: indeed, it would be surprising if it did not. Ultimately, I would submit that – although this may not be of intrinsic interest – this 'reading' vindicates the broader Marxian method of historical materialism (though it should stand because it holds water and not because it is 'Marxian'), no matter how much it may be at odds with putatively 'Marxian' theories, and some statements of Marx himself.

Ricardo's example is also instructive as to the uses (and abuses) of the so-called '*hypothetic-deductive*' method that has, for the longest time, dominated, and disabled, the discipline. The 'premises' of Ricardo so thoroughly over-determined his theoretical conclusions that to place 'assumptions' above reproach, as with Friedman (1953), is to rationalise, uncritically, at the very doorstep of 'science', *a priori politics*: a methodological predilection that, at the very ground floor, reneges on scientific responsibility. *Assumptions are the keys to the scientific kingdom in the social sciences*; their *realism*, or lack of it, is too important an issue to be simply sidestepped in favour of some predictive (social science, at best can only rise to the level of *explanations*, after the fact; 'predictions', in open systems, can mean only very little indeed) or other instrumental capability that a model may be shown to have, *despite counterfactual tendencies known to be contained at the very inception of the analysis*. The economists' strength – as William Maginn, a contemporary of Ricardo pointed out, at the time, with reference to the Ricardians – lay directly proportionate to their *distance from the facts*; as I have tried to make clear, the tendentious nature of the Ricardian enterprise possibly demanded a certain scepticism towards contradictory evidence. But the Ricardian evasion was not a virtue then; and it must not be allowed such a status now.

Although as clever a political economist as any, before or after – indeed cleverer by far! – this reading of Ricardo does soften some of the more exaggerated compliments often paid to the high 'science' of Ricardo, usually, but not exclusively, in the Marxian tradition (in fact, it is quite astonishing how influenced even *mainstream* history of thought traditions are by the original Marxian essays[14] assembled in the posthumously published *Theories of Surplus Value*), for reasons quite obvious; aside from the obvious logical rigour (although equally matched by an awesome obtuseness, not usually commented upon, as represented – for example – in his tortuous exercises over the 'invariable' standard), and the general aura of *scienticity* enveloping Ricardo's work, I submit that it is his embrace of a species of *labour theory* (*of a very different order, though than Marx's version of it*), and his apparent attachment to the notion of class conflict, that endears him to Marx. However, I believe that Marx both overestimated, and misread, Ricardo's attachments to these ideas: the ultimate Ricardian vision of capitalism is *not* one of a society rent hopelessly by class conflict, but quite a harmonious utopia (as Ricardo put it, economic progress is checked only by 'the scarcity and consequent high value, of food and other raw produce'; indeed, with 'free trade', i.e. with cheap imports of corn, '... it is difficult to say where the limit is at which you would cease to accumulate wealth' (Ricardo, 1951–73, 4, p. 179); see also Blaug, 1959, p. 33) – so long as workers submitted to Malthusian 'laws' of nature and both workers and landlords submitted, equally mildly, to the laws authored by a manufacturer-led parliament. And the adoption of a labour standard of value, useful to Ricardo for measuring changes in relative rates of exchange between manufacturing and agricultural goods over time, was mere expediency: as Paglin puts it succinctly, 'without the simple labour theory ... Ricardo would no longer be able to assume that changes in money wages affected only profits and not the price level' (Paglin, 1961, p. 48); in fact, Ricardo was quite happy to retain Smithian value theory until the realisation that the Smithian construction did not yield the required result, with prices rising without any necessary impetus for decline of rates of profit as costs of production rose.

Moreover, the traditional antithesis between 'science' and 'ideology', usually sustained in the Marxian (and some mainstream) tradition, seems to falter if applied to the Ricardian case; taking Ricardo as the 'scientist' and Ms Martineau as the vulgar 'ideologue', for instance – not far from how history (whether written by Marxians or not) has perceived them – it would appear that, in this case, 'science' and 'ideology' were quite *complementary*, differing only in their being 'addressed', as a 'discourse', to different audiences, to the literati, in the first instance, and to the masses in the other; both of them, however, shared identical premises and supported similar policies, *differing only in how they move from premise to policy, i.e. in the mode of argument;* neither, it will be remembered, would brook any 'refutation', either on theoretical or empirical grounds. So, in this instance, it would appear that science was merely formalised ideology, whereas ideology was simply popularised science. Two different languages, but, nevertheless, delivering the same message. Of course, the truth is not that science and ideology are inherently such close cousins, generically speaking, but that Ricardo, rather, was about as far from science, as commonly understood, as the able Ms Martineau.

The policy emphasis, within a materialist problematic, as adopted in this work, does favour some scepticism about many dearly held ideas about Ricardo and his project. In this vein, I think the ordinary interpretation of the famous addition to the chapter 'On Machinery', as representative only of Ricardian 'candour' and intellectual honesty, might have a far simpler explanation (one that nonetheless does not necessarily detract from the common insinuation of the incorruptible integrity of Ricardo) than is normally advanced; now both mainstream and Marxist scholarship are convinced of the intellectual integrity of Ricardo, in 'admitting' that the introduction of machinery is detrimental to the interests of the working class, however temporarily. For instance, Pasinetti (1974, p. 21) believes that:

> ... the chapter 'On Machinery' appears ... an honest acknowledgement by Ricardo of the limitations of this theory.

In a similar vein, Rubin (1979, p. 239) holds that:

> with his great, and characteristic honesty and scientific candour ... he acknowledged that ... machinery is often injurious to the interests of the class of labourers.

In so focusing on the 'science' of Ricardo, *perhaps they fail to appreciate the political significance of the chapter on machinery*: I wish to suggest, and speculatively at that, that it is this chapter which finally clinched the Ricardian argument that the interest of landlords is opposed to all other interests. To explain: the declining net product spells declining rates of profit even as rents rise, so the issue of the diametrically opposed interests of the landlords and manufacturing capitalists was, plain to see, the *consequence* of restrictions on importation of foodstuffs, the impetus compelling recourse to marginal lands. However, why did the Corn Laws necessarily disadvantage the *working class*, aside from the threat of the 'stationary' state, which would put an end to all accumulation, presumably a long-run eventuality in the model (since constant real wages leave workers materially unaffected in the Corn Model, with or without the Laws)? It is the chapter 'On Machinery', I surmise, that securely links the Corn Laws with the *short-run* – i.e. the *immediate* – unemployment and distress of the working class, suggesting that *it was the high price of food that (through its stimulus to wages), was making inevitable the greater substitution of fixed for circulating capital* (so the Luddites, in reality, were not merely the victims of the normal progress of a mechanised, capitalised society, but the special victims of an abnormal speed-up of mechanisation engineered by the existence of the Corn Laws). Ricardo is quick to point out that he is not objecting to technical progress as such – for he could hardly be unaware that this process would survive unchanged after the repeal of the Laws – but merely to the *forced pace* owing to atypical conditions, *conditions which could, at least, be temporarily avoided if the price of food were to sink lower than it was.*

So, the irresistible implication was that the landlords, in the very short run, *distress both workers and capitalists* through their insistence on the Laws. The integrity of Ricardo, I venture, went well beyond the personal – the holy book was to leave no exit possible for the defenders of the English *ancien régime*: the chapter 'On Machinery' closed a gap through which the workers might, otherwise, easily have slipped out of the ranks of the general mobilisation.

11

I believe that this kind of practical understanding of the design of a model prevents the expression of naive 'deductions' from apparently abstract models by those who fail to understand – knowingly or otherwise – their real purpose. A scheme instrumental to one purpose is then taken out of context, whether to defend or to attack the model, the entire exercise being one of splendid irrelevance. Just one instance in this comment, by Pasinetti (1977, p. 17):

> At the beginning of the 19th century, the Ricardian theory ... was a remarkable step forward in the evolution of economic thought. When reconsidered more than a century and a half later, it obviously reveals many shortcomings and deficiencies ... Many of Ricardo's pessimistic conclusions have not been borne out by the economic history of the industrial countries.

Obviously, Professor Pasinetti has not understood the *purposive pessimism* of Ricardo, and sees it as a 'model' applicable, in general, to 'the economic history of the industrial countries'; not seeing the specificity, the model is universalised and then, obviously, found fault with. Now, the 'relevance' of Ricardo to the present stage of capitalism is a problematic issue. In a simple sense, his model, constructed on faulty premises, *has no application whatsoever – no more in our period than in his own.* However, in many 'Third World' contexts, where agrarian capital is pitted against industrial capital, replicating the English experience of the early nineteenth century, his struggles will be well understood, and perhaps his *false theorems* might even be, yet again, invoked. Marx, of course, understood the Ricardian problematic well when he wrote that, under certain conditions, private property in land is an obstacle to *economic growth*[15] and, in particular, to industrialisation. Certainly, the struggle in post-revolutionary Russia, between Kulaks and the state's repressive resolve for accelerated industrialisation was, strikingly, a *repetition* of the Ricardian struggle; at issue then, as in Ricardian times, were the relative prices of agricultural and manufactured goods ('corn' versus 'cotton', in the Ricardian period; peasants versus workers in the Russian case). Partisans of industrialisation – Ricardo as much as Trotsky – were out to subordinate agriculture to industry in order to provide cheap raw materials for the latter. However, the issue must be treated with care, for it cannot simply be assumed, a priori, that high agricultural prices, i.e. agrarian prosperity, is inimical to either economic growth or industrialisation; it is all a matter of context, and the time frame. Perhaps it might be said that, in the very short run, high farm prices might inhibit infant industrialisation efforts, but in the longer run it might provide both the surpluses and the demand for industry. So the paths chosen by Ricardo and Stalin need not be thought of as the *only* ones. *Private property in land, contra Marx, need not be an obstacle to industrialisation.*

Returning to Ricardian prognostications, the *stationary state*, as Professor Blaug has wisely reminded the student of Ricardo, was only a 'methodological fiction to scare the friends of protection' – it is not a *pessimistic anticipation of the course of an ideal capitalism*; indeed, the opposite is true, for the stationary state, as we know, is brought on by the Corn Laws, and in fact turns *progressive* with free importation. The dangers of *generalising* other Ricardian theorems run similarly, and I would urge that the effort itself be abandoned. The 'neo-Ricardian' fashion of 'demonstrating' the 'truth' of the propositions that the profit rate is, in general, dependent upon the conditions of production of wage goods is pure makeshift, for it rests upon assumptions as dubious as those assumed by Ricardo himself. Similarly, the Sraffian distinction between 'basic' and 'non-basic' goods is purely a *definitional* issue bearing no obvious connection with reality. Sraffian 'model-building' – the so-called 'neo-Ricardianism' – in this respect is, practically speaking, as superbly irrelevant as neoclassical architectonics.

Ricardo had the good sense to write theory in service of a cause that excited him; we might do well to emulate his high sense of purpose! The consistency between paradigm and policy is too obvious to be credibly denied, in the case of Ricardo, but I am, of course, arguing for an even stronger case: *that theory was an elaborate rationalisation for policy, i.e. it was policy objectives that prompted the entire 'theoretical' construction*; but the *Kontratheorie* would speak otherwise, as in the opinion of Tribe (1978, p. 146), who argues that:

> It would be quite erroneous ... to conceive this remobilisation of theoretical statements into political argument as the causal [sic] raison d'etre of these statements.

I, of course, do not quite see the 'erroneous' nature of the general argument, at least as applied to Ricardo; the independence of theory from policy is pure delusion in the Ricardian case, and I cannot see how, if at all, such a thesis could be sustained.

12

In conclusion, I wish to quote Toynbee (1928), who, marvelling at Ricardo's finesse in logic, philosophised that '… systems are strong not in proportion to the accuracy of their premises, but to the perfection of their reasoning', even while wondering at the 'curious' contrast, in Ricardo, between the 'looseness and unreality of the premises … and the closeness and vigour of the argument'. Actually, both these facets indicate something quite contrary to Toynbee's observation: that systems are 'strong' *not* in relation to either the 'accuracy' of their premises, or the 'perfection' of their reasoning, but in relation to their ability to answer to the practical needs of the time. Both the success and the failure of Ricardo hinged upon this rather trivial, but sometimes forgotten, fact. For social science, arguably, is generated by social purpose and mediated by social interests; its *findings*, usually, are axiomatically true, i.e. true by definition, pre-given in its premises – predetermined by policy, once we assume away matters of internal inconsistency. Most of the time, however, we, as part of the scientific establishment, are occupied in tracing aspects *internal* to paradigms,[16] either to approve or disprove them; but occasionally, it is enlightening to glance at the social purposes being rationalised by these elegant edifices, for this illuminates a different kind of raison d'être, one existing in a dimension *external* to theory. The strength of a paradigm may then be seen to derive not merely from its correspondence with reality, but from its consonance, also, with practical, social necessity.

It is the *instrumental* nature of social science which renders it a social project, to be judged as critically as any – and all – social institutions.[17] The a priori halo of purity often surrounding 'science' – usually the construct of the beneficiaries themselves, i.e. the *scientists*, something that peaked in England during the Ricardian era, and is with us still in the rampant fetishism of expertise in both bourgeois and 'socialist' societies – needs to be dimmed with far more scepticism than we commonly allow. For social science shifts gears and paradigms change, as social struggles and social relations restructure themselves; ultimately, all theory – like the Ricardian – bears the patent of transience, as new problems render the old archaic. Any notion of 'scientific continuity', thereby, in the evolution of the many schools of economic policy and theory, is possibly both chimerical and delusive; the insights of previous scholarship, engaged in problems and policies past, are then, in ridiculous teleology, seen as fumbling, incomplete anticipations of today's conventional wisdoms. *In the social sciences, the last marginal increment of knowledge does not represent the pinnacle of an absolutely given truth, but only an intuition relative to our own preoccupations*; for, the truth is that, from Smith to Keynes, economics has always been a series of rather submissive offerings to the jealous god of practical relevance.

Notes

1. For the restoration of ontological realism to the human sciences, see the work of Roy Bhaskar, 1989.
2. See, for instance, the mainstream view as articulated by Brewer, 1990, in an exchange between us.
3. For a pious account of young David's preoccupations, see Hollander, 1910.
4. For the full Ricardian story, see Kanth, 1986.
5. A pedestrian description, totally oblivious of both the class struggles of the time, and their importance to this critical period in the evolution of English capitalism, is available in Hilton, 1977.
6. For a vapid chronology, looking generally to the involvement of political economists in Parliament, but quite innocent of any larger agenda involved, see Fetter, 1980 and Gordon, 1976.
7. Of all mainstream analysts, only Professor Blaug, in all wisdom, has appreciated the status of this notion as a 'methodological fiction'; as such, his PhD thesis, published as a book (Blaug, 1958a), will forever stand the test of time.
8. For a devastating critique of the Sraffian interpretation, see the work of Peach, 1984 and 1987.
9. For corrections of this neglect, see Peach, 1987; and my own paper on Malthus in this volume.
10. For a detailed collation of Ricardian theories, totally divorced from their policy context, see, in four volumes, Wood, 1991.
11. As Bhaskar (1986, p. 2) writes, '... Kuhn ... [cannot] explain how there can be a clash between incommensurable descriptions, or to say over what such a descriptions clash'.
12. Smith's straightforward disparagement of merchants and manufacturers might be taken as a simple repudiation of his allegiance to industrial capital in any *direct* sense; however, it remains true that his insistence on laissez-faire, by delegitimising landlord and merchant control over the state, *indirectly – with the help of Ricardian interpretations of the idea* – paved the way for the triumph of industrial capital.

13 To treat the Ricardian system as the ideology of manufacturers would seem trivially obvious, until one confronts the fact that this connection is always disguised in mainstream theorising – as, for instance, in Grampp, 1960. A far more sophisticated veil of discretion is drawn over the subject by Blaug, 1958a, a work which remains one of the clearest treatments of the entire Ricardian oeuvre.

14 Refer again to the work of Schumpeter, 1954a, for illustrative data.

15 This proposition adduced by Marx in *Capital* (1967) was to become the mainstay of subsequent Marxian explorations in what came to be termed the 'Agrarian Question', the other major orthodox contributors being Kautsky and Lenin.

16 Traditionally, commentators – Marxist or mainstream – on the Ricardo question have taken what I term the 'internal' view of the paradigm; the work of Dobb, Sraffa and, more recently, Bharadwaj, 1983, are cases in point – their work, among other things, points to the 'surplus' emphasis in Ricardo (Ricardo being seen as the most important forerunner of Marx). While this approach has its merits, it usually fails to grasp the larger connections between theory and society, and is completely innocent of the real Ricardian project.

17 For the ultimate humanist critique of the project of science, see the unsurpassable essays of Feyerabend, 1987.

8 The Parson and the Plutocrat: Toward Restitution

1

The extraordinary neglect of Malthus (both Marxist and mainstream primers in the history of economic thought – unfailingly reliable indicators of prevailing academic orthodoxy – routinely omit a chapter on Malthus; see, by way of confirmation, the texts of Dobb, Ekelund, Blaug and Rubin, about as wide a spectrum of opinion as can be imagined) in histories of political economy, *outside of 'exogenous' discussions pertaining to demography and ecology*, is a significant indicator of the pervasive intrusion of ideological considerations in economic narratives which, routinely, can only pretend to pedestrian renderings of the straightforward, if somewhat antiquated, divide in the history of the discipline. The prevalence of grid readings and teleological accounts which, anachronistically, view the past history of the subject through the newest lens discovered – as though the marginal increment of knowledge were indeed the most significant one! – have all but guaranteed a certain rigor mortis to the discipline, beset as it is with the deep-running fault of pro and contra capitalist debate. It is this, largely undeclared, war of perspectives that has doomed Malthus to either share the prescribed lot of a grand Satan whose writings constitute a 'libel on the human race', as Marx had it, or to be quietly ignored, disparaged by neglect, on matters considered central to political economy proper (there has been, of course, a third categorisation, far more favourable to Malthus, if foredoomed to remain a minority view, in which he is asked to don unexpected robes as the true fountainhead of a 'correct' political economy – if only tradition had heeded the truth – as Keynes was to eulogise him decades later:

> If only Malthus, instead of Ricardo, had been the parent stem from which ... economics proceeded, what a much wider and richer place the world would be today (Keynes, 1972, pp. 100–01))!

In either case, the real, historical Malthus has been shoved aside, unrecognised and unknown, for the most part, for the critically important part he played in the development of Ricardian political economy, which took lead from Malthus. Almost as much as opposing him, in the grand *political* struggle between the aristocracies of land and capital that was the key setting for the period (and ideas) of both Malthus and Ricardo. This paper is addressed to the issue of this alarming historical indiscretion, not with a view to encapsulating the overall genius of Malthus, in his many capacities as theorist, polemicist, and apologist for special interests (*attributes that Ricardo shared, it is not always recognised, in equivalent measure*), but only to commence the effort of a necessary rethinking of these matters freed from the constricting grids emanating from either of the two grand traditions represented by Marx and Ricardo, and their several epigones, respectively.

2

In earlier work (Kanth, 1985 and 1986), I have argued that it was practical policy objectives that inspired the principal 'theoretical' pronouncements of classical economics in the Ricardian period, with *theory serving merely as a formal restatement of prior policy initiatives*. As Letwin put it succinctly, the Ricardians were prone to 'view economic theory as a particularly elegant way of demonstrating the merits of laissez-faire' (Letwin, 1964, p. v). In this dubious struggle, with politics masquerading as 'science', it was Malthus who, in his 1798 *Essay on Population*[1] (which, in histories of thought, is usually presented as an attack on the radical egalitarianism of William Godwin, although the truth – while certainly inclusive of that assertion – is a trifle more complex), written as a fierce rejoinder to the 1795 declaration of the magistracy of Berkshire (called the 'Speenhamland Amendment' to the Elizabethan Poor Laws) and its follow-through, Pitt's Poor Law Reform Bill of 1796, initiated the intellectual battle – and hence the era, as it were – that was subsequently to be taken up by the Ricardian enthusiasts. Actually (and this is a matter little known), however, the 1798 diatribe was preceded by a pamphlet – which Malthus was not, eventually, to publish – entitled *The Crisis* and penned in 1797 (see the anonymous memoir of Malthus, in Malthus's *Principles*,[2] 1836, p. xxxv), exclusively directed against the measures of William Pitt, particularly as these pertained to poor relief; thus, the *Essay* itself may be viewed as merely the ultimate extension, more fully specified, of Malthus's earlier polemic, one in which the opposition to public relief – welfare – is extended dramatically to encompass a fierce rejection of any and all alternatives to a class-dominated, hierarchical society (read this to mean, of course, England: in Malthus's own words:

> The principal argument of the Essay only goes to prove the necessity of a class of proprietors and a class of labourers ... (*1798 Essay*, p. 177).

The issue, broached by Speenhamland, was simplicity itself. The rural squirearchy, enlightened by the dreaded example of the French Revolution, had decided that they were unwilling to risk anarchy and revolt in their constituencies, facing famine, dearth and commercial crises, as occurred with increasing severity in the latter quarter of the eighteenth century. Setting aside the justly termed 'Laws against the Poor', the magistracy recognised the 'right' of the poor to public relief, with the extent of relief tied to the price of corn. It was this act of enlightened statesmanship (to be derided as 'paternalism'[3] by hostile critics with axes of their own to grind) that was seen as an abomination by manufacturers and their intellectual allies – the political economists – for killing the 'incentive' to labour, i.e. for blunting the cutting edge of starvation, and for raising the tax burden on profits, from which it was assumed, all taxes were ultimately paid. As Ricardo (*Works*, vol. 1, p. 257) was to write in his *Principles*,[4] the poor rates were a:

> Tax which falls with peculiar weight on the profits of the farmer ... it will be a general tax on the profits of stock ...

Less public-spirited – and more bourgeois-minded – landlords, no doubt, similarly felt that the cost of the poor rates far exceeded their social benefit. Evangelical humanitarians – and people of goodwill generally – nationwide, supported this sanction of charity (see Cowherd, 1956 and 1978, for more on this), and for a while their Christian and moral arguments carried public sentiment with them. A pastor himself, Malthus well understood the power of these sentiments; they could only be checked by appeal to sterner imperatives than the dictates of conscience: the 'laws of nature' ('These laws ... appear to have been fixed laws of our nature ...' (*1798 Essay*, p. 70); and further, 'I see no way by which man can escape from the weight of this law ...' (ibid., p. 72), which of course, as he would go on to preach, were the laws of God ('... we turn our eyes to the book of nature, where alone we can read God as he is ...' (ibid., p. 201)). Malthus's 'reading', of course, confirmed readily that the 'Being ... arranged the system of the universe ... according to fixed laws' (ibid., pp. 70–1). The *Essay* was ostensibly written to 'vindicate the ways of God to man' (ibid., p. 200); Malthus was, of course, quite certain that he had accomplished this task: as he writes, '... the principle of population, instead of being inconsistent with (divine) revelation, must be considered as affording strong additional proofs of its truth' (*Summary View of the Principle of Population*, 1830, reprinted in Malthus, 1970, p. 272).

Malthus's position as a Christian minister was, in fact, of critical significance in the public image, for 'Parson Malthus' could not, accordingly, be viewed as 'unchristian', despite his invocation of the laws of the jungle in the treatment of human – i.e. social – adversity. 'The sorrows and distresses of life,' he was to write, blithely, '... soften and humanise the heart ... and ... generate all the christian virtues ...' (*1798 Essay*, p. 209). And his appeal to 'science' suited the fashion of the times,[5] an age (still) of Newton (the specific adulation of the 'grand and consistent theory' of Newton may be found, in pages 126 and 163 of the *1798 Essay*), Hume, and positivism ('... experience, the true source and foundation of all knowledge', ibid., p. 72; and this prepossession was not abounded even later: '... we wish, with M. Say, to make political economy positive science, founded on experience ...' (Malthus, *Principles*, p. 33). Malthus's claims for his 'science' were inexorable indeed: they were, no less, 'incontrovertible truths' (*1798 Essay*, p. 80). It is small wonder, then, as to the centrality of 'mathematical propositions' (those daunting, but dubious ratios!; see ibid., pp. 74–6) in the spurious, if powerfully suggestive argument, made in the *Essay*, to the effect that the power of propagation must exceed – except for intervening catastrophe – productivity in agriculture (*and this in a country, the envy of Europe, that had come through a successful agricultural revolution in both the social and technical senses!*).

Ignoring the specious logic (confusing fecundity with fertility, to name only one issue) – and never mind that Keynes was to offer praise, in this regard, to Malthus's finesse for what he would call, thereby raising an obvious error to the status of a methodological precept, 'inductive verification'– the wild extrapolations (the 'doubling' of population every 25 years, and so on), the policy message, at least, was irresistibly clear: any welfare provided the poor would only increase their numbers, and hence the overall magnitude of wretchedness, instead, it was more humanitarian (Christian?) to simply let nature take its course, thereby 'adjusting' optimal numbers to available capacity. Malthus had provided a 'scientific' case (the less enlightened had not yet learned to fight the bogey of diminishing returns implicitly raised in the analysis by virtue of its reference to the fixed 'supply' of land; economics has since learnt to 'assume' increasing or diminishing returns at will, depending upon the proposition to be proved!) against the Speenhamland Reform and, more generally, against relief to the poor. The first Ricardian lesson had just been taught, and a grand tradition initiated – still extant to our day – *of using the formalism(s) of 'science' as an instrument to serve more murky social designs.*

Science as a cloak for private purposes had been invented for economics, and Ricardo (and his present-day progeny) would carry the idea to still greater lengths in his own work. As Ricardo agitated against the Poor Laws in Parliament, he would invoke Malthusian science as his main prop: 'The pernicious tendency of these laws is no longer a mystery', he was to say, 'since it has been fully developed by the able hand of Mr. Malthus' (Ricardo, *Principles*, p. 196). Indeed, in his own early 'model' of the economy (his

1815 *Essay on Profits*, christened the 'corn-model' by Sraffians for highly debatable reasons) – penned in haste as he sharpened tools with which to deal with his pet policy problem, the Corn Laws – it is Malthusian population dynamics that form, along with the notion of diminishing returns, an implacable scaffolding (Ricardo, like Malthus, would rule out technical progress, at least to the point of seeing it as ultimately unable to thwart the ineffable workings of that irresistible tendency towards abating returns); again, mind you, in English agriculture, easily the most technically advanced agriculture of the time! And in fact, consideration would show that the Ricardian so-called *'corn-model'* is quite inconceivable without Malthusian equipment: the perfectly elastic supply curve of labour at the subsistence wage (to employ the tediously neoclassicist and obviously non-Ricardian terminology), a necessary assumption, is drawn from – and in fact based upon – Malthusian population mechanisms; likewise, agrarian diminishing returns, again a necessary assumption, is an idea touted originally by Malthus in conjunction with his theory of rent – an idea which Ricardo would absorb into his own rival system, albeit with modification ('Mr. Malthus', he would write, '... has satisfactorily explained the principles of rent' (Ricardo, *Principles*, in *Works*, vol. 1, p. 398)). Both of these axial supports of the Ricardian model are fundamentally Malthusian in aspiration, and reflect, even at this early stage, the enormous Ricardian debt to Malthusian ideas.

3

Malthus's contribution to the Ricardian crusade – via his diatribe against the Poor Laws expressed in his pseudo-population theory – would have been quite enough to secure him the role of an original inspirer of the Ricardian project (in fact, Schumpeter's assignation of the *'Ricardian Vice'* – arguing from assumed strong cases – needs correction: it was a Malthusian corruption to being with!). But, in reality, Malthus was to serve Ricardo even more, and better, for it is in his role as defender of the political economy of landlords, against Ricardo's unrelenting antipathy towards the latter, that Malthus distinguished himself as – ultimately – the most profound critic of Ricardian theory in Ricardo's own time. Patiently and persistently, Malthus exposed the specious nature of Ricardian assumptions, and the egregious errors in his reasoning, all the way from the problems with the original 1815 *Essay on Profits*, to the last gasp of the so-called 'invariable standard' in the continually amended – under pressure of Malthusian criticism – versions of the *Principles*. If anyone impressed upon Ricardo the ultimate futility of his search for the 'invariable measure' – a mighty feat considering his doughty stubbornness – it was Malthus; not out of ignorance as to the meaning of Ricardo's quest, as with many (including Ricardo's own loyal following, such as McCulloch, for instance), but secured with a full knowledge of Ricardo's logical and political concerns. In the reshaping of the notion of the invariable measure of value, if not all of the *Principles*, Malthus was the greatest single influence on Ricardo of all economists previous or contemporaneous, in spite – or perhaps because – of the enormous differences between their ideas and interests. And yet both the logical force and the powerful impact of Malthus's criticism of Ricardo have been consistently overlooked in most contemporary discussions of the period.[6]

But whence Ricardo's project? In much the same way as Malthus's 1798 *Essay on Population* was the definitive 'scientific' attack on the Poor Laws, Ricardo's 1815 *Essay on Profits* (subsequently to be rewritten with more care, despite its enduring inadequacies, as the famous *Principles* of 1817 – a work which Winch correctly characterises as an 'ingenious attack on the Corn Laws writ large' (Winch, 'Introduction', in Ricardo, 1974, p. vii)) was intended as an irrefutable cannonade directed against the Corn Laws; it is instructive to note, however, that Ricardo intended his work to be a rejoinder to Malthus's 1815 *Inquiry into the Nature of Progress of Rent*, and 1815 *Grounds of an Opinion* (both following upon the heels of Malthus's 1814 *Observations on the Effects of the Corn Laws*), published earlier, such that even the struggle over the Corn Laws – as with the Poor Laws – was essentially inaugurated by *prior* Malthusian initiatives. The gap between the two separate Malthusian diatribes, which in fact might not have existed otherwise, was most likely due to the Napoleonic threat, which imposed a tactical unity on the warring classes until the resolution of Waterloo. However, the latter even opened up the floodgates of debate and struggle, initiating a battle finally to be won by the industrial legions – massed under the determined, even inveterate, leadership of Monsieur Le Capital: Ricardo.

As viewed by manufacturers, and their allies, the political economists, the case against the Corn Laws was, in truth, simple enough: that the forcible restriction on importation of corn was compelling recourse to poorer domestic lands, thereby raising costs – via the corn wage – and depressing (ultimately) non-agrarian rates of profit. Additionally, and for good measure, the Corn Laws were said to have prevented the development of a foreign market for manufactured English goods, which could be – in a classical, colonial sense – exchanged profitably for cheaper, foreign food. The Portuguese-wine-for-English-cloth idea, presented by Ricardo, and touted ad nauseam in text books ever since as a 'theory' of international trade, thus neatly captured, as in metaphor, how emergent industrial Britain (the scourge of the non-European world for at least a century) was, for quite some time to come, to view the rest of the world – *as it is humbly subordinate colony.*

The matter, of course, was – at least in principle – open to a determinate, empirical test. But it is an index of the political economy of the time (and of the present period as well!) – and the weak, almost nonexistent notion of validation within that tradition – that few such attempts were made with any seriousness. More characteristically, the problem was simply 'assumed' to exist, and a theoretical model, itself built upon untested 'assumptions', was erected to 'prove' (with or without the benefit of any corroborative evidence) that the problem indeed must exist and would, by implication, continue to exist until either the Corn Laws were repealed, or the entire 'neat produce' (sic) of the nation was paid off in the form of rent to the class of landlords – a class whose interest was said to be implacably contrary to the entire national interest.

Ricardo's 1815 *Essay on Profits*, accordingly, had a simple problematic; to connect – or to 'show' – the rise in corn wages (as leading) to a fall in the general profit rate. By extending this 'farm model' to cover the overall economy, Ricardo felt that he had fully demonstrated his proposition that the rate of profit varied with the intensity of the force compelling diminishing returns (Ricardo had quickly predigested the Malthusian theory of rent, published only weeks earlier, seeing its tremendous value for his own ideas on distribution). But Malthus had no difficulty exploding the pretensions of the *Essay* (in fact, Malthus had ruled out the Ricardian idea that it is the 'profits of the farmer which regulates the profits of all other trades' (Ricardo, *Works*, vol. VI, pp. 103–04; as he put it '... I have always maintained that when corn rises, though other commodities would rise they would not rise in proportion' (Malthus, ibid., p. 222)), as well as the notion that there could be a 'material rate of produce' as early as 1814 – 'In no case of production, is the produce exactly of the same nature as the capital advanced. Consequently, we can never properly refer to a material rate of produce ...' (Malthus, ibid., p. 117) – thereby rejecting as improbable the alleged product-capital homogeneity that Ricardo is said to have worked with in the *Essay*,[7] even before the latter had been published in exchange of correspondence. That the discussion could not be conducted outside of a value reckoning in simple physical terms ('exchange value is not ... always proportioned to its quantity' (Malthus, ibid., pp. 140–41)) was, further, made categorically explicit. The Ricardian 'farm' model would not do when reality was otherwise – with dualism at least as far as capital structures went, requiring, therefore, an articulated theory of value, to explain changes in the terms of trade between agricultural and manufactured gods, this connected with the 'diminishing returns in agriculture' argument that buttressed the entire Ricardian analysis.

Ricardo's abandonment of Smith's value theory, and his 'competition of capitals' view of decline of profitability, (still implicitly, if recedingly, assumed by Ricardo in his *Essay*), thus had to do, ultimately, with the force of Malthus's criticism; that is to say, *the search for a labour standard of value was set off by Ricardo's understanding that his case could not be proved within Smithian value and distributive parameters*, a concession forced upon him by the penetration of Malthus's observations regarding the inadequacy of the original

Essay on Profits model of the economy. But Ricardo, in his writing of the *Principles*, where, initially at least (in the first and second editions), a simple labour theory was thought sufficient to establish his critical relationship – such that labour time itself could suffice as an invariable standard, continued in his slumbering ignorance – or avoidance! – or the real issues. Malthus's rejection of the pure labour theory idea was unadornedly straightforward:

> There are ... causes practically in operation which prevent the exchangeable value of commodities from being proportioned to the quantity of labour employed upon them ... It is scarcely possible, indeed to take up two commodities of different kinds, which will be found to exchange with each other in proportion to the quantity of labour worked up in each ... (Malthus, *1836 Principles*, p. 91).

In the first and second editions of his *Principles*, the invariable standard was simply *assumed*: 'if we had then an invariable standard ...' (Ricardo, *Principles*, 1st ed., in *Works*, vol. I, p. 56); again, it took a Malthusian chastisement to rouse Ricardo, grudgingly, from his dogmatic slumbers (underscoring, incidentally, the driving practical necessity, epitomised in the Ricardian endeavour, to arbitrarily 'prove' – regardless of the logical demands involved – a case that was already, a priori, considered to be true; *i.e. when the agenda is not one of science, as normally understood, but of simple political expediency*: regrettably, Ricardian 'findings' uniformly preceded Ricardian investigations).

In fact, Malthus had little difficulty showing that, once divergent capital structures were admitted, price changes could not simply be linked solely to alterations in labour expenditures:

> We can infer nothing respecting the rate of profits from a rise of money wages, if commodities, instead of remaining of the same price, are variously affected, some rising, some falling, and a very small number indeed remaining stationary (Malthus, in Ricardo, *Works*, vol. II, p. 286).

Such a 'perfect' measure simply could not exist. Bit by bit, then, in successive editions of the *Principles*, Ricardo was forced to yield the issue, at least on the limited, and yet vital, question of a measure invariant both to distribution and technical change. The extraordinary success of Malthusian probings may be gauged by the abject, if long-drawn, Ricardian surrender, when the vaunted 'invariable standard' boiled down – in the last edition – to fixing on gold (!) as the least objectionable standard in question (and this from a scholar who had castigated Smith for 'confusion' in value matters; it was Smith, it will be recalled, who had originally shown the unreliability of precious metals as measures of value). As Malthus was to say, in this context:

He is of course compelled to acknowledge in the outset, that a measure so constituted, 'would be a perfect measure of value for all things produced under the same circumstances precisely as itself, but for no others'. But what a prodigious concession this is! What a full and entire acknowledgement is it at once that the measure can be of no use (Malthus, *Principles*, pp. 124–25).

The characteristically Ricardian response to the destruction of his model, and hence of his 'ironclad' case against the Corn Laws, is also instructive: Ricardo continued to believe, to the end, in the correctness of his cause; so much so, that, even having conceded logical defeat ('Of such a measure, it is impossible to be possessed ...' (Ricardo, *Works*, vol. I, p. 43)), he went on to suggest that the real, empirical, significance of Malthusian modifications could not be more than a few percentage points ('The greatest effects ... could not exceed 6 or 7 per cent' (ibid., p. 36) – whence, of course, the Stiglerian 93 per cent theory of value idea), thereby shifting terms, suddenly, on to a very different terrain. Indeed, manufacturers and their political allies, blissfully ignorant of the holes in Ricardo's model, continued to quote him for their cause, as if an oracle were being consulted and held to witness; and they were to win their struggle handsomely, regardless of the correctness of his ideas, even as Malthus would receive short shrift at the hands of the Ricardians. As Malthus was to write to Sismondi (in Ricardo, *Works*, vol. VIII, pp. 376–77):

The Edinburgh Review has so entirely adopted Mr. Ricardo's system of Political Economy it is probable neither you or I shall be mentioned in it ....

Poor Malthus, railing impotently against the Ricardians, had to drink the bitter cup to the dregs, for the phantom of spurious science that he himself had unleashed in his 1798 *Essay on Population* (based as it was on tendentious reasoning and motives political) had now come back to haunt him in the form of Ricardianism – which would now effectively dispossess Malthus's cause (defending the landed interest) just as efficiently as his own arguments had disarmed the friends of Speenhamland. Diminishing returns, which were rallied against the amended Poor Laws, were now effectively being roused against the Corn Laws by his personal friend and political adversary. Ironically, Malthus was to find himself – discreetly – questioning, in Ricardo, the very assumption that he had made in his own 1798 *Essay*, as to the pace and effectiveness of technical change in agriculture:

But unless it could be shown that no improvements were ever to take place either in agriculture or in manufacture ... the [Ricardian] doctrine is evidently not correct in practice (Malthus, in Ricardo, *Works*, vol. VI, pp. 139–40).

The bogey of diminishing returns, raised by Malthus in favour of landlords (as Cannan was to write (1964, p. 231): '... the agriculturalists imagined they were strengthening their case for protection by insisting on the greater cost of growing wheat on the additional land which had recently been turned to that purpose'), was now effectively to be used against that very order by Ricardo, who argued that their effect was merely to depress profits and raise rents – such that rents could be construed a pure and simple (and unjustified) transfer income to landlords. Malthus (*Principles*, p. 152) could only protest this in vain:

> When a given value of capital yields smaller returns, whether on new land or old, the loss is generally divided between the labourers and capitalist, and wages and profits fall at the same time. This is quite contrary to Mr. Ricardo's language.

And, even more pointedly:

> Mr. Ricardo has supposed a case ... of a diminution of fertility ... and he thinks it would increase rents by pushing capital upon less fertile land. I think, on the contrary, that in any well cultivated country it could not fail to lower rents, by occasioning the withdrawal of capital from the poorest soils ... (ibid., p. 144).

So did the biter get bit, on this piece of intellectual sophistry, as unsupported by any decisive evidence in what it denied, as in what it sought to affirm (quite in consonance with the doubtful validity of the Ricardian assertion it sought to refute).

4

Nor was the Malthusian contribution only with respect to criticism of Ricardo's faulty value theory. In fact, via Keynes, Malthus is best remembered – or should be – as an early critic of capitalist complacency about the self-regulating nature of their favourite system. Here, by exploding the myth of Say's Law against the grain of the Ricardian tradition:

> It has been thought by some ... writers, that although there may ... be a glut of particular commodities, there cannot possibly be glut of commodities in general ... This doctrine ... appears to me to be utterly

unfounded and completely to contradict the great principles which regulate supply and demand (Malthus, *Principles*, p. 315).

Or, again, by pointing to structural weakness inherent in a system where the link between production and consumption is both weak and indirect (earning for Malthus the obloquy, from the Marxists, of being an 'undercomsumptionist', while receiving praise from Keynes for the same), thereby showing up the limits to laissez-faire ('It is obviously impossible, therefore, for a government strictly to let things take their natural course ...' (ibid., p. 16)) in favour of legitimate intervention by way of public works:

> It is also of importance to know that, in our endeavours to assist the working classes in a period like the present, it is desirable to employ them in those kinds of labour ... such as roads and public works ... (ibid., p. 429).

Also, by drawing attention to the problem of 'hoarding' as against savings ('No political economist of the present day can by saving mean mere hoarding' (ibid., p. 38)); and, by pointing out the dangers of both ('... the principle of saving, pushed to excess, would destroy the motive to production ...' (ibid., p. 7)); and, by indicating the fiscal aspects of the national debt:

> By greatly reducing the national debt ... we may place ourselves perhaps in a more safe position ... but grievously will those be disappointed who think that, either by greatly reducing or at once destroying it, we can enrich ourselves ... (ibid., p. 427).

In all of these strikingly realist empirical observations about the nature of capitalist reality (profoundly above the ideologically-saturated ignorance of Ricardo), Malthus inaugurated a cautionary, regulative, vision of capitalism that was, in fact, to become the mainstay of the Keynesian mainstream in our own century.

Indeed, in pointing to the demand side weaknesses of classical economics:

> The conversion of revenue into capital pushed beyond a certain point must by diminishing the effectual demand for produce throw the labouring classes out of employment ... accompanied by distressing effects ... and by a marked depression of wealth ... (ibid., p. 326)

And, alluding to the importance of unproductive consumption:

> It is necessary that a country with great powers of production should possess a body of consumers ... not themselves engaged in production (ibid., p. 398).

And, again, in pursuing the theme of underconsumption further, '... the greatest powers of production are rendered comparatively useless without effectual consumption ...' (ibid., p. 411), in a system where realisation is at least as important as production, Malthus was perhaps (within the classical tradition) the greatest forerunner, other than Senior, of the post-classical 'exchange'-based economics that was to supplant the Ricardian school in the late '70s of the century. And, with the exception of the later generation of Senior, no classical economist came closer to the 'three factors of production' vision of the neoclassical tradition, as well as the latter-day insistence on not making invidious distinction between 'productive' and 'unproductive' activities ('Almost every person indeed, must occasionally do some productive labour ...' (ibid., p. 48)), at least to the extent of not seeing 'unproductive' activities as somehow prejudicial to the societal interest:

> It should also be constantly borne in mind, that Adam Smith fully allows the vast importance of many sorts of labour, which he calls unproductive (ibid.).

In fact, the neglect of Malthus possibly has provenance in this paradox, that, in himself, Malthus contained the major ideas of both Keynesian and neoclassical theories, aeons ahead of either tradition – all the more extraordinary when it is remembered that he came to maturity in the age of Smith (last quarter of the eighteenth century), rather than that of Ricardo. Additionally, of course, part of the disrepute that still attaches to Malthus is based upon his championship of agrarian and landed interests in an age that, both in its capitalist and socialist variants, holds up industrialisation as the touchstone of progress – making him out, thereby, as something of a romantic reactionary, rather than the truth (which is closer to the role of the later Bukharin in the Soviet industrialisation effort), which is that of a cautious progressive seeking a compromised capitalist development, reconciling order with change without the necessity for a destructive, internecine, struggle between the two coevals within the same emergent ruling class – the oligarchs of land and the captains of industry, respectively. And lastly, the spurious 1798 *Essay* now has become – deservedly – the relatively permanent millstone around the memory of Malthus, tragically, but inevitably, recalling to the average student the howlers from an ill-conceived propaganda piece, as against the inspired brilliance of his easy disposition of Ricardo's clumsy analytical blunders, or his surprisingly modernist presentation of political economy in his own *Principles*, penned in 1820 as a riposte to the Ricardian work. Although Malthusian ideas are, in content, complementary to – and consistent with – the neoclassical world view, with respect to the form assumed by the latter in our own century, Malthus would have had some misgivings; '... the science of political economy bears a nearer resemblance to the science of morals and politics than to that of mathematics ...' he wrote (*Principles*, p. 1), underscoring his appreciation of economics as a *social* science, in spite of its axiomatic and deductive nature, as presented, in fact – with a hint of contradiction – in his own account: for, in his own words, in economics we are dealing with: 'So variable a being as man' (ibid.).

It is, however, a statement on the policy relevance of economic science that virtually all of the very contemporary-sounding criticisms of Ricardo (on theory, policy, and method) emanating from Malthus were logically necessitated by his own contra policy agenda; the economic importance of landlords ('unproductive consumers'), the challenge to Say's Law, the resistance to laissez-faire, the stress on effective demand, and the plea to make practical correction to all general principles in economics (a wise reminder to our profession given to theoretical recklessness, as it is) were all necessary to obstruct the Ricardian programme, which was itself built upon contrasting positions on these same issues. The fact that he was more correct on these matters than Ricardo – sometimes in logic, sometimes in empirical fact – did little, of course, to establish Malthus's reputation: *social science does not – nor could it – live by its truth content alone.*

In fact, Malthus received 'rough treatment' at the hands of the Ricardians, dizzy in their euphoric adulation of the age of industrial capital. What was useful to the Ricardian cause (the principle of population, diminishing returns in agriculture, etc.) was scavenged happily by their ilk (Ricardo, in all plainness, took essentially Malthusian theories of rents and wages, and added to them only a rather dubious notion of profit decline, under highly controlled, artificial conditions; there is no real 'theory' of profit in Ricardo, only a vaguely implied 'deduction' idea: and that sufficed – amazingly – to constitute his much vaunted 'theory' of distribution; as for his theory of value, it has all the unrequited splendour of a simply labour theory, i.e. it was a grand, but quite total, failure). What did not fit into the great Ricardian programme – or was simply embarrassing – was either rejected with contempt, or ignored with a stony silence. Class struggle then, as now, was the ultimate arbiter of social truth.

What is remarkable about the Ricardo-Malthus encounter is not its secure basis in their diverging support for contrary class interests – which is quite simply irrefutable – but perhaps their rather amicable personal relationship.[8] Of course, uninformed, or merely tendentious, scholarship would seize upon the latter to try and gainsay the former; in fact, Malthus would himself argue thus (*Principles*, pp. 216–17):

> It is somewhat singular that Mr. Ricardo, a considerable receiver of rents, should have so much underrated their national importance while I, who never received, nor expect to receive any, should probably be accused of overrating their importance. Our different opinions, under these

circumstances, may serve at least to show our mutual sincerity, and afford a strong presumption, that to whatever bias our minds may be subjected in the doctrines we have laid down, it has not been that, against which perhaps it is most difficult to guard, the insensible bias of situation and interest.

In what it both affirms and denies, this statement is rather dismally shallow political sociology; firstly, and most importantly, direct class membership is neither a necessary nor a sufficient condition for class affiliation; secondly, and this is trivial, Ricardo's fortune did derive originally from profits – in the bourse – and only subsequently from rents, quite the usual pattern of transition in the England of the time; thirdly, the Church of England – an institution which Malthus served formally – derived its revenue primarily from tithes on landed income – so that Malthus's parsonian entitlements were anything but unconnected to landed property, even though he may not have – as he claims – 'directly' received rents. Finally, it needs to be remembered that the struggle between corn and cotton was not a do-or-die class struggle between the haves and the have-nots, but rather a squabble between the senior and junior partners of the ruling alliance; both had stakes in property ownership, political stability and ultimate stewardship over the labouring classes. In this respect, quite apart from their personal friendship, which need not be doubted, the two orders they defended were not exactly implacable enemies. Profits and rents were at odds only to the extent that the former were attempting to establish suzerainty over the latter, indicating the altered economic and political balance between the two strata; the two ranks, in fact, were to make immediate peace (forming a solid phalanx against workers) once the Reform Act had been passed, and the Corn and Poor Laws repealed (and rents subordinated to profits). Under such circumstances, it is not difficult to appreciate the lack of any bitter blood feud between the two rival champions.

5

The choice between a Malthus and a Ricardo, apologists for landlords and manufacturers respectively, is, accordingly – for one not enamoured of either property-owning order, in the scheme of capitalism – a futile one. It is easy to see, however, why Ricardo has traditionally come off looking better, because *the sympathies of economists – as defenders of the regime of capital – are definitely, now as then, with industrial capital; indeed, economics – excepting some marginal schools – itself may be defined as the crown jewel of the latter's hegemonic ideology.* There are other reasons, of course, why even the critics of capitalism, such as the Marxists, have tended to vote along with their class enemies on this issue: industrial capitalism, through development of productive forces, and the objective socialisation of labour, lays the groundwork for the construction of socialism, in the orthodox, Marxian account – hence, any mechanism that stands in the way of capital performing its allotted tasks, social or technical, is seen (almost automatically) as reactionary. Thereby, peasant modes, tribal societies, and/or native traditions that offer resistance to capitalist advance, all come to be seen as reactionary impediments to the march of progress – with progress defined exclusively in terms of the modalities of the capitalist revolution, the logical limits of which are plumbed, in all their craven depths, in Bill Warren's (1980) inspired 'Marxist' defence of the terrors of colonialism, the slave trade, and imperialism, as necessary, civilising medicine for the historically obsolete peoples of the Third World. Malthus, as well as his favourite social class of paternalist aristocrats, fell afoul of this view – indeed agenda – of progress; hence their championship of Ricardo – despite, it needs be remembered, the latter's single-minded opposition to even minimal relief to the working poor in times of penury, dearth and wretchedness, as sanctioned by the sparse charity of Speenhamland. Ricardo's concrete moves against the working class – even so nominal a political right as suffrage was only to be allowed workers, by Ricardo, on the basis of property ownership and assured loyalty to the capitalist order. As he wrote to Trower:

> In other words ... you [wish for] ... a good choice of representatives and this is precisely what I want. If I cannot obtain it without limiting the elective franchise to the very narrowest bounds, I would so limit it ... but I am persuaded that we should ... get our object ... by extending the electoral franchise – not indeed universally to all people, but to that part of them which cannot be supposed to have any interest in overturning the right of property (Ricardo, *Works*, VII, pp. 369–70).

Under this sound bourgeois prescription, a limited set of workers won the right to vote, after bitter struggle, as late as 1867; women, of course, the other subaltern order within English capitalism, had to wait until 1918 for political membership. Those who automatically see capitalism and democracy as 'Siamese twins' – to use a phrase of Warren's – need to reflect further (specially since Siamese twins are usually separated at the very moment of birth) – are either forgotten or rationalised in view of Ricardo's superior contribution to the maturation of the capitalist revolution in Britain.

Of course, that is not the whole story. Giving implicit credence to the general view that Ricardo was the 'greatest of the political economists' (or as Rubin (1989, p. 244), faithful to his master, puts it even more grandiosely, 'Ricardo's theoretical constructs, once altered and corrected ... are ... one of the great monuments of human thought ...'), Marx insisted upon first inheriting, and then improving upon the Ricardian patrimony – so much so that Marx could be viewed (presumably to his own satisfaction), as he is often termed, as the 'heir' to the classical tradition – the one who had 'bettered' the greatest of the economists. The most politically class-conscious of the bourgeois economists of the classical school was, accordingly, to be singled out by Marx for almost unreservedly lavish compliments for the virtue, ostensibly – if amazingly! – of his analytical insights (something even a 'retrograde' Malthus had shown to be riddled with holes!). But of course the truth is not hard to see: Ricardo had espoused, in Marx's understanding, a 'labour theory' (never mind that Marx did not understand the limited heuristic nature of Ricardo's instrumental use of the idea)– by no stretch of the imagination could Ricardo be conceived as ever being, or even wanting to be, even on the same turnpike as Marx leading to a theory of surplus value; and yet Marxists often argue as if Ricardo were a brilliant, if slightly bumbling, precursor of Marx, coming close, yet missing, the ultimate philosopher's stone. As Rubin writes (1989, p. 260):

> Although Ricardo does not inquire directly ... the general direction of his thinking leads him to the concept of surplus value.

And, again:

> We find in Ricardo the embryonic shoots of a theory ... but it was left to Marx to develop the theory (ibid., p. 255).

Marx himself, of course, paved the way for such a left handed appreciation of Ricardo, wherein Ricardo is reproached for not having followed through with the Marxian agenda. 'Ricardo's writings should have led him to the distinction between surplus value and profit', he writes (Marx, 1969, p. 427); and again, 'Instead of labour, Ricardo should have discussed labour power ...' (ibid., p. 400). Quite innocent of Marxian preoccupations, Ricardo's value theory was, at least initially, no more than a device: more a labour measure than a labour theory, used to help compare changes in agrarian and industrial values over time. Only later in his life, in his reflections on 'absolute' value, did Ricardo ponder the potential importance of the idea of a labour scheme of valuation within a proto-Marxian genre. At any rate, quite amazingly, Marx seems quite unaware of the real reasons for the recourse to a labour valuation in Ricardo:

> But at last Ricardo steps in and calls to science: Halt! The basis, the starting point for the physiology of the bourgeois system ... is the determination of value by labour time ... This then is Ricardo's great historical significance for science ... (ibid., p. 166).

Had Marx compared Ricardo's ideas in his *Essay* with the reformulations in the *Principles*, and had he read Malthus's intervening criticisms of the former, he would have had a better appreciation of the Ricardian attachment to the 'labour' theory, and a sounder understanding of Ricardo's own programme! Aside from harbouring a labour theory, the appeal of Ricardo for Marx lay in his apparent sanction for some form of 'class conflict' in his vision of capitalism (interestingly, Ricardian ideas were mistrusted by class-conscious neo-classicals for this same reason, despite its utter falsity; Ricardo had an essentially harmonious vision of social relations within capitalism, so long as the Corn Laws were repealed and cheap corn could be imported freely; given that, the rate of profit, he argued, would be perpetually buoyant; the bogey of the 'stationary state' was simply, as Blaug wisely notes, a piece of '*methodological fiction*' – like so much of economics! – to scare the friends of protection) principally between landlords against the rest of the 'people', and between capitalist and labourer, at least temporarily, owing to the dislocation caused by the hasty introduction of machinery, itself precipitated by the Corn Laws (never mind that this latter was an afterthought, politically conceived, presented in the third edition of the *Principles*; see the essay on Ricardo in this volume). That was enough; Ricardo could now be conceived as a proto-Marxian 'giant'! It goes without saying that Marx, untrue to this own materialist method (as in the writing of the more dehistoricised sections of capital itself) missed the real agenda underlying Ricardo's theories by a mile; and Marx's loyal epigones, with neither the courage nor the intelligence – not to speak of originality – apparently, to stir beyond Marx's own pronouncements, have loyally stuck to this version to this day. Proof of this proposition may be found by picking up a copy of any Marxist history of thought text, where Marx's working notes in the *Theories of Surplus Value* are faithfully transcribed or reworded – I hesitate to say plagiarised – usually only to the detriment of the original Marxian passion, originality and/or insight.

At any rate, Malthus, therefore, has been slain twice: once by the Ricardians, who ensured that his ideas would be ignored by virtue of their near monopoly of the more popular organs of scholarship in Malthus's own time, and by pro-manufacturers's ideology generally; and, a second time, by the Marxian tradition – with its wont of hailing Ricardo as the superior political economist of the classical school (despite, it will be noted, the latter's shaky position on Say's Law, his notion of the 'impossibility' of a general glut, and the accompanying denial of crises, the tendency towards underconsumption in capitalism etc., viewed in relation to the strong Malthusian criticism of these ideas). Now, the Marxists can well afford to ignore Malthus, for, at least ultimately, their social vision involves – or should involve – a rejection of both Malthus and Ricardo, as well as their social ideologies; but, for mainstream currents, this neglect is a sorry one, for Malthus was one of their own, a brilliant and original intellect – capable both of science and propaganda (the two requirements characteristic, apparently, of every effective economist!) – and wasted only by his arguing in conservative fashion against the stream of gathering capitalist political and social forces. It is only fitting then that, as an enlightened capitalist spokesperson, to employ his own self-description, Keynes would offer public tribute – however opportunistically – to the genius of Malthus for pointing to weaknesses within capitalism – weaknesses that were, apparently, no more admissible in Keynes's time (witness the obduracy of what was to be called the 'Treasury View') than they were in Malthus's own period. *It is perhaps not too late now to own that the greatest political economist of the classical period was the parson (Malthus), not the plutocrat (Ricardo).*

To the toiling poor within capitalism, however, either in the metropolis or in the degrading periphery of world capitalism, Malthus must necessarily remain – given the misdeeds still committed against them in his name – the Archsatan, whose writings on and about them remain, in Marx's unsurpassably eloquent phrase, a 'libel on the human race', all the more vicious for coming from one who occupied the hallowed space of a minister of the anointed church of emergent capitalist, and firmly Christian, England of the early nineteenth century. It is quite appropriate, therefore, that as we pay tribute to Malthus's intellectual genius, belatedly, we nonetheless remind ourselves of its regrettable propinquity to what Southey called, in equally categorical prose, 'bad arithmetic, bad morals and bad theology'.

Notes

1 References to the 1798 *Essay* are drawn from Malthus, 1982.
2 References to Malthus's *Principles* are taken from Malthus, 1964.
3 Capitalist ideology is remarkably consistent across epochs; if the state helps the poor, it is a noxious form of 'paternalism'; if it helps the rich, it's enlightened economic policy.
4 References to Ricardo's *Principles* are drawn from Sraffa (with the collaboration of Dobb), 1951–73.
5 If only the general populace were somehow to become aware of the burlesque parody represented by the pretensions of social science, what a revolution it would inspire!!
6 The work of Terry Peach is a salutary exception to the general disregard of Malthus; see Peach, 1984 and 1987.
7 There is, of course, no explicit evidence of such an assumption in the *Essay*; nor does it appear to be either a necessary or a sufficient one to prove the Ricardian case – but there is no doubt, nonetheless, that Ricardo was working with a notion of the profit share being measured in physical terms, so as to abstract from monetary fluctuations.
8 For a recent comment on this matter, see Dorfman, 1989.

Part V
REVOLUTIONS IN ECONOMIC THEORY: THE PARAMETERS OF PARADIGM SHIFT

9 The Eclipse of Ricardian Ideas: A Primer on Paradigm Shift in Economics

1

The continued resilience of Ricardo criticism, in the history of economic ideas, is almost as striking as the sudden devolution of the original Ricardian paradigm: an inverse proportionality that deservedly demands critical notice. The bête noir of economic theory of over 150 years ago still arouses impassioned debate, as evidenced in his high incidence in current controversy. In this resurgence of antiquity Ricardo, to be sure, is not alone – Marx being the irresistible case in point (though, after the Great Fall of the socialist bloc, there is definitely a sense of debate being on the decline in the latter's case). Perhaps the analogy itself offers at least one clue – that ideology might explain the persistence of certain ideational schemes in history. But one could also posit another case: that both Ricardo and Marx were 'correct' in some suitably refined 'scientific' sense whence it might be argued that their ideas (or ideas about them) endure because, again in some acceptable sense, they are 'true' much as some – not all – Copernican ideas endure for the reason, presumably, that they are still considered scientific, and hence legitimate, if not indeed the other way round. Now these alternative views may only be judged competitive only if it is conceded, a priori, that 'science' and 'ideology' are antinomies in the strong sense; or that they are, in a weaker sense, at least separable and distinct. And this is a claim that is almost axiomatic to both scientists and – at the risk of solecism – to those ideologues who prefer to see themselves as otherwise.

In this paper the clear demarcation of science from ideology in the strong sense of choosing between truth and distortion – as is popularly understood, even by the sophisticates – is viewed as a moot question specifically in the case of Ricardian economics and, by extension, if this is legitimate, in the social sciences generally; *for both the ship of science and the shallop of ideology were grounded securely in the shoals of the Ricardian sea.* Of course it may well be that the Ricardian case was a special case, whence more general analogies may be unwarranted – and that door I leave open to my critics – but as I read the facts there was a Ricardian economics and a Ricardian ideology (itself closely linked to a Ricardian politics) that were reasonably consistent with each other, and if one were to employ, purely hypothetically, the constructs of 'science' and 'ideology' to distinguish between them, it would be found that they differed not so much in what they said but rather in how they said it: a difference only of formalism, which after Kuhn (1962) and Feyerabend (1975) at least, may be thought merely an issue of a given, but not unchanging, set of social conventions. If there was this implicit imbrication between science and ideology, economics and politics, in the Ricardian school, such as I shall argue, then certain explicit implications, for both the historian and the practitioner of economic theory, may be seen to follow; which I shall here adumbrate but not follow through, in the exposition. For my central thesis is that certain practical policy issues native to the early nineteenth century exercised an over-arching influence over the formation (and hence dissolution?) of the Ricardian paradigm, which thereafter was stricken with irrelevance once the policies themselves had been consummated. Somewhat ironically, it was this very practical success that presaged decline – the demise of Ricardian economics being written, irreversibly, in its politics.

The issue of the denouement of Ricardian economics, relatively speaking, has had no dearth of specialist attention, being, after all, a positive axiomatic for the neoclassicals and a negative one for the post-classical classicals, and the Marxians. The split between these traditions has been basically, if not wholly, organised around the issue of the essential rectitude (or its converse) of the Ricardian system whether this veracity (or the lack of it) was seen as vested in theory, methodology, or in empirical confirmation. This form of intellectual positioning, whether a priori or not, has implied its own corollaries which have provided the recurrent – if competing – perspectives that have characterised discussions, virtually unchanged, for well over a century.

For one such as Schumpeter, to identify one pole of argument, Ricardo's ideas lacked 'nothing save sense' (1954a, pp. 473–74), the entire Ricardian trip being seen as a regrettable 'detour', for Ricardo was simply wrong, theoretically, methodologically and empirically; with 'perfectly unambiguous' scientific progress – or what I prefer to call the *law of successive analytical improvement* (happily granted us by a benevolent Providence) – therefore, seeing to its early, but appropriate demise. In this view, which in various distillations is the mainstream one, the decline of Ricardian economics is an open-and-shut case; almost, it would seem, a non-issue. By contrast, in the alternative view as typified, say, in Meek (1950),[1] it was not the putatively apocryphal nature of Ricardian theory – or Ricardian empirics – but its socially dangerous character that provoked, and prolonged, the conservative backlash that was to whip the Ricardians into splendid disrepute. The contrast could not be drawn more starkly; for the mainstream the demolition of Ricardianism was a positive accomplishment in the long march of analytical progress – for the Marxian, and neo-Ricardian, critics, it was a setback to the proper development of science. But these, it will be noticed, are fairly classical positions on the subject, traceable in the one case to Jevons, if not further, and in the other to Marx. And given the nature of the social division, it is clear that neither the Meek, nor the Schumpeterian version, is likely to inherit the earth, entirely.

The contending schools are agreed upon the fact of Ricardian atrophy, and more or less, upon its timing; the latter following from a Marxian suggestion[2] that put it in the early 1830s. However, both have been puzzled by a striking anomaly; if, indeed, the Ricardian paradigm died a classical death in the '30s, then why the unusually long gap between the onset of rigor mortis and the reconstruction of economic theory along neoclassical lines, whether or not on the basis of earlier progenitors, as late as the '70s of the century? And how are we to account for the apparent recrudescence of Ricardian ideas in J.S. Mill in 1848, and even later in the implicit homage to Ricardo in the works of Cairnes and Marshall? Why indeed, did Lazarus return? The schoolmen are not far apart on these questions; for the Marxians,[3] Mill and the others were simply burying Ricardo all the more thoroughly, in a series of ritual ablutions, in the guise of praising him. In the mainstream view, of which, again, Schumpeter (1954a, p. 478) is the principal author, Ricardo outlives himself because of the efforts of his diehard henchmen ('personal piety' as Professor Fetter (1969, p. 80) put it), his considerable personal prestige, the usual lag in public opinion on all matters, and – and this is more negative than the others – through his absorption into the socialist movement (or 'political propaganda' as Professor Fetter (ibid.) characterises it): a view that is not incompatible with the Marxian point.

In recent times, however, there has risen a third view, highly original in its own right, arguing that Lazarus, indeed, had never been put to sleep at all. We were – and are – all Ricardians now! I refer to Professor Hollander's work (1977, pp. 221–57) which has geniously rescued theory from a possible impasse posed by a Ricardo who will not, or cannot, be put to rest, whether in 1830 or 1848, or for that matter in 1977, by suggesting that the Ricardian paradigm, contrary to the schoolmen, was never really subverted in toto; rather that there is a broad continuity in the economic tradition between Ricardian and neoclassical theory, with Ricardo himself placed in apostolic parentage in a splendid, if problematic, anticipation of the house of Walras. In this account Ricardo is legitimised, subsumed as he is within a mainstream continuity; his science rescued, albeit historically relativised.

If only obliquely, all these perceptions implicitly identify the inherent problems associated with any attempt at an assessment of the decline of

Ricardianism – and, by implication the rise of the neoclassical persuasion. In what follows, in stages, I will try to identify a larger accounting system – which I am convinced is possible – within which some of these questions can be posed, and perhaps even resolved: admittedly at a high level of abstraction. Viewed through this looking glass, the received views appear only as partial insights, constituting something less than the whole truth.

2

The Ricardian period, which I situate between Waterloo and the French Revolution, 1848, and regardless of choice of index employed, was one of growth and structural change, conflict and crises, wars and revolutions – or at least one that lived in the shadow of all of these; in short, a turbulent one, following upon the aftermath of two great political and social revolutions, the American and French; two great foreign wars, French revolutionary and Napoleonic; and two great socioeconomic upheavals, the agrarian and industrial metamorphoses, that irrevocably altered the historical destinies of the region, and then, by extension, the rest of the world.[4] The calendar of social unrest, an able barometer of change, was never so crowded as between 1789–1848: the Naval mutiny (1797) and the Irish Rebellion (1798); the Combination Act (1799) and the suspension of Habeas Corpus (1817); the Luddite protests (1816) and the rural revolts (1830); the Chartist revolts (1836–39), the Plug Plot (1842) and the Irish Famine unrest (1846–48) – to mention only a few of the more famous events. Such was the mood at home – defiance provoking repression and vice versa; abroad, the successive 'destabilizing' influences of the episodic French revolutions from 1789 through 1830 to 1848.

State power, on the eve of this tumultuous epoch, was vested in the hands of the agrarian (and commercial) interest – the Commons manned (quite literally) by the squirearchy, the upper house by the landed nobility – an alliance between commercial farmers, merchant capitalists and their aristocratic overlords. The Industrial Revolution, together with the captive colonies and neocolonies (which made so much of the former so very possible), and even the Napoleonic Wars, brought prosperity to these interests which flourished, at least economically, as never before; however, even as the age peaked, the penumbra of new challenges became perceptible in the form, firstly, of the rise to resentment and pique, if not prominence, of the manufacturing middle and not-so-middle classes drawn from various strata with their own interests and hence ideology; and secondly, in the lumbering ascent to self-consciousness of the labouring poor, both rural and urban. Not until 1832 would accommodation be forced upon the landed oligarchy by the first of these entities in the form of significant, if formal, political representation in Parliament; and not until 1867 would the new power amalgam cede the same favour, similarly, to the second of the new social forces. The Ricardian period, and this accounts for much of its effulgence, was overlaid principally by the first of these struggles – although significantly cognisant of the ominous stirrings of the second.[5]

Two issues, both of antique origin, yet largely reshaped by a logic set in motion by the French revolutionary and Napoleonic conflicts, were to crystallize, at this time, into thorny bones of contention between the old order and the new, and their respective political economies: of protectionism, on the one hand, and apparent laissez-faire, on the other. The first was the dispute over the Poor Laws; or, more specifically, the Speenhamland Amendment (1795) to the Laws,[6] in the direction of an intended benevolence toward the rural poor – a hasty concession by the provincial squirearchy to their rural wards in concern for stability, at a time of famine and revolt, in pain of the enlightenment following upon the French Revolution. The second was the struggle over the Corn Laws,[7] whose pernicious effects on the consumer, and, more directly, whose obvious bounty for the farmers and landowners became glaringly transparent, or so the perception ran, during the hard years of the Continental blockade. As the manufacturers were to see it, on both these issues, their interests were inimical to the interests of the landlords and their tenant farmers. Repeal of this perverse protectionism, for that was the principle subjacent to both issues, was only possible given political power, something formally denied them by an unfavourable – and hence illegitimate – electoral system. The Reform Act – and the long drawn agitation leading to it – was the English version of a late bourgeois, though mostly pacific, political revolution, the tool with which to dismantle all legislation contrary to the spirit of sustained capital accumulation.

The threat from abroad – both real and imaginary – kept the internecine, but bitter, struggle within the secure bonds of nationalist sentiment;[8] but success at Waterloo released the long pent-up hostilities as though a dam had burst – and henceforth the agrarian and industrial camps, their princely privileges notwithstanding, were to battle it out in as many fora as were found available. As with the French Revolution, the ubiquitous printing presses were to prove potent political tools: the age of propaganda had matured. But, however uncompromising the intent, in practice the struggle was to be tempered by tactical considerations: for fear, mainly, of inviting the assertion of a similarly rabid ecopolitical identity on the part of the labouring poor, already dangerously politicised by the regrettable example of insurrectionary France.

The middle classes of the industrial bent found themselves with a growing economic power – though more potentially than actually – out of all proportion to their political power, and even more so to their political ambitions. However, their griefs were to be short-lived; for they soon found themselves befriended by a determined school of champions who would employ powerful propaganda to help unseat, or at least unsettle, the two Houses of unreason which, to their minds, were baulking their personal schemes for advancement. Their common ideology would be straitened into a formal idiom – for it was the age of science! – holding up not the limpid pretensions of prejudice, but ostensibly, the immutable axioms of reason: to the detriment of most existing economic policies. As with revolutionary France, it was the solemn stipulations of Science[9] – for she was the deity of these speculative philosophers – that were the great solvent of inconvenient, and hence bad, ideologies; enough to proclaim her name, and one almost achieved the desired effect – at least on people's minds.

It was principally their arguments that served the vital function of delegitimising – in the teeth of fierce, if feckless, opposition – the popular, paternalist ideology that typified the political economy of protectionism that linked the interests of the poor and the rich, however unequally, within the comforting notion of the organic bond of society. And this predatory science would devise its own assurgent battle cry with which the zealots would raze the remaining walls that separated society from the new Jerusalem; and the radical a priori that would unite the manufacturers and their formidable intellectual allies was to be the doctrine of laissez-faire and/or free trade; and so it was that the principle of industrial freedom, and supremacy, would hypothecate its own name to that of a new age of material advance. In carrying out this eminent scientific crusade,[10] the Ricardians were to be supernally successful under the leadership of that great luminary: self-assured plutocrat, supreme rationalist intellectual, and powerful political evangelist – David Ricardo. Not for a long time would political economy triumph again at the barricades until another band of zealots – even more relentless – would seize power directly in another part of the world: in the name of another political economist, who coincidentally, was yet another 'Ricardian', of sorts.

3

The Ricardians were sufficiently consumed by specific political purposes to be thought, at first blush, separable from the tradition of Smith until one recalls that the *Wealth of Nations* itself was a great political tract – possibly the greatest – against the policies of mercantilism. However, it is not inutile to draw a distinction; the difference between Smith and Ricardo approximates to the variance between a prophet and a priesthood – his was a general thesis, theirs a specific preoccupation.[11] Their problematic was simple enough, if farsighted for its time; for, ahead of the manufacturers themselves (who were to organise politically as a class only later, and then too under the guidance of Ricardian ideas – and even more direct Ricardian tutelage: if one recalls one of the principal authors of the Merchant's Petition of 1820[12]), the Ricardians charted the way forward, clearly and directly, engaging in political action – in the widest sense – boldly and forcefully to see this purpose through.[13]

'Progress' was identified critically, almost carelessly, with capital accumulation, which was seen as financed mainly through the abstinence of the manufacturing middle orders; 'comparative advantage' – itself a Ricardian neologism – was conceived as virtually exclusively resident in the sphere of manufacturers. With France safely put in place after Waterloo, the path was clear for England to set up as the workshop of the world – except for two principal obstacles representing the legacy of the past: an idle and parasitic aristocracy wedded to protectionism whose policies, decreed by virtue of its vicious grip on state power, were undermining national advance; and an idle and surplus rural labour force, preempted from proletarian discipline and industrial socialisation by a mistaken charity that allowed them sustenance outside the wage-labour nexus. The Corn Laws and the Poor Laws, it was believed, protected the idle rich and idle poor[14] respectively, based on a pre-modern, reactionary social philosophy, obsolete and anachronistic, that ultimately rationalised the power and privilege of the landed aristocracy and their hangers-on. So the Laws had to go, along with the lawmakers; and their special legatees had to be restructured to find a more appropriate place in the new industrial order.

Accumulation could proceed uninterruptedly only when these relics of a late mercantilist era had been securely entombed. Hence the liturgy of laissez-faire – *the pious mask for a policy mission*: the divestiture of the state from its rationale of support for two of its principal wards – the incipient proletariat, and its late feudal patron, the landed aristocracy: whence its meaning. The political economy of laissez-faire did not abhor the state in general – its self-assured pragmatism being unaccustomed to high principles – for that was a self-serving deduction to be eulogized by others; rather was it a tool, albeit a splendid one, to secure the denudation of a state conceived as irreconcilably hostile to the logic of capital accumulation.

Public opinion was the great battlefield within which the Ricardian troops stormed the bastions of unreason using such media as could be exploited; however, this avenue was found too feeble and inadequate for their rampant energies – so they sought to mould legislation directly. Ricardo purchased into Parliament – as only he could – to be followed by Torrens, and, later J.S. Mill; others such as Senior framed government policy directly when the Whigs were so amenable; still others were involved in open public agitations;[15] and some even assumed such bemusing, but quite unlikely, roles as professors at universities.[16] Their political interest was no mere sideline, a sporadic flirtation with the ever-seductive mistress of the art of the possible, such as might be put down to weakness of character or a lapse from good taste; it was the immediate end, the non plus ultra of their combined efforts, the urgent mission of political economy.

At the risk of overstatement, it must be noted that it was this implicit policy orientation that gave the Ricardians the semblance of unity as a school much more than, as thoughtful researchers continue to discover, usually to their dismay, the labour theory of value, or Say's Law of Markets, or even the so-called 'fundamental theorem of distribution'.[17] To a man – for they were all (honourable) men – the Ricardians – James Mill, Bentham, McCulloch, Senior, Torrens and J.S. Mill, to name only the more prominent among them – maintained a common posture towards the Corn Laws, the Poor Laws and the overriding urgency of reform. But the school is defined even more precisely by its extremities, Malthus to the right and J.S. Mill to the left; for personal proclivities led Malthus to side with conservatism on the issue of the Corn Laws and reform – while similar, or should I say dissimilar, personal predispositions, not unrelated to the times he matured in, swayed Mill, but always uncertainly, to the left of Ricardians. But one must not push this characterisation too far; there was something of the Whig and something of the Tory in Malthus, just as there was Whiggism and Owenism in Mill's own ideology. But this left orientation did not prevent Mill from subscribing to the Ricardian programme, any more than did his late Toryism stop Malthus from opposing the Poor Laws. Both, albeit with different considerations in mind, were only trying to reconcile antagonistic class interests, and hence looked askance at the radical idealism of the Ricardian manifesto.

The most outstanding feature of the Ricardian model – by no means opaque to the naked eye – it might be granted, is its fascinating, if restrictive – or fascinating because restrictive! – set of 'assumptions', thought so outlandish even in his own time as to earn them the caption of Martian economics.[18] The Ricardian complex of assumptions, most fully specified in his *Principles* – diminishing returns in agriculture, a social subsistence wage kept intact through Malthusian mechanisms, the declining rate of profit, or even the impending doom of the 'stationary state' – were not so much derived from 'inspired introspection', as they were the imperious deductions from a stubborn logic wedded to an inexorable policy imperative that would brook no confutation, whether empirical or theoretical, nor concede any argument that would prejudice the general case for laissez-faire and repeal of the Laws. Even his choice of the labour theory – or the labour standard – of value, which so irritates the mainstream and obliges the Marxists, might usefully be construed a matter of pure convenience, for it enabled his model to produce the results expected of it[19] (and intended of it); Smithian value theory, it might be recalled, could not do the job for in it the appreciation of cornwages raised all prices with no necessary or immediate implications for profit decline, thereby vitiating the vital connection between the difficulty of growing corn and the detriment of industrial profits so necessary to debunk the landed interest and deny the Corn Laws. Ricardian dissatisfaction with Smithian value theory needs, therefore, to be placed in perspective. And let it be remembered that the Ricardian theory of distribution – or the general case against the aristocracy – had been worked out prior to his theory of value, the latter being only a supportive but necessary adjunct. The Ricardian value preoccupation had a pressing policy imperative. How did one spell repeal in 1819? I submit, R-i-c-a-r-d-o.

In examining the correspondence – even symmetry – between policy and theory in the Ricardian frame one cannot but be struck by the fine-tuned instrumentality of the key assumptions of Malthusian population theory (mouths multiply at a geometric pace) – which Ricardo made his own – and diminishing returns in agriculture, which constituted the principal axioms of the Ricardian exercise in developing a case against the Poor and Corn Laws.[20] In effect, one set of 'laws' (the law of population and the law of diminishing returns in agriculture) was invoked to revoke another set of 'laws' (Poor Laws, Corn Laws); and it is in these two cardinal tenets that one must rest the Ricardian 'theory'[21] – and, in one form or another, these Ricardian traits characterise the 'school' from James Mill to Cairnes – as one must rest Ricardian policy in the two issues that they helped 'resolve'. Make diametrically contradictory assumptions – in the two specific hypotheses in question – and not only does the Ricardian theoretical model evaporate but also the basis for a 'scientific' case against the Laws; sacrifice in theory, in other words, would have entailed a sacrifice in policy – and neither was to be made, without qualification, by a Ricardian. *It was a science of special assumptions, in a season of special purposes.* Ignore the special pleading, or pretend it didn't exist, and one must regard most of the Ricardian paraphernalia, as in Samuelson's words (1971, p. 404) 'trivial nonsense'; there is simply no point to showing credible alternatives to Malthusian population laws or agricultural diminishing returns or the labour theory only to wonder, in all exasperation, as with Samuelson again, how the Ricardians could have missed so many 'elementary facts' (ibid.); for, in truth, Ricardo exercised admirable care in the selection of his 'facts' given his intent – as, I submit respectfully, even Professor Samuelson must do, in his own chosen area of interest. It could not be otherwise in this specious science of assumptions.

4

The Ricardian mission – at once didactic and political – was invested, with at least constant returns in the short run, in a dazzling array of institutional commissions: from elite clubs, to learned societies, and mass circulation news media. Reforming Tories and progressive Whigs were courted by the Ricardians, as much as vice versa. Lord Essex and Lord Holland elected

Ricardo to the Brooks' Club (1818); Althorp, Chadwick, Hume and Gladstone, in turn, were admitted to the Political Economy Club (founded in 1821). On the public front, the Ricardian propagandists, Marcet and Martineau (apparently it fell to women to dispense the lowbrow stuff), were to enshrine doctrine in popular literature to ensure a mass reception;[22] for besides the various factions within the power elite – Tories, Whigs, and Radicals – the age was one to bear witness to, and not without consternation, the eruption of the poor into politics. The ideology, regardless of origin, was hegemonic; there was something for everyone, everywhere. There was science for the literati, petitions for the activists, formulas for the masses – and, of course, laissez-faire for all.[23] Atop this far-flung apparatus stood the Political Economy Club – the shadow government of economic policy – wherein the magnificos of political leadership received economic counsel under the presiding aegis of the lucent personage of Ricardo, patron saint of the bourgeoisie, the first among the equals. For the haut monde and the hoi polloi, the rubric on the banners stood: let them read Ricardo!

But politics is a fickle mistress; in drafting their plans for the manufacturers, in disembowelling the social philosophy of the landlords, in successfully heaping odium on the aristocracy, the Ricardians had almost forgotten the underclasses. The latter, in viewing the rationale of the agitation for repeal of the Poor Laws, had already grasped the social intent of laissez-faire, assisted in this apocalyptic understanding – for their own purposes – by the ready mouthpieces of the backwoods gentry and their rural overlords. From 1830 on, the Ricardians found themselves dangerously alienated both from the landlords and the labouring poor, the stirrings of the latter particularly impressing upon them the necessity for prudence. Besides, the current was already flowing their way; Tory statesmanship, always alert for stability, had relented and conceded reform; and the Whigs, within two years, had enacted the new Poor Law – thus effectively divaricating the workers' movement from middle class agitation. Of course, the Corn Laws still remained an insulting, if anachronistic, reminder of the power of the oligarchy of land; but repeal, already in the cards, would not – any longer – require pushing the radical case against landlords too far. Henceforth it would be a time for reparation, however cautiously; first to heal the rupture between agriculture and industry, and then to seal the rift between master manufacturer and labourer. In the first context, we see McCulloch and Senior[24] betraying conciliation only too easily, and the dilution of Ricardianism indeed begins with them; in the second we have J.S. Mill, the last Ricardian, overseeing the last lap in the lingering struggle for repeal – already more symbolic than real – and ready to give labourers their due, if within an industrial order sternly supervised by their masters.

1846 saw repeal, again through a statesmanship impressed by instability in and around England: the fulminations of the Anti-Corn Law League and the rattle of Chartism – in its death pangs – within; the Irish famine and the rumbling of revolution in France, without. The triumph of repeal was quickly swamped by the swift aristocratic, rearguard riposte: the passage of the factory acts,[25] bittersweet revenge of conservatism, against the grain of the Ricardian mainstream. Small wonder that, in the Ricardian swan-song of J.S. Mill's principles, final tribute is still paid laissez-faire in spite of the all-total triumph of the practical agenda of the political economy of laissez-faire. A new state had just been won from the past, with laissez-faire as the instrument of attack; it would be defended from the future by laissez-faire as a weapon of defence.

5

1846 marked the completion of the Ricardian problematic in practice, 1848 in theory. The crusades had been won; and rigor mortis set in practically instantaneously. After Mill, the deluge was only to be expected, for the system had quite suddenly outlived its usefulness. Rarely have the mighty fallen so quickly, and from such high standing; in the words of Walter Bagehot,[26] the 'favourite subject of England from about 1810 to 1840' now lay 'rather dead in the public mind'. The Ricardian midwife had delivered; there was nothing more, quite literally, to be done. The science that gloried in tutoring the statesman ceased to be relevant; for the new state had little need for special tuition in what was, after all, to be its own preserve. Like the Marxian, the Ricardian mission was a negative one: laissez-faire – or all hands off profits, the mainspring of capital accumulation; and as in the Marxian case, the new order would find itself hard-pressed – even powerless – to draw sustenance from the source by way of substantive inspiration for positive guidance in tackling the problems of utopia. Only Toynbee, among his contemporaries, grasped this matter clearly:

> But after 1846, the mission of the deductive method was fulfilled. Up to that time economists had seen in the removal of restrictions the solution of every social difficulty. After that time they had no remedy to offer for the difficulties that yet remained. Political economy, in spite of Mill's great work, published two years after the chief triumph of the old method became barren (Toynbee, 1920, pp. 146–47).

After repeal, the Ricardian school went into sudden death; shorn of patronage and practically useless, its intellectual sterility became quickly apparent to the sapient. Sheer irrelevance precipitated decline, not theoretical or empirical weakness. No, it was not the superior sophisms of what followed in the wake of classical economics that explains the transition to neoclassical economics, as the Schumpeterians would have us believe, for there was no such transition, just a radical rupture; nor was the Ricardian dragon slain by a conservative conspiracy for fear of its hazardous nostrums – one system died out, another took its place, more relevant in its choice of techniques to the environment that would succour it, at least for a while. The discontinuity was more practical than logical; nor arbitrarily did the new economics quite literally redefine the science: it was a new science, and a new practice. In its novelty, it was neither a retreat nor an advance, in spite of what the schoolmen say, vis-à-vis the Ricardian paradigm; it had a different set of preoccupations.

6

This thesis of Ricardian decline – and the more general connection it draws between science, ideology, and practical politics – is derived from a larger study (Kanth, 1986) of the Ricardian period wherein the rise and declension of the Ricardian mission is delineated in more detail, and with necessary caveats. However, it is evident, at least to myself, that similar considerations could revealingly be applied to systems such as physiocracy, mercantilism or Keynesian economics with equally telling results; whether in the preliminary choice of assumptions, in the selection of variables and their permissible range of variation, or in the manipulation of evidence, the policy dimension, the practical problematic, the political conjunction cannot, in all intelligence, be ignored – and even more so when treating of major overhauls in intellectual systems.

But first, to essay some implied corollaries of this view. Firstly, despite the schematic flavour, I believe this definition of a policy parameter helps date the Ricardian period – and identify the Ricardians – as never before: historically, between Waterloo, and the Corn Law repeal; textually, between Ricardo's *Essay on Profits* and the publication of the first edition of J.S. Mills' *Principles*. The period itself needs to be further divided in two: a Ricardo *ascendant* – 1815–30 – infused aggressively with radical idealism and self-assurance; and a Ricardo *retrogressive* (or a Ricardo *decadent*) – 1830–48 – laced with a retracting pragmatism, doubt and class caution. The vehicles of this internal turning point within the Ricardian era – and they exist – were McCulloch and Senior whose own political sensitivities, given the threatening social condition, urged a softening of the more inexorable Ricardian rhetoric, in both politics and theory. So, contrary to most impressions, Ricardian influence did not die in the 1830s; it merely took on a more careful – expedient – public image. J.S. Mill's Ricardianism is then not an anomaly requiring either explanation or apology; it was simply the last gasp of the last of the great crusaders.

Secondly, while it is undeniable that the political unpopularity of Ricardian ideas – particularly in the Ricardian retrogressive phase – gave it an unwholesome reputation among both conservatives and working class advocates, this was not the effective cause of the Ricardian demise as Marxists (Meek, 1950; or, more recently, Reich, 1980) are sometimes inclined to maintain; and, by extension, nor was the dangerous character of the Ricardian prospect the primary inspiration for the rise of neoclassicism. Primarily, it was practical irrelevance that provoked its declension, not its politically embarrassing attributes. Contrary to Marx (1967, p. 15), and his epigones, class struggle need not terminate 'science' (however that is conceived) as Marx hinted with respect to classical economics in an oft-quoted passage; it may, on the contrary, actually provoke it and make it possible – as long as it is understood that science is never a neutral enterprise, whether practised by the bourgeoisie or the proletariat. The Ricardians, as a whole, embraced the ether of the new order – industrial capitalism (with reservations, on the part of Malthus and Mill) – and one must not be led to conclude, as the simple Marxian view might lead us to, that an economist such as Senior was a greater 'apologist' (except in a highly personal, and hence irrelevant sense) than Ricardo, the 'scientist'; for both performed both functions – at the same time. Whatever the strengths of the labour theory of value, it cannot be used, as Marx was wont to do, to separate the scientists from the apologists.

Thirdly, neither the Hollander (1977) view of analytical continuity between the Ricardian and neoclassical traditions nor the Schumpeterian (1954b, pp. 189–90) suggestion of analytical advance between them can be seriously entertained, without unaffordable qualifications, for the entities are far too dissimilar to permit such simple comparisons.

Fourthly, and somewhat similarly, I believe Ricardian economics needs to be radically divorced from the work of Adam Smith – being apart in vision, hue and purpose – so as not to collate both, as is altogether too common, under the single rubric of classical economics. Smith should probably be placed at the end of another tradition – the pinnacle of a previous series of cumulative achievement – rather than as a fount of the Ricardian phase (except, perhaps, negatively): for there is no essential continuity between Smith and Ricardo.[27] In fact the distance between them is at least as great as that between Ricardo and Jevons – although in the context of such genealogies it is not difficult to seek – (and find) – links between even contradictory sets of ideas. But the unique specificity of Ricardian system cannot be merged in either what went before or what came after; far more useful, perhaps, to see this phase bounded radically by both – practically and, as will be pointed out, intellectually.

Finally, politics being the warp and woof of the Ricardian system should obviate the naive wonderment[28] at the refractory insouciance of Ricardianism in the face of what was considered by many, in his time no less than ours, to be crushing refutation whether on the theoretical or empirical planes. The Ricardian model was quite immune from such attacks; for a better instrument serving the good cause either could not, or was not to be, devised and apparently nothing less could survive the competition. However, such breed of success could only have been equivocal; for its imminent doom was written in this very triumph of expediency.

7

This thesis of practical import, and the probability of its 'damaging' implications for classical economics, is not a new apprehension – for it is visible in Schumpeter's work where he writes (1954b, p. 84):

> One view ... can be precisely formulated as implying that the theories of the classical economists were nothing else but weapons for practical purposes, that they owed their existence to the requirements of the political controversies of the period and that political tendencies were in fact the premises which determined scientific thought. Is this correct?

He then goes on to deny this, offering us three criteria that establish, in his mind, the alleged 'impartiality' of the school: a) the scientific affinity of all scientific dogmas; b) that practical conclusions do not follow from theoretical premises; and c) that there was no uniform programme at all for which the economists might have taken up the cudgels (ibid.) While point a) is a pure truism, I do believe that my thesis, as advanced here, more than adequately gives the lie to points b) and c).

Unfortunately, Schumpeter only illustrates a more general tendency only too common within the mainstream: of seeing the relevance of political bias everywhere except where it coincides with their own. For the same Schumpeter is quite capable of attacking the putatively 'prescientific' writings of Aristotle and Plato presumably because they 'reflect the attitude of an aristocracy which is confronted by a rising merchant class and has a decided agrarian outlook' (ibid.); or in similar vein, deriding mercantilism for its lack of 'science'. The mainstream, one should note, are all Marxists (i.e. *scientific materialists*) when it comes to analysing pre- or non-capitalist ideologies; the moral could not be clearer: all is science that succours the industrial bourgeois order. While Ricardo is cleared of such intent, in writing of Marx, however, Schumpeter discovered the importance of politics as a relevant variable:

> His importance chiefly rests ... on the enormous vigour with which he created an arsenal of ideas for a political party and a host of slogans which could be used immediately and which were of magnificent effectiveness, of the glowing passion which fascinated members of his party and his

opponents and of the tone of the prophet which made his work unique. This, above all accounts for his success and lifted the discussion of his system out of the realm of science proper ... (ibid.)

Curiously, though, there is little here that could not be applied brilliantly to Ricardo. Politics, I fear, is a double-edged rapier.

8

What of analytical progress, then? Or science? Or ideology? Some comments are clearly in order, with the Ricardian case in mind. Continuous development in the science of economics across the sweep of history, whether conceived in unilinear or multilinear terms, is a chimera: the obvious result of the yearnings of anxious progeny seeking parentage wherever it may, however obscurely, be thought to reside. What we do find passing for economic inquiry are more or less articulated constellations of ideas, essentially discontinuous, which attempt to explain and rationalise the unique, contextually defined, objects of their inquiries – which, accordingly, do not remain the same in different epochs being, usually, overtaken by changes in socioeconomic structures. Contrary to textbooks then, economic writings do not reveal any perception of a *unique economic problem* common to all history. What then the meaning of analytical progress, such as might be assumed to have eventuated between Ricardo and Keynes?

One would have to shy away from the ready Schumpeterian response in the affirmative, despite its reassuring advantage of permitting any of us to feel superior to the best of those who have already been. The answer is ineluctably more complex and dualistic. At the most general level, I submit, systems are incommensurable, being occupied with different problems and armed with dissimilar tools. However, there is a second part to this determination that might be found more encouraging – for those in need of such encouragement. Since analytical tools are presumably designed to analyse social reality, they do grow more complex as the social organisation of production and exchange themselves gain in intricacy; *we invent, and use, such techniques, apparently, as we have a need for*. But is complexity itself advancement? I would argue that the real issue is one of *relevance*. We do not always require a computer to add up two and two; if at all necessary, the abacus may serve just as well. Efficiency also, then, is a matter of relevance. Purpose is the supreme criterion: the marginal calculus may be conceded a useful tool in matters of optimal allocation, but is of diminished relevance when maximisation is not a consideration at all. *So progress, after all, is a value, contingent upon a whole set of other values*. Science, no less than ideology, is close kin of circumstance.

How are we, then, to distinguish between science and ideology, at least in economics? I believe the Ricardian case sheds some interesting light on this question. Let us take, for instance, the common stereotype of Ricardo the scientist contrasted with Ms Martineau, the ideologist, and ask how, or in what, they differed. Both, it will be discovered, held identical first premises, the fundamental assumptions of the appropriateness of a capitalist social order. Both, additionally, held practically identical political goals such as already have been specified. They are seen to vary only, we find, in the intermediate chain of arguments that linked their premises to their policy conclusions. In making the same point, they are speaking different languages; but in what does this language differ?

There are, at least, some criteria. Formally speaking, Ricardo appeals to sustained reasoning, to an implacable logic, while Martineau addresses her appeal to ingrained common sense, intuitive logic, to faith; in Ricardo, further, the plea is for an educated understanding whereas in Martineau the effort is apparently geared only to seducing acceptance; in Ricardo, exceptions to principles are necessarily treated, albeit discarded after being 'proven' illogical – in Martineau, the exceptions are either omitted, glossed over, or simply stated as 'wrong'; in Ricardo, the tone is one of easy, expansive, detached generality; in Martineau we note the restive impatience of partisanship; Martineau speaks simply, Ricardo is rarefied. The implication that leaps at us cannot be ignored; Ricardian science and Ricardian ideology – while entirely complementary, contrary to the interpreters – appear to diverge only in their being addressed to different audiences, however one chooses to distinguish between the latter: whether the division is conceived as running between the critical and the uncritical, the knowledgeable and the ignorant, or the elites and the masses. Social ideology, defined broadly as that social arrangement (whether of the economic or the political life) that one prefers over others, enters, in both Ricardian science and ideology as the first step – the initial presumptions that predetermine, largely, what is to follow in the same way as the highway one chooses usually takes us to where we intended to go in the first place.

It was not that a set of general, hence innocuous, theorems implied certain policy directions in the Ricardian case, as might yet be admitted despite my thesis; it was rather that the putatively 'general' theorems themselves flowed from a priori political orientations which were then presented as though emerging solely from abstract reflection to all the more securely establish their 'objective' validity.[29] *The Ricardian proceeded from assumption, through theory to policy in their consecution: but the assumptions were spawned by an a priori intent.*[30] This is instructive – for then the Friedmanite attempt (Friedman, 1953) to place assumptions beyond reproach may be seen for what it is: a modern ruse to rationalise, at the very doorstop of science, a priori politics.[31] The 'realism' of the assumptions is not the issue – in fact, a red herring; it is the politics of the assumptions that is significant. The first query to put to an economic paradigm, I submit, is not 'is it true?', or even 'is it valid?', but rather 'cui bono?', which established, at the very least, its social basis of acceptance, its relative truth – given the nature of competing material interests.[32]

9

Within this understanding, it is possible to afford an interpretation of the transition to neoclassical theory which undermines, in some respects, the traditional, simpliste explanations as offered, for instance, by Stigler (1950) and Schumpeter (1954b, pp. 189–90); for the former, it is the greater generality and manageability of the marginal school, together with its greater congruence with reality that accounts for both its triumph and inherent superiority over the Ricardian model. Schumpeter is in clear consonance with this reading in his claim for the greater simplicity, generality, 'correctness', and relevance of the marginal persuasion against its classical ancestry. In both these suggestions runs the premise that the *object of analysis* is the same for the Ricardians and the marginalists; for only then can one seriously regard the one set of tools as being clearly superior or inferior to the other, i.e. in relation to the task at hand. But, as remarked earlier, the object of economic inquiry is not an immutable datum; Smith, Ricardo and Jevons were preoccupied with different aspects of the 'economic problem' corresponding to different stages, or moments, in the evolution of capitalism – their analyses, accordingly, are not interchangeable, and hence not comparable.[33] Presumably Newton and Einstein investigated a more or less unchanged universe – so that their theories are comparable, for the object is still arguably much the same; certainly, the definition of the object of the study of physics did not change radically as a result of a switch in paradigms. But *social reality is always in flux*; Smith, Ricardo and Jevons were engaged with different aspects of the process of capital accumulation – and economics found itself redefined, in so doing, by each.

Smith stood at the apex of a long tradition of inquiry, dating perspicuously from the sixteenth century – with capitalism on the ascendant – preoccupied with the question of the source of wealth; drawing upon the cumulative wisdom of previous and contemporaneous schools, he was to be the complete theorist of capitalist production,[34] of *gross* product (which accounts for the almost nonsectarian lack of enthusiasm for the activities of any single social stratum of interest considered in and for itself); productivity, specialisation, division of labour, extent of the market – the terrain was laid bare in a masterly sweep. With Ricardo, the problem of production had already been identified and resolved – a fait accompli to which there was little to add; what remained, however, was the issue of the *net* product, of profits, or surplus, and the problem of relative shares, or distribution; it was left to him to enunciate the necessary hierarchy of incomes under capitalism, and articulate the priority of profit-income; or that part, in capitalism, that is deemed more vital than the whole.

With Jevons, the distributional struggle had been won, with the income parameters structured 'appropriately'; capitalist productions and distribution, practically speaking, were almost non-issues after Smith and Ricardo. The theorist of gross product and the theorist of net product had both come and gone; is it that inconceivable, then, that British political economy, in its mid-Victorian complacency of world mastery, would turn to optimal *allocation* of the now substantial net product as the next great practico-intellectual challenge? Not production, nor distribution, nor growth, but exchange and allocation of given supplies of economic resources; Jevonian economics, as most of neoclassical theory, operated within the scope of this challenge, being intellectually no less original and innovative as Smith and Ricardo – and, certainly, no more.[35] To use discrepancies in value theory as the means of 'choosing' between them is absurd,[36] for the relative weightage of the preoccupation with value – aside from not being the primary object of investigation – was not the same in each. The three major theorists of English capitalism articulated such systems as were relevant to their age; it is this 'problem-orientation' that defines their internal unity – in strength and limitation – as much as it would in the case of Keynesian economics, the other major milestone in the great traditional of English pragmatism.

10

If systems of economic theorising derive as creative responses to practical problems – or crises – then it would seem that they might necessarily carry with them the patent of transience. That is to say that while their falsifiability is a problematic matter, if not an ultimately unresolvable one, their historical eclipse is not. Now, while this has some finite implications for the present run of paradigms, it does leave at least one problem unattended. How do we explain the persistence, or revival, of strains of ideas clearly associated with an obsolete or archaic school of thought (such as the recent efflux of neo-Ricardianism)?[37]

Potentially, several answers are possible; one device might be to see the resurgence as purely anachronistic – the result of the idiosyncrasy of individuals wilfully cast in the role of *laudator temporis acti* – and hence unlikely to have any contextual meaning. Another recourse might be to view it as a deliberate ideological attempt to use the symbols of a bygone age to fight current battles – which fits well into the Marxian argument of class struggle determined ideology. However, in terms of the thesis I am advancing, there is another, more interesting, eventuality: that, in such cases, there may be a prima facie case for wondering whether the grand problem characteristic of the old paradigm had not, once again, reappeared; for it is entirely conceivable that there are recurrent patterns within the capital accumulation process of capitalism that come insistently to the fore under given stimuli; or, in other words, that the 'crisis' may be perceived, at alternate points of time, to be centrally lodged in one of the areas of production, distribution, or allocation, etc., with such shifts in perception – a 'reswitching' of sorts – triggering the terms of previously 'phased out' prepossession.[38] Granting this hypothesis,[39] it follows then that ideas may be not only historically *relative* but also historically *recurrent*; which, again, reveals the sharp contrast with the natural sciences – few points, for instance, indicate the likelihood of a reappearance of Ptolemaic astronomy.

That social science is relevant to social purpose is, obviously neither a novel nor a trivial thesis – but its implications have not been systematically explored, most notably in the case of economic paradigms.[40] Clearly this is the result of the dominant, but peccable, posturing, quite common to most mainstream and some Marxian schools,[41] designed to suggest that their science alone is relatively unfiltered and objective; but this presumption of beatitude, I submit, is a bearing belonging to prehistory, drawn from the reckless age of Newton and the empyrean reification of positive science into something akin to state religion. Science, like politics, is a social enterprise, wherein we are free to choose our preoccupations, our goals and our modes of struggle – subject, always, to the constraints of the given situation which, in the last instance, exercises its own stringent selectivity and imposes its own binding definitions. Social science, like the class struggle itself, is not above history; its success – such as it is – accordingly, being altogether variable, and only too evanescent.

Notes

1   For a more qualified statement of the same position, see Reich, 1980.
2   This is to be found in Marx, 1967, Vol. 1, pp. 14–15.
3   See, for instance, Dobb, 1973, chs 4 and 5.
4   Hobsbawm, fittingly, terms the entire period between 1789 and 1848 'The Age of Revolution' in a book so titled (1962).
5   That these were the principal class/power struggles of the age seems accepted by Marxian and non-Marxian historians alike; the former exemplified in Hobsbawm, 1962 and the latter in Thomson, 1978.
6   For an account of the Laws and the rationale behind the 'Speenhamland Amendment' see Mantoux, 1961.

7   The definitive chronicler of the Corn Laws is Barnes, 1930.
8   Is it this that explains the curious gap between the *Wealth of Nations* and the opening salvoes of the Ricardians after Waterloo, i.e. the long hiatus between Smith and Ricardo punctuated only by Malthus's *Essay on Population*, written close of the heels of Speenhamland?
9   And thus even that skilled corrupter of artless minds, Harriet Martineau, found it politic to stoutly claim the ultimate defence on behalf of her didactic fantasies: 'I take my stand upon *Science*' (quoted in Blaug, 1958a, p. 135, emphasis mine).
10 In the writing of what I choose to term the new school of revisionism, every effort has been made to disengage the Ricardians from their policy affiliations, the authors being Robbins, 1953; Coats, 1971; O'Brien, 1975; Blaug, 1958a, Grampp, 1960; and others. In this attempt Grampp makes by far the boldest case for separating laissez-faire from free trade, both from the Ricardian school, and the latter from the agitation for repeal of the Corn Laws. However, see Kanth, 1986, for a rebuttal of these views.
11 Smith's impassioned plea for industrial freedom – fencing off the traditional poaching grounds of court favourites – argued as a general principle in his macroscopic diatribe against the political economy of mercantilism bears scanty resemblance to the more concrete policy undertakings of the Ricardians whose class politics were much more explicit and specific. Laissez-faire, accordingly, was aggressively motivated pleading for Ricardo; it stemmed not from any finer appreciation of natural law or of any other such lofty philosophical tenet drawn from either the French or the Scottish Enlightenment as might still be attributed to Smith. Not high idealism but ruthlessly practical political sense enjoined the tendentious Ricardian embrace of the slogans of laissez-faire with this ideology skilfully manipulated as an instrumental tool to secure the reform/repeal of the Poor and Corn Laws. To put it bluntly, the Ricardian harboured few fantasies as to the mythical ill-effects of 'state intervention'. For greater elucidation of the idea, see Kanth, 1986.
12 Thomas Tooke: one of the founder members of the Political Economy Club.
13 In the history of economic discourse – 'discourse' is a useful term, here borrowed from the work of Tribe, 1978, for it seems to avoid the appearance of evolutionary continuity suggested by the more familiar 'history of economy thought' categorization – the Ricardian school occupies a special place. It is the first systematic instance of an economic discourse self-consciously rationalising explicit class politics in a situationally-determined political context.
14 In the strict Ricardian reckoning, the Poor Laws were an intolerable burden on the net revenue of the nation, a sum in imminent danger of

being swallowed whole by the poor rates (as Ricardo himself portrayed it); aside from being 'bad' for profits (which, it might be surmised was reason enough), Ricardo noted astutely that the Laws gave the poor the dangerous illusion of a 'right' to relief outside of any services to employers – a concern for the mandatory institutionalisation of the work ethic among the fledgling proletariat that is only too contemporary. Actually, the conflict over the Laws also appears to have been a struggle between industrial and agricultural employers over control of the labour force – for Speenhamland had let the poor languish, but at near-subsistence, and in their accustomed rural habitat; the manufacturers, it would seem, would have preferred to have seen the rural 'surplus' driven, adventitiously, by penury, to the gates of their 'satanic' mills. As for the Corn Laws, Ricardian perceptions located their consequences in inflated wage bills, declining rates of profit and rising rents – a pure transfer payment into the coffers of the landlords. Aside from this it was also felt that reduced importation of corn was restricting the market for manufactured goods abroad thereby prejudicing the manufacturing interest in the long run as well. A denuded, but disciplined, workforce and an aristocracy stripped of state power; thus was industrial capitalism to be consecrated within the Ricardian vision.

15 If Tooke helped draft the Merchant's petition, young John Stuart Mill publicly supported the Anti-Corn Law League, earning the appellation of 'His Satanic Free-Trade Majesty' in the process.

16 James Mill helped the Benthamites found University College, in London, to carry out the machinations of 'counter-education'.

17 In point of fact, the Ricardians shared few purely 'theoretical' orientations in common. Aside from James Mill, who devotedly adjusted his own ideas in line with his master's voice, Senior, Torrens and John Stuart Mill maintained theories of value quite apart from the labour theory. Even McCulloch, another devout Ricardian, fell out with Ricardo over the addition of the chapter on machinery in the third edition of the *Principles*. Splendidly unmindful of the importance of the point uncovered, Blaug 'explains' such facts as follows (1958a, pp. 51–52): 'Whatever one may thing of the ethics [sic!] involved it is probable that both Mill and McCulloch feared that political economy could not command a respectful hearing if its exponents differed point-blank on first principles ... tactical considerations called for consolidation and suppression of difference'. On the issue of Say's Law, Meek, 1950, makes the very suggestive point that Say's Law was more of a politically expedient device to defend industry-led capitalism against Malthus and other critics than an analytical tool intrinsic to the Ricardian apparatus. (Blaug, 1958a, pp. 2–3, similarly, comments on the unimportance of Say's Law to the basic Ricardian model with the statement that it 'was

never a vital feature of the Ricardian outlook, much less its keystone'.) I am, of course, arguing that expediency explains a lot more of the Ricardian model than is commonly allowed.

18 It was Henry Brougham, Member in the Commons for Winchelsea, who was not particularly ill-disposed toward Ricardo, who is reported to have remarked during a debate in 1820, 'Where has the Honourable Member [Mr Ricardo] been? Has he just descended from some other planet?' (quoted in Sraffa, 1952, vol. V, p. 85).

19 In Smith's 'Wages Theory of Value' (as characterised by Dobb, 1973) a rise in the price of corn raises all prices uniformly. For Ricardo, with the Corn Laws in mind, this was quite unsatisfactory, for he was concerned with showing the advance impact of a rise in corn prices on the rate of profit. Smith's 'adding-up' theory of value did not produce consequences that could serve the strong case against the Laws. (Actually, Smith had his own theory of the declining rate of profits, but one that had little to do with scheming landlords and rising corn prices.) However, the labour theory of value, together with Malthusian differential rents/diminishing returns, produced the necessary effects: now a declining net product coupled with rising labour costs squeeze profits, raise the price of corn, but leave the price of other commodities unchanged! (Value being proportional to labour embodied rather than corn prices or corn wages; and the value of (commodity) money, of course, being 'held' constant under the strictures of the same value theory.) Contrary to Smith, Ricardo is now able to 'show' the growing differential between agricultural and industrial commodity prices to drive home his patiently contrived point (the 'duality' of Ricardo's value theory has not gone unnoticed: in agriculture, the labour theory plus diminishing returns/differential fertility; in industry, the labour theory, plus implicitly constant returns). Value theory only duly consecrated this prior 'understanding' of the distributional structure.

20 This interpretation necessarily deflates Professor Stigler's reassurance that it was Ricardo who helped establish 'a professional frame of mind', and further, that it was his influence that helped reduce 'ad hoc theorising' and 'promiscuous fact gathering', which, claims Stigler, was the basic 'Ricardo effect'. See Stigler, 1952.

21 These two ideas are found at the core of Senior's four 'general' propositions constituting, in his opinion, the 'science' of economics. See Bowley, 1949, pp. 46–48; they take pride of place again in one as late as Cairnes, 1965.

22 The 'revisionists' such as Robbins, 1953; Coats, 1971; and Grampp, 1960 – even, but to a lesser extent, Blaug, 1958a – attempt to delicately distance the economists from these propagandists to preserve the integrity of the former; but the facts speak otherwise. See Kanth, 1986.

23 The propagation was visited upon many different fora such as the Society for the Diffusion of Useful Knowledge and the Utilitarian Society; or journals such as the *Westminster Review*, the *Edinburgh Review*, the *Scotsman*, and the *Globe and Traveller* (the last actually owned by Torrens).
24 For a sample of McCulloch's predispositions see O'Brien, 1970; for Senior, Bowley, 1949, provides a full account. Senior's attempted reconciliation, in theory, of profits and rents as subspecies of the same genus is highly significant of this political accommodation; for the relevant passages, see Senior, 1928, vol. I, p. 54.
25 Blaug, 1958b, in the tradition of revisionism, attempts to blunt the popular perception of the economists' hostility to the Factory Acts – but unconvincingly.
26 *The Fortnightly Review*, 1876, p. 216 (quoted in Shove, 1942).
27 Even more appropriately, Smith is better conceived as a splendid and self-collected isolate who inspired Ricardo only by provoking his relentless criticism. Continuity between them is entirely open to definition; much stronger links can easily be established with Malthus and perhaps even John Stuart Mill. It cannot be overemphasized that Ricardo disagreed profoundly with Smith's conclusions, his method of working, and even his mode of exposition: there can be no school of economics conceivable where the two could coexist as coevals. In this context, I am reproached by Paul Sweezy (1984), a renowned authority on Marxian economics, for having gone 'too far in denying any continuity between Smith and Ricardo', because both of them were theorists of 'manufacture' as opposed to 'machinofacture' (despite the 'afterthought' on the machinery issue in Ricardo) and thus were both students of the same 'phase' of capitalism. Doubtless, this argument is important and has some merit; however, as with Ricardo taken in relation to Marx, I prefer to see discontinuity rather than continuity, the matter clearly being one of emphasis.
28 Blaug, in this vein, finds the 'separation' between 'abstract theory' and what must be conceived as contradictory 'empirical work' – 'curious' (Blaug, 1958a, p. 185). Stigler, 1952, likewise, puts it down to a Ricardian lack of 'common sense'. More perceptive is the comment by William Maginn, a contemporary of the Ricardians, to the effect that the 'strength of the economists' lay in keeping 'at a distance from facts' – for the quote, see De Marchi, 1974, p. 124.
29 To believe in the a priori innocence of theory is a great error and Tribe is decidedly mistaken, in my view, when he writes (and one should note the congruity of opinion between mainstream and radical critic, Schumpeter and Tribe, on this issue) that, 'It would be quite erroneous, however, to conceive the remobilisation of theoretical statements into

political arguments as the causal raison d'être of these statements', mistaken because he has, in effect, put the cart before the horse. In Ricardo's economics it was policy intent that was 'remobilised' into 'theoretical statements'! The independence of the Ricardian model from the social struggles of the period is, I maintain, pure delusion (Tribe, 1978, p. 146).

30 Contrary to Max Weber, therefore, fundamental assumptions are never arbitrary in the social sciences; in the Ricardian case, which may be more general than many would conceded, they were conceived in partisanship – there being deep method to his brand of madness. Contrary to the posture of having dropped 'from some other planet' (quoted in Sraffa, 1952, p. 85), he had his feet planted firmly upon the earth of his seeking.

31 Social science is constituted for the most part by systems of more or less coherently organised assumptions, fundamental premises that load the subsequent analysis with a strongly predetermined posture. To forbid close questioning of such powerful fabricators of the scientific enterprise is to completely renege on the very possibility of a sociology of science, i.e. in determining why we assume what we do in fact assume. (For most practical purposes, knowledge of a researcher's primary assumptions is sufficient to permit a very close appreciation of the likely results of the research.) What very different research programmes, for instance, are likely to emerge from the assumption of 'exploitation' in capitalism as against its disassumption! Thus, contrary to Friedman, assumptions in social science are far too vital to be placed beyond a critical review, and the attempt to do just that would seem to be to engage in a recreant form of evasion.

32 Social 'truths' are relative to material interests and thereby lack the enduring finality of physical 'facts'; where these interests are in conflict, or are contradictory, the validity of a general proposition cannot be assessed independently of the sectional interests that are diversely affected by it. Economic paradigms are, accordingly, 'partial' truths (in the double sense of the word); and a purely theoretical adjudication between them on formal grounds, even if possible, would leave the practitioners highly unimpressed. The inconclusiveness of the 'capital theory' debate between the two Cambridges, while a poor example for many reasons, is a case in point: what is at issue is two different political views of capitalism.

33 In this context, one would have to agree with Tribe (1978, p. 2), and his criticism of writers in whose work 'the economists of the later 18th and 19th centuries are constructed as predecessors of Marx in which it is only the discourse of Marx that provides the rationality for judging their statements'.

34 Contrary to mainstream understanding, Marx always stressed the tradition between Petty and Smith, via the Physiocrats, as one devoted to the analysis of production; the allocation of parametric inputs, on the other hand, has always been a singularly neoclassical preoccupation. For confirmation of this idea from a non-Marxian source, see Myint, 1946; also Walsh and Gram, 1980.

35 It is commonplace, of course, in some strands of opinion, to see Ricardian economics as 'bourgeois' economics, this categorisation usually being a reference to the class vantage point of the Ricardian vision; however, this way of defining the discourse does pose some difficulties. For instance, Jevonian or neoclassical economics may also easily be seen as bourgeois economics; wherein then the difference, and a self-perceived difference at that, between the two schools? Why, then, does a common class standpoint take on such distinctly different hues? Obviously, even common class visions are profoundly influenced by the situational conjuncture in an evolving historical process. More specifically, the policy imperatives, at different points of time, are indeed different – and economic theorising, consciously or unconsciously, has taken the form of responding to such challenges, and also rationalising them. So, in trying to understand a Ricardo, a Jevons, or a Keynes, one must attempt a definition of the policy preoccupations of the time, for it appears that the 'real problematic', the so-called economic 'problem', is redefined periodically even from the perspective of the same class interest. One day production, another day distribution, a third day optimal allocation; the focus of interest keeps shifting, a sort of 'reswitching' that is not arbitrary but defined rather precisely by concrete practice and empirical experience.

36 Value theory, while perhaps always an intellectual curiosity, was never, in non-Marxian economic theory, or at least among the classical economists, an overriding preoccupation; Marx, on the contrary, considered it relevant to establish his theory of exploitation and, give his sweeping influence on the writing of the history of economic thought – for his was the giant beginning in this genre – it is not surprising that so many others have followed suit. Of course, classical, Ricardian, and neoclassical theories differ in their standards, measures, and even sources of value; but to define the object of inquiry in each case as a satisfactory theory of value is absurd. It is at least partly ironic that Marxian value theory, considered by Marx so very vital to his theory of exploitation, should now appear, after Sraffa, not strictly necessary to establish the latter. In any case, value theory, for Marx as much as Ricardo, was a purposive preoccupation.

37 There is something not wholesomely Ricardian about the so-called Ricardian revival after Sraffa; certainly many of the Ricardian

fundamental assumptions in theory are irrelevant to Sraffian models – and Ricardian policies, I would hope, are outside of their intent. If the Sraffian enterprise is strictly an exercise in value theory – by its demonstration of the irrelevance of demand for price determination – then it is a splendid tool with which to debunk the neoclassical models, even if its appeal to Ricardo fails to seize upon the gist of the Ricardian apparatus. However, the fact that it may be – and has been – used to deride Marxian theorising also brings it a step closer to the original Ricardian political agenda, which may be of some significance. If, on the other hand, it elaborates but one aspect of Ricardian theory – shorn completely of Ricardian politics – i.e. value theory, it becomes only an intellectual curiosum, destined to desuetude. For more on the issue, see Rowthorn, 1974. For an even bolder categorisation of the impending extinction of the Sraffian effort, see Hunt, 1983.

38 The prior identification of the specific economic 'crises', that are the usual provocation for major redefinitions of the scope of economic theory, qualifies them as almost the very first task to undertake in any effective examination of the material, policy rationale of 'schools' of economic theorising.

39 As correctly pointed out by an anonymous reviewer, this position constituted a 'theory' too: so whose interests does it serve? My response pinpoints the dilemma I have been trying to outline all along: if this 'theory' does not serve either side of the political divide, it might well be doomed to unacceptance, even if it were 'valid' as a plausible explanation of the course of intellectual evolution. Actually, this position, of what can only be termed 'materialist relativism', for which I am arguing, is likely to be rejected by most mainstream and Marxian perspectives; that may not, however, impinge on its inherent 'validity'.

40 At least one effort, bold if isolated, exists in the literature of economic thought, linking ideas to practical politics: see Rogin, 1971. I hope that my own analysis of the demise of Ricardianism will provoke further research – if only for the sake of rebuttal – in this direction.

41 Here I am duly corrected by Paul Sweezy, 1984, who writes, '... you lump together mainstream and Marxian schools as suggesting that "their science is relatively unfiltered and objective". Perhaps you can find passages from the writings of Marxists to back this up, but if so they are quite unMarxian. Marx never claimed objectivity in the sense that bourgeois economics does – quite the contrary. What he did claim was a bias in favour of the working class, which for him, however, meant, *in the long run*, bias in favour of humanity as a whole – a bias which bourgeois theory also would have no reason to disclaim. Here there really is a question of which of the two is in a meaningful sense "truer"'. Thus chastised, I reread Marx and found a fitting statement in his *Second*

Theses on Feuerbach (1970, p. 121), where he writes: 'the question whether objective truth can be attributed to human thinking is not a question of theory but is a *practical question*. Man must prove the truth, i.e. the reality and power, the this-sidedness of his thinking in practice. The dispute over the reality or non-reality of thinking that is isolated from practice is a purely *scholastic* question'. Perhaps inevitably, this passage is at once revealing and opaque. While Marx's impatience with scholastic disputes is understandable, it is not obviously clear how 'practice' can conclusively vindicate the 'correctness' of theory. Where Sweezy is immensely sustained, of course, is in the fact that Marx indeed does not claim any superior objectivity for his ideas (although confident that history will absolve them). I am willing to stake the claim, however, that Marx would not have disagreed with the idea that his intellectual system might also be subject to historical situation; but the sustained effort to subject the Marxian system itself to a materialist, historical, scrutiny remains to be made.

Part VI
OTIOSE CONTROVERSIES IN MARXISM: AGAINST ORTHODOXY

10 The Falling Rate of Profit: Clarifying a Conjecture

1

In the chapter entitled 'The Law as Such', in Volume 3 of *Capital*, Marx introduces what has often been considered by Marxians to be the 'primary law of motion' of capitalism, simply, if somewhat abruptly; in his words:

> The gradual growth of constant capital in relation to variable capital must necessarily lead to a gradual fall of the general rate of profit so long as the rate of surplus value ... remain[s] the same (Marx, 1967, p. 212).

The disproportionate growth of constant capital vis-à-vis variable capital was no special discovery of Marx, however; as he himself acknowledged (Marx, 1935, p. 60) elsewhere, many others like Sismondi, Ricardo, Barton, and Richard Jones, had already observed and recorded the phenomenon in a 'more or less accurate' manner. On the other hand, with reference to the causation implied by Marx, there is indeed a radical departure from the conventional economic wisdom of the time. True, his notions of 'constant' and 'variable' capitals were only an emendation of the Ricardian 'fixed' and 'circulating' nomenclature, but they were qualitatively different enough from Ricardo's categories to enable Marx to define the rate of profit as something other than the ratio of profit to wages (in Dobb, 1937, pp. 94–97). Equally true, of course, that virtually all of classical political economy, from Adam Smith to Ricardo, had already made the uncomfortable discovery that profit, for one reason or other, apparently eventually tended to fall, from the saturation of capitals hypothesis of Smith to the Malthusian diminishing returns argument in Ricardo. As viewed by Marx, all these attempts were either indeterminate, incomplete, or simply false (quoted in Koshimura, 1975, p. 117) explanations of a real, observable tendency, despite the fact that the classical economists 'perceived the phenomenon and cudgelled their brains in tortuous attempts to interpret it' (Marx, 1967, p. 213).

In the elaboration of this so-called 'law', Marx felt that he had resolved a thorny classical dilemma in two easy steps: one, by defining and distinguishing between constant and variable capital; and two, by disaggregating surplus value from profit. Since profits are surplus value calculated in relation to total social capital, in the Marxian account, and since it is living labour that is value producing, it followed that surplus value declined with a shrinkage in its *primary source*, i.e. in variable capital, relative to the means of labour. To illustrate, algebraically: given the rate of surplus value (s/v), and the rate of profit $[s/(c+v)]$, it followed that, assuming constancy in the rate of exploitation (s/v), the rate of profit must fall as the degree of 'organic composition' (c/v) increases.[1]

The 'composition of capital', i.e. the ratio between petrified and living labour power, undergoes transformations in the historical process of the accumulation of capital. When, occasionally, the requirements of accumulation exceed the given supply of labour, competition between capitals for its services bids up the price, i.e. wages. Marx himself offered evidence of such long term disequilibria in England during the fifteenth century and the first half of the eighteenth century, but these clearly were conceived as exceptional, the market normally 'correcting' such unfavourable imbalances, under competition, with its customary, impersonal ruthlessness. At any rate, the consequent rise in wages depresses the rate of surplus value leading to the substitution of machinery for living labour, thereby aggravating the organic ratio.

Under 'competitive' conditions of accumulation (an achitectonic assumption, shared in many regards by neoclassicism as well, belonging only to an epistemological capitalism of thoroughbred fantasies), capital flows from areas of less-than-average profits to sectors of higher-than-average profits; which, in terms of the discussion, would be from higher to lower levels of organic composition, intensifying competition in industries with low organic rations, and compelling the latter under threat of extinction to rationalise and raise their organic ratios ultimately. Aside from an equalisation of the rate of profit, a more important transformation takes place, viz., the average rise of organic ratios across the economy, leading to sagging profit rates universally. The paradox, of course, and *Marx loved nothing so much as paradox*!, is that the rate of profit falls precisely when social productivity is at its height, illustrating in striking fashion the *contradiction*, in capitalism, between the forces of production (productivity, machinery, technology, etc.) and the relations of production (private appropriation of surplus value as rents, profits, interest, etc.) that inhibits social production generally. The implication that the 'barrier to capitalism is capital itself' had, it must be admitted in addition, a splendid dialectical relish to it.

In broad terms, this is roughly the sketch of the argument Marx presents in the third volume of *Capital*. Now it is of course well known that the draft of what was to constitute Volume 3 had been written well before Volume 1 had gone to the printers (Mandel, 1970) – so the question as to why the rate of profit discussion (and discussion as to the limits of capitalism generally) is 'postponed' to Volume 3 raises the hoary debate as to the modus operandi of *Capital*, the staple of a certain species of Marxology. Without putting too fine a point on it, it might be suggested that the macro effects of real life competition are only detailed in Volume 3, whereas Volume 1 was intentionally a modular sketch of the 'pure' capitalist mode of production, which, when taken together with its constituent categories, would represent a sort of an 'ideal type' of the system. And clearly, Volume 3, rightly or wrongly, deals with the myriad complications introduced by the competitive reality of the system as a whole. Stated differently, the 'law' in question could only be posed *after* the process of capitalist production and circulation had first been elaborated and understood comprehensively – it was not simply an inspired afterthought.

Almost more than the law itself, it is the set of qualifying/counteracting/limiting tendencies provided by Marx that has attracted the justifiable attention of both apologists and critics. Marx lists six of the 'most general counterbalancing forces' that run counter to the implications of the law and which give it 'merely the characteristics of a tendency'. They are:

1 increasing intensity of exploitation;
2 depression of wages below the value of labour power;
3 cheapening of the elements of constant capital;
4 relative overpopulation;
5 foreign trade;
6 the increase of stock capital (Marx, 1967, pp. 232–40).

These counter-agents, of course, pose unavoidable problems for the 'normal' workings of this fundamental law, as Marx well understood.

Even in the original formulation of the FRP hypothesis, the key condition that the rate of surplus value remains unchanged, catches the eye – prompting a long line of critics from Bohm Bawerk to Paul Sweezy[2] to argue that such an assumption, carried through logically, would not only bring down the law of the rate of profit, but also the law of value itself, by implying the empirically untenable condition of an *equalisation* of the organic composition of capital across all industries (Sweezy, 1970, pp. 98–99). Marx himself argued thus:

> The same influences which raise the rate of surplus value ... tend to decrease the labour power employed by ... capital ... [and] tend to reduce the rate of profit (Marx, 1967, p. 235).

In other words, the very increase in the means of labour that raises productivity, decreases proportionally necessary variable capital; in effect, Marx seems to have believed that an equivalent increase in the rate of surplus value and the organic composition, in the long run, was not feasible – as Mandel (1970, p. 167) puts it:

> Because with the increase in the productivity of labour there often comes an extension of workers' needs and a corresponding increase in the value of labour power which ... encourages the development of the labour movement ... thus restricting ... the rate of surplus value.

The technical, sociopolitical and economic elements of the causation involved are thus intertwined in 'dialectical' fashion to make of the law a tendency subject to counteraction by precisely equivalent processes.

The fall per unit of the value of constant capital, because of increased productivity, need not necessarily be a corrective since, as both Dobb and Mandel argue, the value ratio between constant and variable capital need not change if the mass of constant capital increases due to a fall in price. The depression of wages below value, through wage-cutting and other 'interferences' with the market determination of prices, while empirically feasible, are excluded by Marx for not belonging to the province of a *general* analysis of capital. Under conditions of an infinitely elastic labour supply to industry ('relative overpopulation'), the 'field of exploitation could extend *pari passu* with capital accumulation' (Dobb, 1937, p. 111), as it apparently did in the early industrial stage of 'primitive accumulation', securing the rate of profit with no need for any alteration in the organic composition. And foreign trade might be similarly conducive if it cheapened workers' consumption goods and constant capital.

Whether the rate of profit will fall, or suffer modifications, through the reasons enumerated, is ultimately an *empirical* question: one can adduce no 'proof' in the abstract that would suffice. Marx's own caution, though frustrating for the hasty Marxist, is quite instructive: there can be no a priori logical proof of the proposition. As Dobb (ibid., p. 109) puts it:

> It would have been alien to his whole historical method to suggest that any answer could be abstractly given or that any conclusion of universal application could be deduced mechanically from data concerning technical change treated *in vacuo*.

Ultimately, then, it would seem that it is the intensity of the antagonism of the two great historically opposed orders, capital and labour, and a host of factors, including technical changes and the size and compositions of market demand, that determines the rise and fall of profits in the aggregate.[3] Under current conditions, various such 'determinants' serve to either reinforce or offset Marx's stated tendency: trade unionism, political class struggle, and social-democratic governments sometimes dampen profits, and the morale of capitalists generally. On the other hand, the growth of monopolies, and the migration of capital internationally, and the forcible subjugation of working class movements, through both legal and extra-legal state actions, plus imperialist control over captive world markets, might all assist in keeping the rate of profit artificially afloat. Empirically speaking, the data is far from sufficient to make irrefutable statements in this area, despite some efforts on the part of orthodoxy, as by Mandel, to 'conclusively' prove its existence.

2

Empirically, of course, it is impossible to distinguish decline in rates of profit occasioned by capital composition factors as opposed to factors making for 'Smithian', or 'Ricardian', or any other declensions, so the entire issue is not of much moment in that domain, nor can actual evidence of a fall in the rate of profit be taken as evidence of the validity of the theory, in the light of the same objection. In theory the argument is both weak and simplistic: stated simply, *a single tendency that is counteracted by several tendencies cannot be treated as a strong force in any domain*; this is especially so when the counteracting factors seem to be more easily verifiable, on a routine basis, than the presumed central tendency. Ultimately, the Marxist claim of having discovered the fatal flaw in capitalist accumulation remains an unsupported proposition, based on assumptions about capitalism that are as dubious as neoclassical assumptions about the nature of competition (indeed without 'orderly' competitive conditions, the Marxian theory of value itself runs aground; not that it fares much better *with* those assumptions).

The cardinal error here is in deriving propositions axiomatically from a 'model', rather than from careful observation of historical data: as in so many areas, *Marx did not remain true to his own methodology of historical materialism* given his eagerness to subvert classical political economy from *within*, that is on the basis of its own assumptions. In so doing Marx fell into a carefully laid trap – of his own design: 'economics', whether Marxian or neoclassical, can simply not be a science of deductive propositions drawn from given assumptions about the nature of socioeconomic reality. In thus isolating the 'economy' from its cultural and political shackles, Marx made possible the very neoclassical fantasy of imagining economics as having 'laws' of its own, independent of more primal social causation(s). The mechanistic world view of materialism leads just as easily to Stalinism as it does to Reaganism; small wonder, since Smith and Marx, in common, shared so many of the presumptions of the capitalist Enlightenment.[4] In the task of rethinking Marxism, issues of philosophy and methodology would appear to be the fundamentally inescapable, and necessary, tools of correction.

3

However, there are aspects to the falling rate of profit discussion much more salutary to the problematic issue of Marxian methodology. If one accepts the realist proposition (as in Bhaskar's work (1989)) that society is an 'open' system where invariant, hence determinist, regularities do not obtain, then it is an eye opener to examine the tenor of Marx's discussion in this context. The fact that, in reality, it is always a case of *tendency pitted against counter-tendency* (as with the rate of profit discussion), *with the outcome always a question of conjunctural determinations*, gives the lie to any and all attributions of mechanistic determinism to the original Marxian impulse in political economy (no matter how often Marx himself breached that precept). The falling rate of profit is then only an, albeit interesting, *hypothesis* – as indeed is all of Marxism itself; no more, no less.

Further, there is a definite confoundment of the macro and micro domains in the manner in which Marx begins with a micro model of the 'Law as Such' and then blows it up to make it measure up to a scale model of the capitalist 'economy' as a whole. This will not do; capitals as whole do not behave like a single capitalist, nor do they face identical ecopolitical circumstances. As with the Keynesian 'paradox of thrift' idea, the macro implications of micro problems are not necessarily of the same order, sign, or magnitude; the economy is not simply an aggregated version of the individual firm (as neoclassicism assumes all the time). In fact, in general, micro tendencies are antipodal to macro tendencies: moreover, there are far more degrees of freedom operating at the micro level than at the macro, which, as a totality, is far more constrained. Even within the abstract scenarios of economic fancies, if a capitalist firm discovers that its rate of profit is slumping (for whatever reason), it should either (eventually) go out of business, or seek counteracting measures that shore it up. Either way, the initial 'tendency', or the firm itself – rather than 'capitalism' – disappears – thereby vitiating a theory posited upon its rather curious stasis.

Finally, Marx was heroically wrong, leastways in the long run, to imagine that the 'barrier to capital is capital itself': the ultimate barrier to capital is the inspired resistance – political, moral, and spiritual – of its victims, and the inherent natural limitations of planetary resources and social bondings. It can only be hoped that the first, and not the second, set of factors will finally, and soon!, spell the needed limits to its predacious expansionism. It can only take a complete capitulation to the renegade and mechanistic philosophy of materialism to seriously imagine that capital would succumb, quite naturally and mechanically, to a falling rate of profit, *without being able to shift the burden of correction on to other social orders and classes*; such are the risks of living solely inside artificial 'models' (where the 'economy' is viewed as having a life of its own, divorced from its cultural and political correlates), with reality serving only as a remotely distal, 'exogenous', variable. In this, as in other regards, Marx subverted his own deep sociopolitical insights into the functioning of capitalism in favour of abstract theorising on the lines of classical political economy, so keen was he to hang it on its own petard.

The real tensions in capital derive not so much from 'inadequate' rates of profit, barring the periodic collapses endemic to business cycles, but from inflated expectation of profits that far exceed the capacity of reality to yield them: i.e. the restless effulgence of the psyche of capital stems from a relentless greed that will not accept a 'satisfactory' level of profits, and from a corresponding readiness to go to any extent (pillage and rapine, devastation of ecological and human resources, etc.) to make the latter measure up to its insatiable demands. Stated simply, capital is ready and willing, on a daily basis, to risk natural and social catastrophe in order to appease a werewolf appetite that is, inherently, quite unrequitable. As such, if the moon tomorrow were to be harnessed, as yet another 'colonial' production site, it is not because the great mass of average consumers desperately 'need' such additional resources to sustain their hunger for happiness, but because it is necessary to shore up ever higher and higher returns to capital. The end process of such a demented logic, pitting class against class, capital against capital, and state against state, is simply the extinction of the planet as a habitable, hospitable home for the myriad species that dwell on it; as such, to cry halt to this scrofulous despoliation is the first political duty of responsible humanity; and the very preliminary basis for such a stand would involve a total rejection of the expansionary, appropriative, ideology of economics, which today stands as the epistemic court jester and soothsayer of the regime of capital.

Notes

1 Paul Sweezy takes the organic composition to read $c/c+v$; Marx uses c/v.
2 Sweezy further subdivides these into two categories: factors that tend to lower the organic composition of capital (item 3) and factors that tend to raise the rate of surplus value (items 1, 2 and 4), with foreign trade being common to both. See Sweezy, 1970, ch. VI, pp. 98–99.
3 This is precisely how Nobuo Okishio (author of the celebrated Okishio theorem) ends his 1961 paper, entitled 'Technical Changes and the Rate of Profit'.
4 My forthcoming book (Kanth, 1997) treats this matter in some detail.

11 The 'Asiatic' Mode of Production: Eclipse of a Notion

1

The notion of the 'Asiatic' mode of production (AMP), as raised in Marx's original writings, poses critical questions as to the nature of traditional Marxist historiographical analytics, its Eurocentric vision, and its untenable reductionism. Stated baldly, the assumption of an 'Asiatic' mode, defined only the lapidary, and wanton, ignorance of Europe (Marx included) about the nature of society and economy in the non-European world. For a long time, debate over the so-called 'Asiatic' mode spilled over the bounds of Marxist scholarship, into both bourgeois and socialist 'ideology' (understood as political propaganda, pure and simple), sensitive, as always, to the more immediate policy implications flowing from intellectual positions, and this did little, of course, to further the aim of historical accuracy. The search for even a residue of historical 'truth' underlying the 'Asiatic' mode may well prove inconclusive: for the means of research are, in themselves, critically circumscribed, in the case of ancient economic history, by their availability and authenticity. Controversy and debate apart, however, the discussion over the AMP illustrates yet another historical fact: the failure of subsequent Marxist scholarship to match up, in this area as in others, to the historical energy, and impulse, of the meanest of Marx's speculations – and few Marxians realise the extent to which Marxian ideas were *speculative* – to say nothing of going beyond them.

The (Marxian) study of pre-capitalist formations has been far from exhaustive for a variety of reasons, not the least of which was the comparatively late publication, and availability to a mass audience, of the *Grundrisse*, clarifying so many Marxian notions and intentions. And the AMP mode, of course, had all but vanished from view after Lenin, strapped in the straitjacket of the so-called 'Law of Four Stages', first in the Soviet Union, and later in China, although pockets of resistance did survive elsewhere.[1] In the West, Karl Wittfogel's infamous *Oriental Despotism*, based supposedly on a schemata of 'hydraulic' societies, claimed to be in direct, unedited, line of descent from Marx himself – indeed criticising the latter for 'retreating' from his own established position on the AMP. Stalinism, on the other hand, quite disingenuously, saw 'feudalism' everywhere, and history became a straight line to be drawn at will (and imposed by force!). Nonetheless, the notion of the AMP refused to be routed, destined to rear its ill-defined head, if in sometimes startling forms.

Postwar European discussion of the subject, though a mite more sophisticated, was not necessarily more illustrative. 'De-Stalinisation' was claimed to have 'rescued' the concept: but the ends of the enterprise still remained quite dubious. Admittedly drawing his 'definitions' from '... three letters of 1853 ... and four articles published in the *New York Daily Tribune*', Ernest Mandel,[2] to cite but one instance of a major EuroMarxist, had the following to say about the AMP:

1   what is above all characteristic of the Asiatic mode of production is the absence of private property in land;

2   as a result, the village community retains an essential cohesive force which has withstood the bloodiest of conquests through the ages;

3   this internal cohesion of the ancient village community is further increased by the close union of agriculture and craft industry that exists in it;

4   for geographical and climatic reasons, however, the prosperity of agriculture in these regions requires impressive hydraulic works: 'artificial irrigation here is the first condition of agriculture'. This irrigation requires nearly everywhere a central authority to regulate it and to undertake large-scale works;

5   for this reason, the state succeeds in concentrating the greater part of the social surplus product in its own hands, which causes the appearance of social strata maintained by this surplus and constituting the dominant power in society (whence the expression 'oriental despotism'). The internal logic of a society of this kind works in favour of a very great degree of stability of production relations.

In addition to these 'five characteristics' of the Asiatic mode, Mandel suggests that the distinctive structure of this mode was the 'subordination of the towns' to agriculture and the 'central authority', leading, apparently, to 'retarded development'. It is quite unnecessary to dispute the canonical authority being casually vested in Marx's 'three letters and four articles' here; enough instead to examine the putative 'characteristics', to note the elisions therein.

The 'absence of private property' in land, item one, if taken as a 'by and large' statement is perhaps admissible, although significant divergences from this norm are well recorded both in India and in China, the allegedly 'classic' Asiatic types. And it does not do, as has been quite customary, to circumvent the latter empirical piece of discomfort by suggesting that these were in the nature of 'illegal' appropriations – i.e. the work of 'guilty' parties 'cheating' the system.

In item two, the explanation is a bit more foggy. The relative 'cohesiveness' (endurance need not always be equated with cohesion) of the village community – though hopelessly exaggerated – might be admissible in contrast, say, to the anomie of capitalist society, but what is one to make of the idea of its having 'withstood' conquest? Perhaps the village was indifferent, culturally, to the varying moods of the conquering authority, as a matter of course, since there were so many of them?; but this might just as much suggest something about the nature of the 'conquerors' rather than the village – it might in fact have been the conqueror who was regally indifferent to the tribute-paying village. All this is in the realm of supposition, of course – for, in the actual Mandel discussion, as is usual, the precise social nature of the 'conqueror(s)' side is left magisterially undisclosed. In addition, the presumption that the 'self-sufficient village' is a uniquely 'Asiatic' institution is highly doubtful, such characteristics abounding in other pre-capitalist formations as well.

In item three, we find a similar situation. There is nothing specifically Asiatic about the combination of agriculture and craft within the individual units of production, together with the presumed absence of a social division of labour between them: a little reflection would discover parallels in early European ('feudal') history.[3]

The fourth characteristic races breathlessly from geography and climate, through irrigation, to a centralised 'state'! Here, then, is a 'functional necessity', indeed one imposed by a *geography and climate*, that brings into an ill-defined coexistence the specific kind of state adequate to it, aside from the implied teleology suggesting that 'needs', in a simple sense, create 'appropriate' institutions.[4] Even so, granting that the ineffable necessity for an agency of coordination did exist, then why not a form of organisation other than the state? The state, should one already exist, might well perform this or that function, including the organisation of waterworks: but is the reverse also true? Does the state arise out of a need to 'irrigate' (by that logic, in monsoon-stricken areas, an umbrella-providing state must arise out of the 'need' to seek protection from rain)? Like all functional explanations, this glibly presupposes what it must first prove.

The fifth point merely completes the confusion. It is this 'state' that creates the class structure (the use of the term 'strata' is rather a clever evasion of the issue), in embryo. Further, it is for the function of organising irrigation ('for this reason') that the state concentrates the greater part of the social surplus into its hands. So, here was a state, undifferentiated from society to begin with, which, for the generous purpose of coordinating irrigation, at some point, detaches itself from society and begins to appropriate social wealth. Obviously, the question remains as to what breed of animal this state was before it decided to set off on its productive mission? On the other hand, if it is argued that this is not a 'state', in a 'true' sense, but rather a mere 'political functionary' (as the entire muddled logic seems to imply), then it is no more an 'Asiatic' type: no classes, no state, plus communal organisation adds up, leastways in Marxian discourse, to something more akin to primitive communism! Mandel is by no means ignorant – but quite illustrative of a tendency amongst Marxist is his refusal to break with the fatal 'three letters of Marx', in spite of their obvious sketchiness.

2

Now to consider Marx's own (few) ideas on the subject of the AMP. He did not invent the term, Lichtheim (in Avineri, 1973) tells us; James Mill (in *History of British India*), in 1820, with India in mind, had already written of the 'Asiatic model' of government. And similar conceptions no doubt abound in the writings of Adam Smith, Montesquieu, and John Stuart Mill. But the stronger influence may well have been Hegelian[5] notions of the 'East' as opposed to the 'West': notions marking a radical separation between Europe and the *Other*, shared by European scholarship, Marxists or not, at least since the so-called Enlightenment. Indeed, even in the late twentieth century, fashionable French anthropology, in the 'anthropologist-as-hero' guise of Levi-Strauss, could speak glibly of 'hot' and 'cold' societies (meaning societies with and without history!), in demarcating Europe from the non-European world (so as to better assert the uniqueness of European civilisation).

In any case, in *essence* (to use of Hegelianism), Marx seemed to have been convinced as to the static and unchanging nature of the basic socioeconomic structure of the Orient. 'Asiatic' society was conceived by Marx as a cellular structure, each cell being unaffected by the presence of the other, and all being quite indifferent to the many dissolutions and reformations of the despotic central authorities that ruled over them. Marx was quite unequivocal about the *stasis* of Asiatic communities: they had no history,[6] except a succession of conquests that were *external* to them, which in any case supposedly did not occasion any changes in the village structure. This becomes all the more incredible, when we find Mandel, interpreting Marx, suggesting that these notions were not meant to apply to some benighted 'Asian' society, in some archaic times past, but *Asian society as encountered by colonial powers in the eighteenth century*! To bolster the canonical authority of Marxian speculations in this regard, yet another EuroMarxist, Eric Hobsbawm (Marx, 1965, 'Introduction'), mentions a not unimpressive list of 'sources' consulted by Marx in his 'oriental' studies, suggesting also that, given Marx's genius, it did not require a massive consumption of literature (even presuming anything like that was available to him) to digest the essentials of the subject at hand. Perhaps Marx was a whiz kid who 'figured' things out rather quickly; but, equally undeniably, he also made a bunch of egregious howlers, en route.

From what he did read, Marx did apparently feel that he had extracted the essentials of the 'Asiatic' socioeconomic structure as presented in the literature. But, from here on, the qualifications take over: first, the informed nature of the literature itself; second, Marx's own limited interest in the subject, quite apart from the immediate requirements of a casual (potboiler) journalism; third, it is not usually appreciated that the entire passage on Indian village communities, so gleefully anthologised by Marxist orientalists, was an outright plagiarism from Hegel's *Philosophy of History* (the same Hegel who, lecturing in Jena in 1830, on the eve of the French conquest of Algeria, could ignorantly assert, to a devotedly convinced European audience, that Africa has no 'history' of its own, with Africans being at the very 'infancy' of humankind, representing 'natural man in his completely wild and untamed state'!). When it came to characterising the non-European world, Hegel and Marx were obviously close (ideological) brethren!

At any rate, two different (or not so different) explanations are forwarded as to the real interest of Marx (and Engels) in pre-capitalist formations. Hobsbawm (Marx, 1965) suggests that Marx was basically concerned with *capitalism*, and that he:

Dealt with the rest of history in varying degrees of detail, but mainly in so far as it bore on the origins and development of capitalism.

Mandel (1971), on the other hand, believes that Marx's original interest was in:

Explaining the peculiarities of the historical development of India, China, Egypt, and the Islamic world, as compared with the historical development of Western Europe.

At first glance, the two statements seem quite similar; but there is a subtle difference. Mandel is explicitly referring to the supposed *'duality'* in the history of the world, and therefore, in EuroMarxist theoretical explanation, between the West ('development' toward the 'self-realisation' of humanity through contradiction) and the East (static and repetitive social structure dominated by despotism, in a 'history' consisting mainly of stagnation), whereas Hobsbawm, prudently, steers clear of such a contentious interpretation. Such a duality is, of course, admissible in a Hegelian philosophy of history: but what of Marx? Does he, too, rationalise *essentialist* differences between East and West, on the basis of a dimly conceived 'necessity' — geographic, or otherwise?

An apology for Marx would run thus: for Marx, the separate and essential nature of the East, coupled with its distinctive geographic existence, is not a necessary moment of a self-evident teleology; he takes the differences as being given (based on the literature available to him) and then proceeds to explain (not rationalise) why. His reasons are not primarily 'geographic', as understood by Wittfogel[7] and Lichtheim, or even Mandel, however unwittingly: rather, Marx, in magisterial objectivity, locates the fundamental distinctiveness in the sphere of *production*.

The unity of crafts and agriculture in each community makes it possible for each unit to contain within it all of the necessary conditions for its reproduction. Hence the economic continuity and political repetitiveness of 'Asiatic' society. Far from abounding in geographical determinations and functional necessities, Marx's own views, rightly or wrongly, focused on production as the determining instance of the 'unchanging' East. Geography and the 'need for irrigation by a central authority', did not and could not 'determine' motion or stasis in society, by itself. To put it simply, Marx remained true to Marxism (*regardless of the truth of the latter*) even when he was patently wrong, for being ignorant, or simply misinformed, about 'Asiatic' society. Marx was wrong to conceive of pre-colonial India as a society without a history; but Marxism, with the benefit of hindsight, need not make the same error.

A bolder, and more accurate, characterisation, on the other hand, would be that Marx does not come off entirely clean on the charge of nurturing (unconsciously?) an ethnocentric vision of world history: if one is to turn to the doubtful authority of the 'three letters and four articles' once again, there are numerous suggestions that Marx seemed to believe in the world-historic role of the West, and of the 'necessity of subjecting the unfree and unchanging East to Western tutelage', something that leads clever reactionaries like Shlomo Avineri[8] to crow about how Marx was really justifying colonialism as the only means of shaking the sleeping Orient out of its lethargy and inertia (a thesis pushed to all its reactionary limits by the late Bill Warren). Of course, analytically speaking, Marxists would argue that it is 'capitalism', and the bourgeoisie, neutrally conceived as between East and West, that 'modernises' the world, regardless of where it originates; but his does not gainsay the fact that *actual history did present us with the capitalist West as the prime mover, shaker, and destroyer of non-European cultures, societies and economies, for better or for worse.*

It may be true that, viewed in a materialist discourse, Europe[9] itself is explained by the category of the mode of production and not vice versa; that is to say, a mode of production is no more 'Western' than it could be male, or sweet. But, in point of fact, European capitalist elites were androcentric, misogynist, racist, and anthropocentric; *and little of the social history of coloniser and colonised can be understood without a deep appreciation of these characteristics.* The 'materialist' viewpoint eliminates these considerations from analysis, *ex definitione*, so that we are left only with technicist, and economistic, 'forces' that 'drive' a carriage, called 'history', willy-nilly. This exonerates, and exculpates, the sexist and racist miseries inflicted on women and non-Europeans by European (capitalist) men, since they are now abstracted into an impersonal 'force of history'; worse, into a 'progressive' force that gives 'us' the benefits of capitalism and modernism. It is in this dehumanised *scientism* that Marxism itself turns into a grotesque, cowardly, apology for the depredations of European capital and patriarchy. Yes, the record needs to be set right: Marx was inescapably Eurocentric.

3

The writings of the so-called 'French' school, Godelier, Suret-Canale and Chesneaux, read the Asiatic mode, generally, as a system combining the production activity of village communities with the economic intervention of an exploiting state. In this view, the specific 'Asiatic' denomination is generalised to a wide variety of geographic, and historical situations. Mandel charges that Pierre Boiteau sees it as a *universal* stage through which all societies have passed – which, of course, raises yet again the spectre of the 'succession of stage', and here Mandel is on solid ground (as much as Hobsbawm) in charging these writers for first rejecting the law of stages and then resurrecting it again, surreptitiously. But our criticism is more basic: rather than seeking empirical demonstrations of an idea (a curious reversal of the Marxian method), it is urged that we need: a) *evidence* vis-à-vis the empirics; and b) *clarity* vis-à-vis the theory.

Beginning with item b), it may be helpful to attempt to define the AMP, within the historical materialist problematic, in contradistinction to other analytical types. In this purely logical exercise, the first premise would have to be that the term 'Asiatic' should not be understood geographically, or else its homogeneity disappears considering the sheer variety involved in a continent the size of Asia. The only constraint, of course, in such a construction of the definition of the AMP (again, as a rational exercise) is the Marxian grid, irrespective of empirical confirmation. Briefly, this becomes a theoretical exercise of building a model, a sort of an 'ideal type', in order to illustrate differences from other 'known' types.

A mode of production, to pursue the matter within the traditional Marxian schema, may perhaps be defined as an articulated combination of a specific mode of appropriation of the product and a specific mode of appropriation of nature; it is a 'unity' (by definition) of relations and forces of production. The mode of appropriation of the product, which is our concern here, is 'determined' by the relations of production, by the distribution of the means of production, and the consequent relation established between the labourer and the labour process. A distinct mode of appropriation of the surplus product supposes, accordingly, a distinct structure of relations of production. Now we stretch Marx's writing on this Procrustean bed: what is the mode of appropriation of the surplus product in the AMP? By way of an answer, to turn to a rapid summary of the more recurring characteristics that appear in Marx's 'Asiatic' writings:

1   it is the 'state' that extracts the surplus product;
2   there is no ruling class or exploiting class, other than the state;
3   there is an absence of private property in land: i.e. land is state property;
4   the dominant form of production is non-commodity production in agriculture.

We are dealing, then, with a pre-capitalist form of agricultural production where the direct producers have the effective possession (this of course would be invalid in the case of at least one pre-capitalist mode: slavery) of the means of reproduction of their labour power (implying the non-separation of the labourer from the means of production). The mode of extraction of the surplus product should, to follow the Marxist theory of rent, be: rent. Now to turn to Marx (1967, p. 791):

> Should the direct producers not be confronted by a private landowner, but rather, as in Asia [be] under the direct subordination of the state which stands over them as their landlord and simultaneously as sovereign, then rent and taxes coincide or rather, there exists no tax which differs from this form of ground rent.

The mode of appropriation of the surplus product, in this case, takes the 'form' of taxation which is also simultaneously payment for the right of possession and use of land (rent). Do we then have a specific mode of production according to the terms of our definition? Not quite, because a distinct structure of relations of production corresponding to the 'Asiatic' type is not demanded by the mode of appropriation of the surplus product, which is no different from the general form of state taxation. Apparently, even the *logos* of the AMP does not answer to the mode of production prescription common to Marxian analytics.

As far as the 'empirical' evidence goes (which is not very far) the debate is far from exhausted. Most 'Asiatic' writers tend[10] to imply that the self-sufficiency of the oriental commune is largely mythical and the alleged 'stagnation', even if ever true, was no different from other pre-capitalist forms of stasis. The real challenge, of course, comes with the rival concept of 'feudalism', and it is interesting to make a comparison, analytically, between the two modes of appropriation of the surplus. Under feudalism, it is agreed that there is a class of landlords distinct from the state: also feudal rent requires that the direct producers be politically and legally bound as subordinates of the landlords. If it can be shown that a landlord class, distinct from the state, did develop appropriating 'ownership' or land and claiming jural authority, then the AMP dissolves in a happy, or unhappy, 'feudal' mess.

Of course, Marx himself repeatedly pointed out that such intermediaries did often arise in oriental history; but, usually, the problem is wished away by suggesting that such intermediate classes never acquired the 'degree' of social and political power assumed in Europe by similar classes, in the face of the 'hypertrophy' of state authority. On the other hand, the writings of Marc Bloch (1962) indicate that, at least in the case of Japan, and maybe even China, 'feudalism' is the more appropriate characterisation, although with 'inevitable and deep seated difference' – 'semi-feudal', perhaps, and even 'semi-Asiatic'! But such speculations are only a reflection of a peculiar intellectual stubbornness that sees an 'all or nothing' in every field. Since the historical evidence is so diverse and conflicting, why is it necessary to force an analytical straitjacket on it? After all, considering the extent of time, and space, and peoples covered by the concept, surely it is altogether simplistic to insist on one, immanent, institutional type?

4

Stated simply, Asian history, not unlike European history, suggests the coexistence of a bewildering variety of modes of production, and social forms, in a complex and interacting evolution: instances include tribal, independent peasant, tributary, communal, slave, and even 'feudal' formations, with rich pockets of flourishing merchant capital.[11] Far from an unchanging and unbroken, monotonous chain of 'nonevents', as in silly European constructions (wherein all 'Asiatics', apparently, look alike), we find a rich and variegated history full of advances and regressions, growth and decay. Far from there being an undifferentiated 'subject' population vis-à-vis an omnipotent and alien state, there was a highly elaborate social division of labour (caste was by no means a purely 'ritual' hierarchy) both in villages, and within linguistic and kinship regions: if never else, *most certainly at the time of colonial conquest*. Commodity production, far from being absent, flourished at periods well known to historians in Europe of the time, and guilds and artisanates rose to prominence in towns. Asia's pre-capitalist forms were diverse and variegated in its turbulent history of continuous superimposition of conquering modes of production: more precise historical data, and less ideologically- (and Eurocentrically-) charged research, is needed to identify the dominant modes, and their specific relations with other modes extant in the period of history in question – isolated and fragmentary evidence, drawn of hasty judgment and careless research – not to mention outright ignorance and prejudice – can hardly suffice. It is time that, at least, 'Asiatics' put aside this European fantasy, as they go about reconstructing themselves outside of the myths of colonialist historiography; but that would first require, or so it would seem, a clean break with the European Enlightenment, the provenance of all our modernist miseries.

Notes

1. The prewar writings of R. Palme-Dutt are a case in point; also see Namboodripad, 1952.
2. As it appears in *The Formation of the Economic Thought of Karl Marx*, 1971.
3. Eleventh century Île de France and ancient Germany are suggested for a favourable comparison.
4. Small wonder functionalist sociology and vulgar Marxism are mutually attracted to one another.
5. Hegel's notorious 'theorising', as to the differences between East and West, are to be found in his *Philosophy of World History*, New York, 1956 – a permanent testament to the monumental ignorance and prejudice of the European literati.
6. This argument appears in his article entitled 'The Future Results of British Rule in India', 1853.
7. References to Wittfogel's ideas are drawn from Wittfogel, 1957.
8. S. Avineri, in his 'Introduction', 1969. Avineri delights in discovering 'malicious irony' in all or most of Marx's pronouncements on the Orient, thereby revealing his own smug and insufferable Eurocentrism, if not outright chauvinism.
9. One is entitled to wonder why 'Europe' is designated a separate continent when it is obviously part of a continuous land mass that includes Asia? It wouldn't matter whether the single continent were called Europe or Asia, but not *both*: obviously, Europeans wished to have not merely their own history, but also their own geography as well. This, their ideology of separateness.

10 This is aside from 'official' Soviet and Chinese ideology; see the works of D.D. Kosambi, Amiya Bagchi, Bipan Chandra – and even M N. Srinivas.
11 As suggested in the writings of Lenin and Trotsky.

12 The 'Transition' to Socialism: In Dubious Debate

1

Few Marxian debates have been as dreadfully tedious, despite their portentous implications for the subaltern orders living under socialist regimes, as the matter of the 'correct' modality of a transition to socialism (as if, in all gravity, there were some golden tablets from which the truth could be canonically deciphered). Post-Stalinist discussion on the nature of the putative 'transition' in the European genre, though richly varied, was nonetheless, inevitably, highly contradictory. One way or another, the controversy, wholly sterile now with the swift evaporation of Eastern bloc regimes, put to critical scrutiny almost every serious precept of the system Marxians identify, self-assuredly, as *historical materialism*. As it was, the debate fluctuated, unevenly, between an elaboration of the general, and an examination of the particular, between theoretical projection and enduring empirical circumstance, so that the dialectic/distinction between the two was quite often blurred. That default, however, was only incidental; more refreshing, given the times, was the fact of the extant historical conjuncture where the object of enquiry, long buried beneath the debilitating debris of Stalinism, had been declared open once again, in the ideological thaw of the '60s and '70s.

At any rate, in retrospect, it is astonishing how much of critical import was actually left *unsaid* by the front-rank Marxist intellectuals of the time, on a subject whose interpretation directly affected the welfare of millions. In this short piece, I trace only the outline of the debate, before pointing to way(s) of transcending the near-stupefying vacuity of the Marxian dream of social amelioration.

2

As noted, the general and the particular on the question had become closely entwined: either one proceeded from a 'theory' of the transition to a criticism of the Soviet Union, or vice versa – the preoccupation with the Soviet Union taking precedence over all else, as in this near-extraordinary pronouncement from (the late) Chairman Mao, to be later echoed by Western Maoists:[1]

> The rise to power of revisionism means the rise to power of the bourgeoisie. The Soviet Union today is under the dictatorship of the bourgeoisie, a dictatorship of the big bourgeoisie, a dictatorship of the German fascist type, a dictatorship of the Hitler type.

The putative theoretical 'explanation' for the overarching rhetoric ran as follows: what was once a 'socialist state' had now degenerated into a 'social-imperialist' state, as soon as the 'renegade Kruschev-Brezhnev clique' had grabbed state power, supposedly to restore 'capitalism'. Aside from the generous abuse of categories, what was curious was the implication that 'socialism', having once been achieved, in a manner (under the regime of Stalin, no less!), had then been overthrown by a 'revisionist renegade' clique. Charles Bettelheim, who took on the formidable task of building a theoretical framework wherein such formulœ could be outfitted with a garb of respectability, was necessarily more guarded:[2]

> In my opinion the decisive factor – i.e. the dominant factor – is not economic but political. This decisive political factor results from the fact that the proletariat has lost its power to a new bourgeoisie, with the result that the revisionist leadership of the Communist Party of the Soviet Union is today the instrument of this new bourgeoisie.

Aside from the idea of a *new* bourgeoisie (as distinct from the old), Bettelheim used the term 'state bourgeoisie' (reminiscent of Djilas) to describe the new 'ruling class' of Soviet society, and 'state capitalism' as the theoretical characterisation of the latter. Since all this was putatively a 'political' creation, the Twentieth Congress of the CPSU – a political event – became the historical watershed between two systems, one that was allegedly transitionally to socialism (under Stalin), and one that had *changed course* to take the 'road', if not there already, to 'state capitalism', or 'state-bureaucrat-monopoly-capitalism' (!), as Mao would have it. Of course, the facility of inventing novel concepts, requiring double-hyphenation, is that one can define them at will, by fiat – and for this very reason, there is little point to disputing them. But what of historical materialism, in such an analysis – which, at least in Marxian discourse, is considered determining, in the last instance, of the mode of analysis itself, irrespective of the specific concepts that are its resultants?; enough, for now, to note that it appeared powerless, in the times, to prevent the egregious abuse inherent in such arguably tendentious formulations. At any rate, the European defenders of Maoism tended to see the question of the transition to socialism as decisively, and hence determinately, a *political* question.

Paul Sweezy, much like Bettelheim, was a Mao sympathiser and a critic of the Soviet Union – though possessed of a little more socialist caution. His analyses of the Soviet Union were, on the whole, quite incidental, in a sort of uneasy compromise with Bettelheim. He argued that, in the USSR: the '... socialist ownership by the whole people had degenerated into ownership by a privileged stratum ...' – with the emphasis on 'de facto' ownership – suggesting that a new 'state-bourgeoisie' now controlled the means of production. The chain of logic was, then, quite irresistible: 'privileged stratum' equals 'state bourgeoisie', which equals 'control over means of production'; and that equalled, finally, to the thesis of 'capitalist restoration' in the Soviet Union (no less, on the authority of Lin Piao)! Nonetheless, the remarks of Sweezy on the nature of the transition were interesting, offering the following four 'assumptions', of an appropriate discourse, as follows (Sweezy and Bettelheim, 1971):

1. there is no such thing as a *general* theory of the transition between social systems;

2. nevertheless, a *comparative* study of transitions can be extremely valuable;

3. transitions are never simple or brief processes ... they are *multidirectional*;

4. transitions from one social order to another involve the most difficult and profound problems of historical materialism.

Two point did emerge from this preamble, which, in essence, were contained also in the original Marx-Engels: that the question of transition was historically *specific*, and that all revolutions are, at least potentially, subject to counter-revolutions (the Paris Commune being only one case in point). On the other hand, even between historically specific instances, there are, or might be, *general differences*: for instance, the transition to socialism was perhaps quite a different process than the transition, say, from feudalism to capitalism.

Ernest Mandel, anti-Maoist and Trotskyite (the once competing current in EuroMarxism to Maoism, and traditional pro-Sovietism), sought to clearly differentiate between the formulation of 'laws of motion' (a favourite phrase of orthodoxy) of transitional societies – a theoretical issue – and generalising from the rather limited Soviet experience of such a transition. His so-called 'ten theses' (stretching, in effect, to thirteen) offered a broad reference for discussion, as follows:

1   even 'transitional' epochs are characterised by *definite* relations of production;

2   the structural stability of such relations, however, is an open question, and a retrogression is possible;

3   these relations are not a simple *combination* of capitalist past and socialist future: they are specific to the transitional period;

4   the socialist potential of these relations is *not* to be judged by the prevailing consciousness, prevailing political leadership or ideology: rather, it is to be judged by an investigation into the nature of the production relations *themselves* (which is contrary to Maoism);

5   only the actual experience of a mature, transitional society between capitalism and socialism will provide us with the *pure* 'theory' of the transitional society;

6   in other words, present analysis is confounded by the absence of *decisive* historical material;

7   transitional production relations are a hybrid combination of non-capitalist economic planning and the elements of commodity production;

8   the social character of labour in the USSR is realised even in the absence of a 'technical integration' of enterprise (contrary to Bettelheim, Poulanzas, etc.);

9   a full appropriation of all produced goods is not necessary to establish the social ownership of the means of production (contrary to Bettelheim);

10 capitalism has not been restored in the USSR because: a) if this is a post-Stalinist phenomenon, then it needs to be proved that production relations have radically changed after Stalin; b) capitalist production relations cannot be reduced to relations of superordination or subordination *within* the enterprise; c) on this reckoning, China is not too far behind the USSR;

11 to deduce from official Soviet 'ideology' that capitalism exists is to make the mistake of idealism: to judge an epoch by its consciousness;

12 the USSR is a bureaucratically-deformed workers' state;

13 ultimately it is a matter of creating the economic, political, social and cultural conditions for the withering away of commodity production, of money, classes, and the state (Mandel, 1974).

Here, as is evident, a critique of the Soviet Union, and by extension China, was interwoven with a general theoretical framework strongly linked to historical materialism, though interpreted in the usual formulaic mode. Of course Mandel had added little, a measure of his devotion to his political guru, to the original observations of Trotsky made repeatedly in the '30s. Yet the critique, given the prevailing standards, remained compelling and was to be used with telling effect against the simpliste formulations of Maoism, by virtue of its being less arbitrary, and more securely orthodox (rightly or wrongly), in its use/abuse of classical Marxism-Leninism. Its most penetrating criticism concerned the issue of the critical *absence* of a critique of Stalinism in Mao, in whose vision there was a radical break in the USSR after Stalin toward capitalism, while Stalin's own period was viewed as 'socialist' (as was to be standardised in the Bettelheim version of things).

The Mandel account had located an important parameter in the discussion: that the issue was not 'theoretical' but, rather, *concrete* – a complete theory being only possible post factum. Two additional issues were to be highlighted in this rendering:

1 the question of property relations/production relations/class relations/ social ownership/exploitation, etc.;

2 the question of the state/dictatorship of the proletariat/revolutionary ideology and politics/workers' control, etc.

These two problems might be simplified as the *'economic'* and *'political'* moments, respectively, or, even more vulgarly, as problems of the *base* and problems of the *superstructure*, though such bimodal schemes, when used to imply a determinate causality lead usually, as understood in classical Marxian litany, to the 'errors' of *economism* in one direction and *idealism* in the other.

In the first instance, the data on the Soviet Union, in respect to ownership, was fairly unambiguous: the means of production, for the most part, were under 'social' ownership (state property), and did not circulate as *commodities*; and there was no class of capitalists privately appropriating surplus labour. Capital did not flow towards sectors with a higher rate of profit, neither domestically nor abroad; nor were there periodic crises of overproduction – in short, nothing remotely resembling any of the phases of capitalism with which we were historically familiar. Hence, it followed, on first principles alone, that the USSR had, at the very least, a *non-capitalist 'economic'* base.

The second issue posed problems both empirical (in relation to the Soviet socioeconomic formation) and methodological (in relation to Marxist theory, Leninist practice, etc.). The Soviet state was a sprawling leviathan, with a party that, for most purposes, saw itself as co-terminous with a giant bureaucracy, with a pronounced centralism that quite subdued any pretence at democracy – exercising, with few qualifications, dictatorship over the proletariat, albeit in its name. The political ideology of revisionism, which, since the Twentieth Congress had become more conciliatory toward imperialism, was combined, at home, with a benign (and sometimes not so benign) paternalism leading, in general, to a *depoliticisation* (a critical element preordaining the subsequent collapse) of all Soviet citizenry – producing in the main, an apathetic, submissive, working class accustomed to the strictest obedience to bureaucratic diktats. Workers' control, even participation, in production decisions was minimal, with the managerial elite in increasing possession of all aspects of the production unit. Here, then, was an apparently 'non-*socialist*' '*political*' superstructure, to say the least.

What is the resultant configuration when a 'non-capitalist' economic structure is tied to a 'non-socialist' political apparatus? Herein lay answers, if at all, to the riddle of the USSR, but there was still a residual issue: the '*plan-value*' contradiction, which was real enough in the Soviet system, and over which commentators had conducted do-or-die struggles for decades. On this matter, it appeared that:

a) the mere presence or survival of the categories of price, money, commodity (the law of value) in a transitional society was no great indictment so long as it did not replace national planning entirely (since Marx had been quite explicit about that); and

b) a final judgement was only possible, again, *after the fact*, as the struggle between the two, a class struggle, was fought to the finish, when one replaced the other, which was not yet the case at the time (but is so, of course, today).

The Mandelsian 'resolution' of the question of 'theory' was itself, thereby, necessarily quite irresolute.

3

But what of Marx himself, on the transition? It is clear that he recognised the need for the survival of what might be termed *bourgeois right* in post-capitalist society (like the state, this too was supposed to wither away as the class struggle drew to a final close in the abolition of class society): the primary, initial, emphasis was on socialising *production, not distribution.* Indeed, Engels had already given us, in a little noted, and seldom quoted, tract, a detailed enumeration of the first requirements of a transitional society, both economic and political. Here, the economic preconditions for a successful transition:

1. limitation of private property through taxation;

2. gradual expropriation of landlords and industrialists through state competition and compensation (bonds);

3. confiscation of property of rebels and emigrants;

4. organisation of labour in public factories;

5. equal obligation on all members of society to work until private property was completely abolished;

6. centralisation of money and credit in the hands of the state;

7. expansion of production, both agricultural and industrial;

8. education of all children;

9. construction of communal dwellings;

10. destruction of all unhealthy accommodations;

11. equal inheritance of all children regardless of legitimacy;

12. concentration of all means of transport in the hands of the nation (Marx and Engels, 1964).

Next, follows a highly illuminating passage:

> It is impossible, of course, to carry through all these measures at once. But one will always bring others in its wake. Once the first radical attack

on private property has been launched, the proletariat will find itself forced to go even further, to concentrate increasingly in the hands of the state all capital, all agriculture, all transport, all trade. All the foregoing measures are directed to this end; and they will become practicable and feasible, capable of producing their centralising effects to precisely the degree that the proletariat through its labour, multiplies the country's productive forces. Finally, when all capital, all production, all exchange have been brought together in the hands of the nation, private property will disappear of its own accord, money will become superfluous, and production will so expand and man so change that society will be able to slough off whatever of its old economic habits that may remain (ibid.)

Critics of the Soviet Union from Maoist perspectives will find little support for their positions in the foregoing. In the strictly 'economic' sense, certainly the Soviet Republic was well on track, if Engels is to be believed. On the other hand, the *political requirements* were spelt out thus:

Above all [the transitional society] will establish a democratic constitution and through this the direct or indirect dominance of the proletariat (ibid.)

Notice the quite flexible 'direct or indirect' dominance of the proletariat and the 'democratic' constitution; at any rate, the Engelsian definition of a socialist polity begins to look quite radically *minimalist* compared to the purist demands of both Trotskyism and Maoism.

Add to this minimalism Lenin and the theory of the vanguard party – a party of and for the proletariat exercising dictatorship – a role that the Bolshevik Party assumed under the leadership of Lenin in 1917, and scale in the historical circumstances of the USSR, where within a decade, most of the original party, and a good bit of the proletariat was decimated by civil war, imperial aggression, and Stalinist purges, and we appreciate the Bolshevik reality. The close link between party and proletariat steadily weakened, with only official ideology providing a tenuous link; in other words, the salient – and simple – 'lesson' of history is that even a victorious party and a proletariat can still be easily estranged by ordinary, material circumstances. The Soviets, on paper, retained a more or less 'democratic' constitution (despite the far greater weight given to workers against the peasantry, initially, in terms of votes), and a party that claimed to represent the proletariat, 'directly or indirectly', vindicating Engelsian claims to be sure, but little else of consequence.

The Mandelsian solution for the Soviet muddle was a *political revolution* in the Soviet Union, so that power could be returned to the Soviets, representing a struggle by the proletariat against the revisionism of the party and the domination of the bureaucracy. That would have constituted a concrete, empirical 'solution', true – but the larger theoretical problem remained for addicts of Marxism-Leninism: *that under certain, not unusual, circumstances the power of the real producers can be ruthlessly appropriated by a party that rules over them and the functionaries to whom the party delegates power.* No subterfuge can gainsay, or escape, this conclusion; Sweezy and Bettelheim (and even Mandel, despite, or because of, the Marxist trappings of his critique) obviously had little conception of what was to be done, or even what needed to be *undone* – aside from a mild 'warning' of what could happen to a 'transitional' formation in the light of the negative example of the USSR. Instead of institutional suggestions, and structural political reforms, the critical offerings in the period in question were merely admonitions, of the following kind, as with Sweezy (Sweezy and Bettelheim, 1971, p. 73):

> The existence, at any given time, of a party whose activity and organisational forms incorporates the collective knowledge acquired by the proletariat through its revolutionary struggles does not provide a 'definite' guarantee that the socialist road will not be abandoned. The only guarantee of progress along the road to socialism is the real capacity of the ruling party not to become separated from the masses. This capacity must be constantly renewed; this also implies that the renewal of the party – a continuous effort to avoid the sterile repetitions of ready-made formulations, and repeated concrete analyses of every new situation, which is always unique. Such a capacity in turn requires that the party of the proletariat remain in fact the servant of the labouring masses, that it be capable of drawing lessons from all their revolutionary initiatives, and to commit itself to these initiatives and assist in their development.

Platitudinous pieties, obviously, but little else.

On the other hand, it is also necessary to dismiss Mandel's repeated contention, another favourite theme in Marxian orthodoxy, that everything that was wrong about the Soviet Union was due to '*scarcity*', i.e. a low level of development of productive forces, for this is simply apologetics, 'economic determinism' style, particularly when the question is raised in the context of the possibility of the formation of more representative political instruments in 'socialist' societies. The truth of the matter is that since Lenin, with the exception of Mao, and perhaps even Che Guevara, the problem of proletariat political organisations received scant attention, the very success of the Bolshevik and Maoist revolutions apparently discouraging any further thinking in this direction. This is not to debunk Leninist and Maoist contributions to revolutionary Marxist practice, for better or for worse: Lenin and Mao succeeded supremely, at least in their own terms, if somewhat transiently. But further, and deep, examination is necessary of the fruits of that success, and the nature of the socialist agenda itself.

It is, of course, necessary to recognise the trivial fact of the combined pressure of imperial capital against any and all forms of socialist experiments (which can hardly be conducted *in vacuo*), and the resulting distortions in the political practices of 'transitional' societies forced to walk the tightrope of war and nuclear annihilation in their struggle to survive (quite seriously speaking, only the West had the nuclear *option*; socialism could only hold out a nuclear *deterrent*). Other than this, all we can say about transitional societies, Marx had already said about the Commune:

> The working class did not expect miracles from the Commune. They have no ready-made Utopias to introduce *par decret du peuple*. They know that in order to work out their own emancipation, and along with it that higher form to which present society is irresistibly tending by its own economic agencies, they will have to pass through long struggles, through a series of historical processes, transforming circumstances and men. They have no ideals to realise but to set free the elements of the new society with which old collapsing bourgeois society itself is pregnant. In the full consciousness of their historical mission, and with the heroic resolve to act up to it, the working class can afford to smile at the coarse invective of the gentleman's gentleman with the pen and inkhorn, and at the didactic patronage of well-wishing bourgeois doctrinaires pouring forth their ignorant platitudes and sectarian crotchets in the oracular tone of scientific infallibility (Marx, in Draper, 1971, p. 77).

No ideals to realise! – Marx at his materialist best, no doubt, but what an utterly vacuous guide to human *praxis*!

To summarise: the debate over a 'general' theory of the transition in the dominant Marxian literature tended to be unduly influenced by the specific Soviet experience. It is true, as Sweezy says, that a 'general theory of the transition' between social systems does not exist (indeed could not exist); but such a theoretical *overview*, right or wrong, did exist in the case of the transition to socialism: what else is the Marxist theory of revolution, historical materialism, and putatively 'scientific' socialism? Marx and Engels sketched the outer trajectory of this movement from its beginnings (the overthrow of capitalism) to its end (the establishment of communist society), which mark, at the poles, the full life of a 'theory' of transition. So Mandel is quite off the mark when he implies that such a theory is to be constructed only when the 'socialist society' is first established: but how is this configuration to be determined if not with reference to theory?

Secondly, were such a socialist society to be established, then the empirical data so revealed would remain, by necessity, *particularistic* and would not yield, again, a general theory. We are obviously on false terrain here; it is not that we lacked a Marxist theory of the transition, it is really how this theory could be put into practice, given the constraints of reality. The theory, like all Marxist theories, was rich (almost overburdened!) in conceptual content: revolution, dictatorship of the proletariat, expropriation of the bourgeoisie, class struggle, withering away of the state, social ownership of production, production of use-values based on human needs, and their allotment as per the same principle, removal of the antithesis between mental and physical labour, a democracy of real producers, and ultimately, the dissolution of class society! Admittedly, these concepts were supposed to find their application in different phases of the transition – but the *direction* of the movement was quite clear and unambiguous. Not all of these features were duly exhibited in all the socialist countries, but this is hardly for want of a 'theoretical' apparatus within classical Marxism.

4

In plain fact, the real crux of the issue, astonishingly overlooked by all commentators in this discourse, is that Marx had more to say on the nature of the *transition* (the socialist revolution) than on the *constitution of socialism* itself, particularly its all-critical political form(s). The penchant for *economic reductionism*, common to Marx and Marxists alike, was to prove suicidal when it was referred to on matters political, legal, and constitutional, where Lenin and Mao simply played catch-as-catch-can with institutional forms, thereby leaving millions vulnerable, on a daily basis, to the oppressions of absolute/and-or/arbitrary power (what could be more eloquent than the Berlin Wall as to the hollowness of the socialist polity?) Add to this vacuity the dissembling doctrines of historical *determinism*, to be used at will to suit any and all expedients, and you had the potent formula for outright disaster.

It is obvious, today, that socialism(s), in all its/their plurality, needs to be fought for and built by those who wish it – it may not be imposed on a disenfranchised majority by an elite minority empowered with physical force, as was the case with many of the erstwhile 'socialist' societies. These have been the great outstanding corruptions of all 'socialisms' to date – it is these crushing anomalies, apart from ever-present imperial intrigues, that brought the system crashing down, when it did, like a house of cards. *It is all this that must be undone*, if any such 'transition' is ever going to be on the popular agenda, again, in the foreseeable future. In short, while Marxist diagnostics of the ills of capitalism remain relevant and meaningful (if *incomplete*, as, e.g., with respect to feminist and ecological critiques), Marxist 'cures' (as witnessed in practice) remain an unsavoury, and quite hopeless, muddle. Finally, it is worth, at this critical stage of a new millennium, pondering the idea that materialist critiques are perhaps always inherently self-immolating: only moral critiques carry the potential of transcendence.

Socialism started out as a moral critique of capitalism (devolving into 'materialist' dialectics soon after); it were best if it were now to return to the founts of that great heritage. It is still not too late; classical socialism was only the imperfect ancestor of the drive for generalised *self-determination*, which stands poised to replace it in the age to come. It is important to note, *contra* Marx, that there is no teleology or 'necessity' to history; neither capitalism nor socialism were 'inevitable'; there is no script to the human story – and nothing that human society creates, wilfully or by accident, that may not be undone, again, by human will(s). Materialism is an inherently reactionary philosophy that enchains the human genius in the catechism of laws, determinisms, and straitjackets; but it is precisely human wills that always have the potential to shake off such entrapments. Max Weber was right: charisma, when understood as the ineluctable force of the human spirit, has the power to unseat the most powerful materialist tyranny. All of the decisive, enduring, changes in history pertain to cultural, not material, forces: as such, Christ, Gautama, and Mohammad, were far more important in delineating the course of human evolution than the spinning jenny, the marvels of hydroelectric power, or other such artefacts of technical invention; the latter are all perishable, tawdry, wares – but the former may never be annulled. In the last instance, it is not material forces, but cultural and spiritual forces that always prevail. For a while, socialism channelled this powerful force into a secular version of religion; only on that energy did it last even as long as it did. Only when its dissimulating charlatanry became obvious to the many did it abide, on borrowed time, purely, if temporarily, by the sword.

Marx's mature ideas on socialism and the 'transition' period were inspired by two facts. First, the Paris Commune whose organisational spontaneity he idealised at first, only to reject it when the Commune fell, gleaning from the latter (rightly or wrongly) the dangers of decentralisation when facing a centralised enemy (hence the iron tone of the 'dictatorship of the proletariat'). Secondly, facing with competition from Bakunin in the International, Marx yielded to the essentially anarchist conception of a state that 'withers away'. Of course, in theory at least, the fact that these two conceptions fit ill with each other explains the conceptual mess inherited by would-be socialist governors. Easy to see, however, which way all governors, socialist or otherwise, tend to when given by half a chance (gleefully embracing dictatorship as a 'Marxian' godsend!)!

5

Today, emancipatory movements, if merely to pre-empt auto-subversion, need to reject both alienated society and an alien state, the twin evils of modernism, and any notion of 'government' that is not, first and last, *direct self-*

government. Only by moving toward self-determination, in the political domain, and *self-provisioning* in the material one (and not the artificial level of 'state', 'nation', etc., but at the most enabling, affective, and creatively inspired, 'micro' levels of socio-personal existence, homesteads, communes, etc.; this would approximate to a *revolutionary individualism*, a far cry from the reactionary variant dear to capitalism), can we hope to escape the ravages of modernism, and its notion of (an imposed) order (both social and political). Important also to recognise that there is no privileged constituency ('working class', etc.) in the drive for a *human* emancipation; freedom, cannot, by its very nature, be corporatist, or exclusive.

Traditional (mainstream and radical; i.e. 'modernist') emphases on *aggregate* (social) phenomena, vis-à-vis the modalities of social change, rest on fundamental misperceptions about the nature of the ontological distinction between the individual and social moments. In realist analysis, the two levels are not distinguished by any ontological *priority* between the two domains (as reflected in the paradigms both of methodological individualism and Marxism, polar antipodes in this respect) as much as by a *radical hiatus* between them. *It is almost a law of ontology – both social and natural – that macro phenomena always appear to be 'law governed' and (thereby) predictable while micro phenomena seem to be 'free' and less predictable.* An example, or two, may perhaps suffice: any individual worker is potentially capable of turning into a 'capitalist', given the right assemblage of opportunities and attributes, but the working class as a whole cannot turn 'capitalist' without violating the structural norms of capitalist society. For not dissimilar reasons, crowd behaviour, given someone shouting 'fire' in an auditorium, is more or less predictable, but how any particular individual in that hall will behave (to stay put or to rush out, being the alternatives) is far less predictable. The point should be clear; individuals are led by apparently 'free' wills, whilst aggregates of individuals seem more bound to the expectations of normalcy (i.e. patterned behaviour). Stated differently, aggregate behaviour is more 'controllable', (for) being more predictable, (for) being more determinable; individuals, au contraire, can slip through the cracks of the (any) system. Summing up, individuals have more 'options', more degrees of freedom, than societies and other such aggregates. From a dim perception of this truth, the 'reasonable' inference drawn by the sociologically-minded, in Eurosociology (Durkheim, Spencer, Marx, etc.), seems to be that the social moment is the *more important* one, both in terms of the general analytics of a social science, and in terms of the prospects, themselves, for social change. The unreasonable corollary of this position, on the other hand, has been that the individual placement is a relatively unimportant one in discussing the moment of emancipation.

This, however, is simply false, both ontologically, and in terms of human morality. There is no doubt that individuals can behave *contra* to social norms (be they socialist, or capitalist, norms; hence the conservative restraint of social 'deviance' in both social forms), thereby annulling all theories of sociological determinism (conservative or radical). If that's the case, then emancipatory movements can just as easily, in fact far more likely, given the inevitably inertia of aggregate social entities, rest their faith in *individuals* to initiate the dynamics of societal change. *If contra behaviour is possible for any one individual in society it is, ipso facto, possible for any and all individuals (but only to the extent that they are behaving qua individuals)* making individual choices), because society, while a larger organon than the individual, nonetheless *also* exists at the ontic level of a simple aggregation of individuals. Individual *delinking* from social norms can just as easily (in point of fact, far more easily) initiate social change, as much as the vaunted Marxian faith in mass-conscious class action. Individual delinking from the *logos* of capitalist production and consumption is, therefore, neither reactionary nor retrograde, as the social determinists would have us believe; indeed in the many instances of the virtual nonexistence of class based resolves, it is the only way to proceed. In point of fact, even more rests on this understanding; *individuals may not only be catalytic institutors of alternate ways, as might still be admitted in a weakened Marxian framework, but actually constitute, all on their own, those ways.*

The truth is quite paradoxical; one has only to examine the role of influential individuals in history, Mohammad, or Gandhi, or Lenin, to realise that individual determination often prevails over formidable social restraints (like the other way around). It is now possible to understand all forms of sociological determinisms (stemming from 'social science', of Left or Right) as profoundly reactionary ideologies, geared to stifling individual initiatives in the area of *self direction*, so as to maintain the power and control of mini-elites at the head of putative 'mass' movements. Both Marxists and capitalist planners wish only to 'lead' the less privileged, or the more gullible, 'masses', like to many cattle, into pre-selected social corrals where they are permanently dispossessed of the will and capacity for self-determination. The mass movement, a herd phenomenon, is quite ideally suited to their purposes, because, being aggregate behaviour, it lends itself to both *predictability and control*. The emancipatory impulse needs to shun all such mass frenzies: it is the regrettable lesson of history that mobs will, ultimately, fall prey to the rule of mobsters. *Any move toward self-direction is, by its very nature, an individual, even personal resolve; there is no imperative to carry the world with one (least of all to demand compliance!), on that journey – each has to discover, and decide, for oneself.*

Notes

1 Quoted by Liang Hsiao, in *Peking Review*, No. 45, 1975.
2 In his paper entitled 'On the Transition between Capitalism and Socialism', Sweezy and Bettelheim, 1971.

13 Beyond Marx: *Contra Theses on Feuerbach*

Marx's *Theses on Feuerbach* (1970), though merely jottings, are often said to constitute the philosophical underpinnings of Marxism. Here, I offer some theses, mere jottings again!, on the *Theses*, in the same order as Marx presents them, as a means of both comprehending and transcending the limitations of the latter.

1

Human activity is subjective, and practical, sensuous activity; the fact that it is, occasionally, embodied in *things* does not give the latter domain precedence over the former. Ideas are both objective and subjective, and there is no practice that is not informed by the former.

2

Truth is both objective and subjective; it is not merely a practical question, but an episteme as well. It cannot be 'proved' – merely *expressed*, both in practice and in passionate moral evaluation. Indeed, it is materialist scholastics that divorces practice from ideas, much as idealism itself.

3

Social change is not merely a function of a materialist, even 'revolutionary', activity, but is the set of intended and unintended consequences of normal, everyday, continuous human activities which include deeply spiritual, emancipatory drives *as a matter of course*.

4

The rift between the sacred and the profane is a function of the modernist, bourgeois Enlightenment (both in ideology and in practice), and an expression of its alienation. It cannot survive that regime and outlook, and will be reunited again. Neither aspect of life can be parsed, merged, or reduced, into the other; together, they constitute the unity of human existence.

5

Sensuousness is expressed not merely in practical activity but also in moral, intellectual, and spiritual speculations as well; the mind-body, materialist-idealist rift, again the baneful gift of the Enlightenment, is false and one-sided.

6

The human essence, be that as it may, is not reducible to any particular 'ensemble of social relations', nor can it suffer mutation as a consequence of changes in the latter.

7

Sentiments are both human reflexes and, socially-mediated, *productions*. Religiosity is a spiritual drive, and cannot be reduced to the 'social' fact of religion.

8

All social life is neither 'practical', nor 'contemplative', considered apart from each other. It is, rather, the *contextual* unity of both moral and practical energies.

9

European materialism may have peaked in the bourgeois Enlightenment, with its open celebration of that social order; but the contemplation of 'single individuals' need not be materialist, nor even bourgeois, at all, as in non-European (e.g. ancient Indian) philosophies.

10

The standpoint of the 'old' materialism was not civil society per se, but of the *bourgeois interest* within it; the 'new', 'proletarian', standpoint did *not* include all of social humanity; orders left questioning the new order would be women, tribals, 'other' cultures, and various minorities, both within and without the working class.

11

The 'point' is neither to change nor to 'interpret' the world (although both, entirely normal, human activities are quite interdependent), but to live hospitably and nonviolently in both society and nature, within and without such processes.

Part VII
NEW HORIZONS: AGAINST PATRIARCHY

14 Feminist Horizons: Toward Cultural Revolution

1

Feminism, in the European tradition, is to the twentieth century what Marxism aspired to be, at its best, in the late nineteenth: i.e., *an inclusive programme of general emancipation*, a programme subsuming, encompassing, and superseding, all other agendas of liberation. The social, legal, and cultural, status of women is arguably perhaps among the principal touchstones of the degree of civilisation attained in a given social formation; for sexism is easily the most ubiquitous form of social oppression known to human society, yesterday as much as today, making of *patriarchy*, however variable in form and function, one of the dominant, universal, abominations of social evolution. It is a chastening reminder of the glaring blind spots of European civilisation, putative heir of the Enlightenment, and the many vacuous declarations of human rights contained therein, that the usually venerated, near-ideal, bourgeois democracy, Switzerland, would have denied its women – over half the nation! – even nominal voting rights as late as *1981*. And yet, despite the horrific injustice of this elementary denial of the most inane basics of civil society, Europe could still proudly pass itself off as the very acme of high civilisation.

True, feminists are as fiercely divided today into diverse clans and sects (*the real, and encompassing, divide being, of course, almost all but unnoticed, between First World and Third World feminism*; the one driven by materialist, rationalist discourse, the other by affective, emotive impulse), as Marxists were in the past (and are still); in one sense, perhaps, dissension is probably only reflective of the growing maturity of the movement, rather than any obvious weakness within it: *for the struggle for ideas, representing different ideals, is always inherently more divisive* than the rather mundane, even banal, struggles for *power and domination*. Recognition of a plurality of interests, and a plurality of struggles – in general – would seem to be the derivative lesson to be learnt from this diversity and heterodoxy. Indeed, it is probably to the credit of serious feminism that it has not, usually, invoked the traditional Marxist *formula/metaphor/event* of a cataclysmic seizure of the citadel, or the capture of the winter palace, as the indispensable desideratum of emancipation, focusing attention instead on an epistemic unravelment of the incredibly tangled mosaic of language, culture, and tradition, which works as an unconscious social prison within which both oppressor and victim lie critically, even mortally, trapped. In so pointing to the reality and efficacy of structures beyond, and below, simpler, and more transparent, *material* structures of domination, feminist criticism has served the more general function of a revolutionary *cultural* critique, a necessary correction to the all too schematic, and mechanistic, materialist dialectics of vulgar Marxism (is there another kind? Perhaps ...) with its permanent accent on *economism*, and its childlike faith in the apocalyptic 'revolution' as the ultimate act of absolution.

However, in another sense, feminism needs to heal its own internal breaches as well. In this respect, rationalist, and materialist feminism, characteristic of European modernism, is destined, I fear, to fail quite unhappily for reproducing, within its own ranks, the epistemic misery (self-interestedness, atomism, aggression, divisiveness, and intolerance) of the very spirit of *patriarchy* that it opposes; *affective* feminism, as indubitably expressive of the genius of the bonding cement of pre-capitalist, 'Third World' cultures, offers, instead, the inspiration of drawing men and women together in a common struggle *to affirm the values of warmth, felicity, and hospitality, toward all forms of planetary life* (instead of the self-conscious anthropocentrism of Western discourse). It is this latter perspective, sometimes termed *ecofeminism*, that possesses the native hue and resolution to *respiritualise* reality, for all of us, regardless of our specific agendas.

At any rate, the abolition of sexism (as a mode of social control, rather than simply as a prejudice) is inherently far more complex than the abolition of class society, because no single set of institutional changes, let alone alterations in a simple set of parameters, can serve either as a necessary, or even a sufficient condition for it; it seems to demand, by its very nature, a *total transformation* of our values, drives, practices and motivations. Worse, I have the apprehension that such a revolution would involve, at a deep, fathomless remove, also a transcendent victory over the machinations of Nature that have apparently endowed men and women with rather powerful instinctual drives. This is by no means to cast a pall of gloom over the question of the ultimate success of feminist objectives, *within which all other emancipatory objectives find their place*, but rather to indicate the involute nature of the problematic itself, and the inherent promise contained therein of a redemption beyond the dreams of idle radical rhetoric. *A feminist world would be the decisively antipodal antithesis to the entire frame of alien social life as we have come to know it* within the treacherous minefields of *modernism*, representing, in its grandest form, the capitulation of nature to culture. In physics we use nature to tame nature (as, say, in counteracting gravity); but, in this area, we can only be armed with the high, if all too transient, impulse of human self-consciousness: stated simply, nothing short of a spiritual revolution could assure the exalted affirmation of the feminine principle over the brute instincts of masculinity lying none too deep under the surface skin of socialisation. However, be that as it may, the first, initial – even embryonic – steps in that direction, will still involve chipping away at the grand bastille of patriarchy, erected through centuries of indurate, repressive socialisation; at steadfastly removing the various economic, legal, and political disabilities of women, while devising strategies to fight the cultural revolution *simultaneously* (reform and revolution being quite *complementary* in this context); razing the ideological superstructures, one might say, while digging deep to expose, and dissolve, the substructures upon which they rest.

My own small effort, within this struggle, by way of my 'study'[1] of Utah women houseworkers, was extraordinarily simple, even trivial: to expose the ineradicably sexist *dualism* that inhabits formal, economic theory – *part and parcel of the general ideology of capitalism* – which is able, by deft sleight of hand, to critically devalue the traditionally designated sphere of *female* labour, and its produce, while conferring honorific title, and high bounty, on the (traditionally-designated) domain of productivity of *male* labour. The Utah study revealed, quite unambiguously, the critical contribution of women houseworkers toward the general economic health of the public and private economy, boosting employer rates of profit, and the wellbeing of the proletarian (and non-proletarian) household simultaneously. The blind disregard for *housework*, *contra* its critical economic significance, shows up clearly the role of patriarchal ideology in disguising this social form as innocuous forms of expression of the 'private' sphere where values do not intrude. The strength of this invidious ideology is evident in the case of even well-meaning (orthodox) Marxists who idealise the heroic proletarian (usually male) while reserving little comment on the unpaid slave (usually female) at home, who keeps our emancipatory proletarian hero, and his progeny, alive and well during both good and bad times; and whose ragged trousered philanthropy, constituting the very *irreducible social basis of wage-labour*, has been all but ignored in both mainstream and Marxian forms of social theorising. Far from the vaunted 'welfare state', it is the transcendental philanthropy of women, i.e. *unremunerated women's labour*, that provides the vital, and vast, social dividend allowing for generalised social subsistence. Indeed, our very notion of *productivity*, stemming from the class and gender bias of economics – and, in fact, even the line demarcating the putatively 'public' from the 'private' sphere – needs be seriously called into question, while addressing this egregious default that still passes for 'normal science' in the discipline.

In the case of European history, in the modernist period, the formal dispossession of the *productive* functions of women (skills, crafts, knowledge, property, etc.) seems to be a fairly recent process, dating its beginnings from roughly 300–400 years ago (the organised witch hunts being only the highly symbolic forms of such depredations), when the coercively-imposed transition to the '*woman-as-housewife-consumer*' – wherein the largesse of women's social being was radically, and ruthlessly, reduced to their reproductive roles – became pronounced, as capitalism consolidated its social (and military) victories within all spheres of social conduct, and across all areas of the globe. Indeed, the same process was to be inflicted, even more grievously, upon *non-European women*, in the colonised world, in much the same period of history, and by the same social forces; in fact, to this day, the famous fleshmarkets of Asia, now made even more invidious by the new ubiquity of child sex and pornography (of which the major clients remain European men), are still the peak centres of *Western* influence, grim reminders of the dubious gifts of European civilisation. Women fought back and resisted then, as best they could; they are doing so still, here and now, but in ways that are uniquely, and inescapably, feminine.

2

At another remove, and involving considerable tragic irony, it appears that '*housework*', the allotted preserve of women, is now turning into almost the preferred model of work in the so-called *New World Order*, with select industry and capital (textiles and electronics) steadily shifting to the Third World, from the '70s onwards, to South Asia and the Far East particularly, looking for a docile, passive, manipulable, underpaid work force, remarkably akin to the '*houseworker*' as a genus (the ideal worker for capital is not one that needs to be supported by burdensomely inflated wages, benefits, and rights, but one that will slave devotedly, supplicating only for the irreducible minima of a crypto-social existence; indeed, if capitalists could somehow both invest in, and consume, *all* resources, slavery would be back in a trice as the preferred labour regime) in which the female component is very high. Paralleling this tendency within the First World itself, and its peerless paragon the United States, is the noticeable shift towards the fragmentation of work, the atomisation of the worker, the break-up of unions, and the dispersal of industry (through out-sourcing, subcontracting, relocations, etc.), the erasure of job security, dissolution of benefits, and the general shrinkage of the old model of the unionised worker as developed during the heyday of the pre-Reaganite, *Fordist*, postwar, welfare state. Certainly, there has been a narrowing of the traditional differences between wage labour and housework, with the burden placed squarely on the *self-provisioning* activities of the work force (within which the labour of women has always been of altogether critical importance), reminiscent of the hoary era of the transitional form of the *peasant-worker*, to ensure the social reproduction of the working class. Stated differently, the ideal worker under capitalism may not be the classical proletarian, as originally conceptualised by Ricardo and Marx, any more, as much as the *housewife*; the basis of exploitation being not so much *paid labour* but *unpaid labour* – such that the so-called 'primitive accumulation', far from being archaic and anachronistic, may well be quite an advanced, and advancing, form of social deprivation as capital consolidates its victories globally.

I have always suspected that women have always been intuitively aware of their incredible oppressions in the domestic sphere (to say nothing of the public domain), quite regardless of their susceptibility to the hegemony of male ideology, institutions, and constructs. And, after much direct observation in diverse cultural settings, East and West, in capitalist and non-capitalist societies, I am now convinced, at some distance from some Marxian and materialist theories of ideology, that while ideology might well aid in rationalising and 'explaining', in duly soporific form, the fact of oppressions, *it is never able to blunt the critical 'felt' edge of their appreciation on the part of their victims*. I remember my own stepmother, in India, who was as 'feudal' as anyone about her role within the household (and, by inference, in society), a role that she appeared to play ('play' is quite the antipodal verb, of course) to the hilt; asked what she prayed for every evening, though, for she was very religious, after the day's chores were done, she said simply, but emphatically: *'to be born a man, in my next life'*. Even as a child, I remember being struck by the world of meaning in that simple statement.

Similarly, the mainly Mormon women, who constituted the principal respondents in my Utah study, may have been quite conservative and religious in their convictions, true to popular stereotype; but they certainly betrayed no ignorance of their daily burdens, and no single one was identified who cheerfully whistled a happy tune, in total delight at their servitude, right through the almost interminably long domestic working day (on *average*, in Utah, houseworkers put in a *15* hour working day, every day of the year, without rest or respite, until sheer physical incapacity intervenes). Put another way, *women are fully aware*, I think, *in all societies, as to the invidious nature of the exactions placed upon them*; their difficulty, usually, seems to lie in not knowing what to do about it – and one can empathise quite easily: for I doubt if all the feminist theory in the world, of which there is not an inconsiderable amount, actually points the way, in any simple sense, to their general emancipation from such travails, even today, *in the foreseeable short run*.

However, there is a far more important element to their acquiescence to serfdom which materialist dialectics tendentiously refuses to acknowledge;

that, being disinclined to be perfectly rational, and 'maximising', greed machines, and involved in the *non-alienating domain of the production and consumption of use-values*, women have, by and large, assumed the burdens of their self-inflicted affections more or less cheerfully. It is this selfless largesse, this warm-spirited nobility, this *idyll of generosity*, that holds out the definite promise, to human society more generally, of a higher humanity. *It is women, therefore, who have virtually embodied – almost unnoticed by male ideologies – almost inconceivably noble ideals of human civility.* Utopia needs no wild flights of fancy, as men have imagined: it has always stood beside them within the embalming matrix of domesticity; it requires no forces of production to be transformed, no factories to be built, no towers to be razed. The male concept of justice, usually, is *retributive* (and most radical agendas, socialism included, have been marred by the mean, materialist, spirit of vengefulness): the female spirit, albeit nurtured by force in the repressive matrix of patriarchy, has been one of peaceableness and cooperativeness, searching instead for mutually sustaining bases of harmony and complementarity. As must be obvious, much of Gandhian political philosophy, quite ingenuously, has taken cue from this near surreal *'politics of femininity'*; indeed, in any reckoning, Gandhi would have to be the true, and prophetic, precursor of all the planet-sustaining, nonviolent, and convivial modes of emancipation that are likely to define the struggles of the new millennium. He *practised*, in the modern era, alone but unruffled, an age ahead of his time, what we are only starting now, belatedly and awkwardly, to *think* about; but what women have *lived*, within the effusive eloquence of silence, and the sibylline passion of patience, for aeons. There are no *material* final solutions to the so-called 'woman question' (indeed, women are not the *question*, except in a male-centred discourse: they are, on the other hand, in a critically important sense, the historically inspiring *'answer'* to the violence of the modernist order of patriarchy); only in the affective, spiritual, domain can the *revolutionary pacifism* of women, sustained across any and every 'mode of production' and social formation, tame the otherwise hopelessly incurable tensions of masculinity, and bind us all in the healing warmth of a *social economy of affection* (it is true that patriarchy imposes the values of nurturance forcibly on women, imprisoning them within that structure of roles, but two aspects of this cry out for comment: nurturance was not merely a social demand on women, but appears to be a natural one as well; besides, if women can be so pacified, albeit by force, into care, civility and grace, there is, prima facie, the charter of hope for men as well). As such, it would not be an exaggeration to see the vital poser for our times as, simply: *Feminism or Barbarism*!

At any rate, my task in the Utah study was remarkably simple: to reveal, in all concreteness, the true *obligations and values of domestic services*, as they pertained to *houseworkers*, and to show how this *hidden economy* (hidden, that is, only from the blind and the unseeing) – unscaled by our corporatist accountants – *sustains the formal one*, humbly, continuously, and without fanfare. No ideological camouflage can disguise the fact of the real values generated within the household (which, in my study, ranged from 87 per cent to 143 per cent of her spouse's wage), although opinions might differ as to the methods of valuation chosen. I found what we must all intuitively know: *that women are the true welfare donors of human society* – that it is their ceaseless, unsung, and Herculean toils that allow society to both produce and reproduce with all ensuing 'charges' written off to the impulses of love and generosity alone; indeed, the houseworker would have to be almost the obverse of the capitalist whose entrepreneurial spirit economics celebrates in shameless abandon – *she gives, and gives, without thought of taking*! The challenge is then posed unambiguously to formal economics, and economists, to show why they continue to understate the real value of the GDP (to point to but a trifling elision), belittling housework, befogging – and befogged by – their own, pervasive, almost wholly unconscious, *sexism* that is embedded deep in the ideological foundations, at the very core of the 'discipline'; and, more to the point, why they don't impassionately sanction a '*wages-for-housework*' policy given their own penchant for materialism (that is quite impotent to understand either altruism or charity as *human* impulses; being philosophical Hobbesians, economics worships only the brute in all of us), and their lip service to the idea of a quid pro quo in the economic realm.

3

The road to emancipation, conceived as a *process* and not an *event*, is necessarily fed by multiple byways; significant amongst these would have to be the efforts to reveal and expose, and not only in an intellectual sense, the full range of ideological and material disabilities inflicted upon women. As it is, we are still on the threshold of such revelations, on the brink of vistas still obscured by custom, veiled by language, shrouded by prejudice. Of course, the way things are, theory does not necessarily lead to appropriate action; nor is appropriate action necessarily informed by true theory. *But ideas and practices, when sufficiently far apart, do generate the critical, creative, tension that drive emancipatory movements, and create the vital emancipatory potential for self-reflexive passions.* I can only hope that studies like my Utah project reveal the *radical critical distance*, the sheer dissonance, that exists between ideology and reality when it comes to how society perceives, portrays, and values *housework* – and the perennial labours of women. As in so many areas of social theory and practice, it is very small comfort to note exactly how much that still needs, unhappily, to be *undone*.

Note

1 In book form this study is entitled *Devaluing Women: the Uncharted Domain of Domestic Drudgery* (awaiting publication).

Postface: Rethinking Political Economy

1

Do we need economics?; given its present constitution, only as much a we need a hole in the ozone layer, the disappearance of the rainforest, and the extinction of the blue whale. And who would miss it, were it suddenly to be expunged from the annals of self-inflicted human misery? The ruling class would be bereft of its most formidable apparatus of ideological camouflage; ranks of arrogant, well-heeled, formula-toting, parasitic, technocrats would be looking for some more communally useful avenue of employment; corporations, and the state, would be hard-pressed to find an equal rank of dumbly loyal dissemblers and apologists for the status quo; additionally, universities would have one less monotonous stream of irredeemable drivel to inflict upon the hapless student on her way to a licensed form of politically (in)correct knowledge. The damage to the populace at large, in other words, would be slight, almost marginal. Of course, the ilk of those who believe that the invention of double-entry bookkeeping is the critical watershed of civilisational accomplishment (and the great European gift to the world) are unlikely to fare so well; and they will cry apocalyptic doom, even as they bring it down upon themselves – and all of us.

Economic ideology has dried the lifeblood of the human genius at least since the capitalist 'Enlightenment' (a curious enlightenment, where Europe doffed one mode of ideological slavery only to capitulate, almost simultaneously, to another), reversing almost all the normal, decorous polarities of human society. Virtues were hurriedly transmuted into vices, and vice versa; morality was put paid to, culture debased, and the arts of life turned into so many drab and dreary avenues of pecuniary advancement. The alienation of capitalist state and society was reproduced in economic ideology; to beggar thy neighbour, and to let the devil take the hindmost were now enshrined as the very highest precepts of civilised human accomplishment. To cite the inimitable Bentham, one of the patron saints of this vulgar utilitarianism, pushpin would henceforth be as good as poetry (if not quite as good as political economy); economics, with unerring instinct, would seek out the lowest denominator in human drives and revel in it in an orgy of self-satisfying stupefaction – it would similarly serve as eager counsellor to captains of industry and masters of state, exhorting them to go forth and sunder the communal tie anywhere, and everywhere, replacing it with the tawdry, dissimulating, attachments of the cash nexus. To forcibly create *market dependency*, to impose the paradigm of unrequitable work, to exult in the global celebration of predacious regimes of profiteers, privateers and pirates, to destroy self-provisioning, to annihilate self-determination, to extirpate the ingenuous diversity of the variegated cultural economies of this planet, to reify production and consumption as the overriding objectives of the societal life, to craft a homogenous, uniform world, driven by the werewolf lusts for accumulation (private and public) would only be a few of the contributions of this metaphysics of Mammon to the devolution of the species. A genuine political economy needs be concerned not merely with the mundane manufacture of the *means* of material sustenance, but also the larger ends of life within which the vital *meanings* of such activity are given; as such, the cosmos of culturally ordained values are its necessary, ontic, parametric, guides. Instead, neoclassicism surreptitiously substitutes its own aridly amoral *episteme* of calculating selfishness for prevailing ontic norms in the social universe; in so usurping the manifest of culture, neoclassicism functions as the *paradigmatic metaphysics of the age of capital*.

Thous shalt truck and barter, to the nethermost limits of thine energies, all that may be grasped, till the end of thine days! That, the sovereign commandment of this degenerate pseudo-science of the ascendancy of capital; and so, a reluctant humankind, forced into servitude, ended up almost trading away its inalienable birthright of conviviality, grace, and cooperative contentment. In this lucrative enterprise of despoliation by *conscriptive exchange*, free-spirited tribals and ethnic minorities were transmogrified into dismal chattels, peasants into wage slaves, women into sexual commodities, self-renewing use-values into cornered, price-tagged, and scarce, monopolies, and the very planet into a giant workshop, mill and foundry. And yet, even as the social world was being ravished into a wasteland, and the natural into a graveyard, the huckstering ideology of modernism – economics – would have us all live in the delusion that things were getting better all the time, that progress was ubiquitous, and that, no matter what the havoc of the present, there were always new, uncharted frontiers still remaining to be torched and ravaged, raped and pillaged. And, equally dumbly, both conservative and radical *loyalists* (e.g. Marxists, who, for aeons, have celebrated the ravages of capital as a necessary step toward human advancement) of the *nouvelle régime* would console themselves that this was the best of all possible worlds, only to be made better by being made bigger, and even more predatory, toward all forms of life than hitherto.

Economics, as ideology, cannot be 'reformed', or made more 'realist', or more 'relevant', as many internal critiques (liberal and radical) have tried to do for over a century. By its very nature, it embodies the crassly incorrigible triumphalism of capital unchained: *it is the grand illusion of the epoch of modernism*; the only bulwark that is inherently loaded with a primeval, intractable, resistance to its venomous vapours is the sentient, affective, consilient bonding of sentiment and morality, the very hallmark of *premodernist* cultures (expressed, variously, in the richness of their religion, magic, kinship, etc.) with roots deep into the very psyche of the species being of humanity. As such, it is the vestigial human agents still vested, however marginally, with the anachronic memory of the past (women, ethnic minorities, tribals, aboriginals, etc.), and/or the structurally ill-fated groups like workers, permanently designed to be cannon fodder (to a lesser extent, even aristocracies – and some sections of the intelligentsia not totally drugged by the spurious slogans of modernism – disaffected by social disfigurement and turmoil) that represent the last, and lasting, pockets of radical rejection of the malignant mindset of Mammon.

It is amongst such orders, wrought within that normative, unchained, and unyielding, world of human resolve, that capital, and economics, encounters what it cannot buy, or co-opt; *it must either destroy them, or be destroyed by them* (it is this intuitive understanding of the 'Third World' that keeps imperialist armies permanently poised to swoop down on them). But, despite all its virulently depraved expression of energies, political, military, and economic, in this area, this is one battle *it cannot win*. As with the gathering revolt of Islam, it is the moral fire of sensual, and sensate, *culture* that will first withstand, then prevail over the insensate armies of the night. Modernism will be overturned, inch by inch, sector by sector, province by province; almost as if the planet were a living thing gifted with its own instinct of self-preservation. European capital, and its many satellites (within and without its periphery) have brought the world to the very brink of extinction, physical and cultural, through reckless adventurism, primitive piracy, and a coruscating greed beyond the scope of even the most satyric lusts (that the 'civilisation' that gave us two world wars, and almost fought a third, and final, one, could yet think of itself as the very acme of humane civilisation must surely rank amongst the most egregious of hallucinations of humankind). With apocalyptic modernism upon us as it is, can the reckoning be far behind?

2

It is easy now to see the lapidary errors of the hoary critics of capital: they premised their critiques, firstly, upon the very ontological terrain of the former, accepting its crippling confines of alien 'society', 'nation' and the 'state' – *even when these alienations were the very cause of the 'false consciousness' they deplored* – thereby being trapped forever within the irreconcilable contradictions of modernism (accept the bourgeois social order as the norm for communal living and we are enchained forever in its paralytic deformities of competition, structural conflict, and irresolvable contrarieties of interest, paradigm, and power). Secondly, they were epistemically locked into the materialist straitjacket of Eurocapitalist ideology, still venerating production and consumption as the orgiastic end-all of societal evolution, regardless of its consequences for living, being, etc. Given this, the socialist dream could only be what it turned out to be, a grim nightmare of a prison, entombing the freedoms of the millions in favour of the ghoulish treadmill of implacable slavery that reduced entire, living, social forms into hopeless gulags of human debasement. (Wo)Man does not live by bread – nor by dread – alone. Our deepest, most ingenuous, urges have not one materialist swirl to them; we are familial, tribal entities, seeking warmth, affection and love within a culturally woven cocoon of self-social fulfilment. The rationalism of the Enlightenment, thereby, inaugurated only the dark age of artificial passions within contrived societal and political boundaries where we would all, in desperate anomie, wallow in our collective rootlessness, while the masters of the economy and the polity, and their many servile hangers-on, fed their inexorable ambitions with forever escalating extortions.

To break with that ideology of expansion, to embalm the eternal attributes of human covetousness, and aggression, once again within a restraining matrix of organic affection, and corespective empathy (as all pre-capitalist, particularly tribal, entities were/are able to do), is the vital requirement today if there is to be any hope of emancipation from the dire incubus of capital. Its ever-present, ineffable, possibility is vouchsafed by the near-eternal *politics of femininity* that, across any and all modes of production, has assured, for tyrant and toddler, the daily reminder of a domestic economy of care, consideration, and conviviality. *Indeed, it is the family, and the familiar – within which we have forcibly imprisoned the grace of femininity – that is the eternal provenance of all visions of emancipation.* It is this *feminine principle* that needs to be set free, so it may envelope all of us within its nurturing warmth. It is not that evil, injustice, and grief will ever disappear, no matter how we design and redesign the material domain; but we can – as in the past – ensure that such infelicities are bounded and checked by the overpowering force of human sentiments. The 'social' may then yet once more be what it was before the baneful European, capitalist assault upon convivial social forms: a nurturing *balance of affections*, rather than a corrosive balance of interests (or terror).

The truth about 'economics' is that it is wholly subservient to our will; despite the cant of the pharisees, there are no iron laws, no ineluctable catechisms, no inexorable necessities: production, consumption, distribution are all societal/communal/familial/individual activities subject to the logic of our preferences, moods, and idiosyncrasies, ranging (as humans will) from crass self-regard to lofty altruism, from competition to cooperation, from distrust to empathy. As such *there are no laws of economics that do not first derive metaphysically from our epistemic orientations*; it is in this vital regard that Marxists are as wrong in their speculations as the neoclassicists for eking out a squalid existence solely *within* the ontological premises of capital (and alienated societal forms, generally). The human laboratory of social forms, in the material domain as in others, is a glittering array of diversitude, invention and adaptive facility; easy to see how the modernists lie mortally trapped in one regressive paradigm – the regime of generalised commodity production – the feculent gift of the capitalist 'Enlightenment', which then eradicates even the very memory of other modes of living. *The 'open' society of modernism is a cruel, mordant hoax: all the putative pluralities of its political spectrum – designed to co-opt, and/or extrude, any and all forms of resistance – succeed only in a de facto affirmation of its essentially constrained and constraining discourse, forced to subsist under the guardian shadow of the institutional needs of capital.* How we can continue to celebrate an epoch that has granted us the execrations of the factory, the workhouse, and the gulag, in 'exchange' for almost the entire range of our convivial freedoms, will remain a wonder all in itself.

3

Political economy is not a science; it is the uninspired, demotic, liturgy of covetous conduct, commodity production, technological fetishism, and wage slavery. Its maxims are not merely dissembling nostrums, but arguably ruinous to the animate and inanimate world; *modes of living* are not irresistible 'technologies', as the economist would have us believe, to be studied from manuals fabricated in the charnels of human depravity, but stem from the artless choices of the untutored imagination; they belong to us, autonomous humans, not to the 'experts', the scientists, and other such menial, insensible retinue of capital. Nor is science, in its impersonal, misanthropic, objectivist, unfeeling, Eurocentric form, the only meaningful form of human knowledge; to the cumulative wisdom of humankind, modern science has added nothing, and subtracted a great deal. *It is not 'better' to think rather than feel, to analyse rather than empathise, to calculate rather than care. I write this* book out of my own vulnerable store of *personal, subjective, affective, intuitions;* but the latter are not inferior to the dissimulating cast of third person speculations that scientism thrives in. Organised science, the tool of domination, hopes to forcibly suppress this store of native ingenuity, given to all of us, and replace it with its own catechism of duly licensed, instrumentally adequate charlatanry, so we may all function like robots in the big machine. Science strips us of our own lived experience, the permanent source of all worthwhile empirical knowledge, preferring to smother our recalcitrant intuitions with putative 'truths' gleaned in remote, inaccessible, laboratories where the system, safely in command, can produce the enervating sop of rote, routine, and normalcy. Science itself – as a corporate tool seeking information for the sake of control – is a form of alienation, *viewing people as a means to proprietary ends*, spawned by modernist drives. Against its tyrannical, misanthropic sway, we need to emphasize the felicities of *personal knowledge*, our own personal purchase on the alembic of human *wisdom* cumulating for aeons; it's time we regained confidence in our own sovereign, critical faculties, so savagely repressed by the commissars of technocracy. The native shrewdness of the human race, underestimated by tyrants past and present, is still the best antidote to the varying oppressions of the relentlessly inventive impostures of capital.

We are not better off, in the modern epoch, than our forebears; we do not know more than they (indeed, they are what we know; except in the novel domain of threatening planetary survival); science and technology have not made life better for the populace; we are not more happy, nor more content, nor better read, nor more civil, nor more caring, nor more benign to life-forms. Instead, we are more powerless over our immediate environs, more critically dependent on others for daily needs; more de-skilled, and depersonalised; more resigned to an unrequited life; more lonely, and more disenchanted with our place in the scheme of things than at any epoch in history. The so-called 'romantics' of the past (much like the ilk of Gandhi in our own age) Carlyle, Ruskin, Southey, etc., were the true realist revolutionaries who fulminated (alongside peasants, workers, and others), in all hapless rage, against the falling dusk of modernist political economy, only to be savagely scorned as reactionaries, fools, and madmen, by an age won over to materialist wiles. It is their fears, and presentiments, that have been amply vindicated today; market forces, actively encouraged by the ruling orders, have ruthlessly desolated sociability, ravaging the most delicate balances of planetary existence. They called then for a banishment of the pernicious gospels of political economy; the time is ripe, nay overdue, now, to act upon that prophetic, but unheeded, call. All it takes, as a first step, is a personal, epistemic, break with the *logos* of modernism; the rest will follow like dawn after dusk.

We could choose to act now to preserve what still remains of the ravished treasure trove of our cultural heritage, and its eternal (but culturally-shaped) values of pluralism, autonomy, freedom, and coexistence. If we so choose, the material moment could be chained, once more, to moral preoccupations, economics yet again leashed to communal needs, power to cooperative coexistence. It is a globe that spins helplessly outside, apparently, of our wills; we, its benighted, transient time travellers; best not to reproduce that grand impotence within our own, malleable, communal relations, nor to pit force against force, will upon will, class to class, and order to order, in a profligate expense of wasteful energies. We may yet return to the great aboriginal understandings of our place in the fleeting universe; against the grim litany of modernist dehumanisations let us seek not analysis, but empathy; not science, but wisdom; not iron necessity and implacable propensities, red in tooth and claw, but human choices made by fallible, self-realising humans (to choose not to resist is also a human choice; as such, the roots of oppression lie not merely without, but within us as well: there is no 'enemy' that is other than of our own design and/or acquiescence), in the full scope of their free, if mediated, wills; not alien labour, but self-fulfilling, self-directed, corespective creations. In that sensual, easeful world, of simple exultation in the boundless bounty of *being*, economics will be, indeed can be, no more. *Imagine.*

Bibliography

Alchian, A.A. and Allen, W.R. (1964), *University Economics*, Wadsworth Publishing Co.: Belmont.
Althusser, L. (1971), *Lenin and Philosophy*, New Left Books: London.
Amin, S. (1976), *Unequal Development*, Monthly Review Press: New York.
Amin, S. (1988), *Eurocentrism*, Monthly Review Press: New York.
Amin, S. (1990a), *Delinking*, Zed Books: London.
Amin, S. (1990b), *Maldevelopment: Anatomy of a Global Failure*, Zed Books: London.
Amsden, A. (1990), 'Third World Industrialization: "Global Fordism" or New Model?', *New Left Review*, No. 182.
Arrow, K.J. (1987), 'Economic Theory and the Hypothesis of Rationality', in Eatwell, J. et al. (eds), (1987a, q.v.), pp. 69–74.
Avineri, S. (1969), *Karl Marx on Colonialism and Modernisation*, Lieber-Atherton: New York.
Avineri, S. (ed.) (1973), *Marx's Socialism*, Lieber-Atherton: New York.
Ayer, A.J. (1952), *Language, Truth and Logic*, Dover: New York.
Bachelard, G. (1970), *Le Rationalisme Applique*, Bibliotheque de Philosophie Contemporaine: Paris.
Bachelard, G. (1968), *The Philosophy of the New Scientific Mind*, Orion Press: New York.
Backhouse, R.E. (1994), *New Directions in Economic Methodology*, Routledge: London.
Bagchi, A. (1982), *Political Economy of Development and Underdevelopment*, Cambridge University Press: Cambridge.
Bahro, R. (1989), 'The Alternative in Eastern Europe', *New Left Review*, No. 177.
Banaji (1972), 'For a Theory of Colonial Modes of Production', *Economic and Political Weekly*, Vol. 7, No. 52, pp. 2498–502.

Bandhopadhyaya, J. and Shiva, V. (1987), 'Chipko: Politics of Ecology', *Seminar*, No. 330.

Baran, P. (1957), *The Political Economy of Growth*, Monthly Review Press: New York.

Baran, P. (1969), *The Longer View*, Monthly Review Press: New York.

Baran, P. and Sweezy, P. (1968), *Monopoly Capital*, Monthly Review Press: New York.

Barnes, D.G. (1930), *A History of the English Corn Laws from 1660–1848*, Routledge: London.

Benoit, E. (1968), 'The Monetary and Real Costs of National Defense', *American Economics Review*.

Berger, P. (1967), *The Social Construction of Reality*, Anchor Books: New York.

Bernal, M. (1987), *Black Athena: The Afroasiatic Roots of Classical Civilisation*, Vol. 1, Free Association Books: London.

Bhaskar, R. (1979), *The Possibility of Naturalism*, Harvester: Brighton.

Bhaskar, R. (1986), *Scientific Realism and Human Emancipation*, Verso: London.

Bhaskar, R. (1989a), *Reclaiming Reality*, Verso: London.

Bhaskar, R. (1989b), *The Possibility of Naturalism*, 2nd ed., Verso: London.

Blake, J. (1958), 'Jacob Morris on Unproductive Employment', *Science and Society*, 22.

Blaug, M. (1958a), *Ricardian Economics*, Yale University Press: New Haven.

Blaug, M. (1958b), 'The Classical Economists and the Factory Acts – A Re-examination', *Quarterly Journal of Economics*, 72, pp. 211–26.

Blaug, M. (1980), *The Methodology of Economics*, Cambridge University Press: Cambridge.

Blaug, M. (1990), *Economic Theories: True or False?*, Edward Elgar: Aldershot, Hants.

Blaug, M. (1992), *The Methodology of Economics*, 2nd ed., Cambridge University Press: Cambridge.

Bloch, M. (1962), *Feudal Society*, London: Routledge.

Blomstrom, M. and Hettne, B. (1984), *Development Theory in Transition*, Zed Books: London.

Bodley, J.H. (1982), *Victims of Progress*, Menlo Park: California.

Boland, L. (1981), 'On the Futility of Criticising the Neoclassical Maximisation Hypothesis', *American Economic Review*, 71.

Bolton, R. (1966), *Defense and Disarmament*, Prentice Hall: Englewood Cliffs.

Bowley, M. (1949), *Nassau Senior and Classical Economics*, Kelley: New York.

Branford, S. and Kucinski, B. (1988), *The Debt Squads*, Zed Books: London.

Brenner, R. (1977), 'The Origins of Capitalist Development: A Critique of Neo-Smithian Marxism', *New Left Review*, 104, pp. 25–92.

Brewer (1990), 'On Ricardo and All That: A Reply', *The Review of Radical Political Economy*.

Bronfenbrenner, M. (1970), 'Radical Economics in America: A 1970 Survey', *Journal of Economic Literature*, 9, pp. 747–66.

Brown, A. and Deaton, A. (1972), 'Models of Consumer Behaviour: A Survey', *Economic Journal*, 82, pp. 1145–66.

Bukharin (1926), *Historical Materialism: A System of Sociology*, International Publishers: New York.

Cairnes, J.E. (1965), *The Character and Logical Method of Political Economy*, Frank Cass: London.

Cannan, E. (1964), *A Review of Economic Theory*, 3rd ed., A.M. Kelley: New York.

Chomsky, N. (1986), *Towards a New Cold War*, Pantheon: New York.

Cleaver, H. (1979), *Reading Capital Politically*, University of Texas Press: Austin.

Coats, A.W. (ed.) (1971), *The Classical Economists and Economic Policy*, Methuen: London.

Coddington, A. (1972), 'Positive Economics', *Canadian Journal of Economics*, 5.

Comte, A. (1893), *The Positive Philosophy*, 2 vols, trans. Martineau, H., Kegan Paul: London.

Cowherd, R. (1956), *The Politics of English Dissent: the Religious Aspects of Liberal and Humanitarian Reform Movements from 1815 to 1848*, New York University Press: New York.

Cowherd, R. (1978), *Political Economists and the English Poor Laws*, Ohio University Press: Athens.

Davidson, B. (1987), 'The Ancient World and Africa: Whose Roots?', *Race and Class*, Vol. XXIX, No. 2, pp. 1–15.

De Grasse Jr., R.W. (1983), *Military Expansion and Economic Decline*, Council on Economic Priorities: New York.

De Marchi, N.B. (1974), 'The Success of Mill's Principles', *History of Political Economy*, 6, pp. 119–57.

Dobb, M. (1937), *Political Economy and Capitalism*, Routledge and Kegan Paul: London.

Dobb, M. (1963), *Studies in the Development of Capitalism*, International Publishers: New York.

Dobb, M. (1973), *Theories of Value and Distribution since Adam Smith*, Cambridge University Press: Cambridge.

Dorfman, R. (1989), 'Thomas Robert Malthus and David Ricardo', *Journal of Economic Perspectives*, Vol. 3, No. 3, pp. 153–64.

Draper, H. (ed.) (1971), *Marx and Engels' Writings on the Paris Commune*, Monthly Review Press: New York.

Durkheim, E. (1964), *The Rules of Sociological Method*, The Free Press: New York.

Eatwell, J. (1986), 'Notes on Effective Demand and Accumulation', submitted as a conference paper to the Department of Economics, University of Utah.

Eatwell, J., Milgate, M. and Newman, P. (eds) (1987a), *The New Palgrave: A Dictionary of Economics*, 4 vols, Macmillan: London.

Eatwell, J., Milgate, M., and Newman, P. (eds) (1987b), *Farewell to Reason*, Verso: London.

Edwards, R.E., Reich, M. and Weisskopf, T. (eds) (1978), *The Capitalist System*, 2nd ed., Prentice Hall: Englewood Cliffs.

Fetter, F.W. (1969), 'The Rise and Decline of Ricardian Economics', *History of Political Economy*, pp. 67–84.

Fetter, F.W. (1980), *The Economist in Parliament 1780–1868*, Duke University Press: Durham.

Feyerabend, P. (1975), *Against Method*, New Left Books: London.

Feyerabend, P. (1978), *Science in a Free Society*, Verso: London.

Feyerabend, P. (1987), *Farewell to Reason*, Verso: London.

Fisher, S. (1991), 'Recent Developments in Macroeconomics', in Oswald, A.J. (ed.), *Surveys in Economics*, Vol. 1, pp. 1–47.

Fleetwood, S. (forthcoming, 1997), 'Order Without Equilibrium: A Critical Realist Interpretation of Hayek's Notion of Spontaneous Order', *Cambridge Journal of Economics*.

Frank, A.G. (1966), 'The Development of Underdevelopment', *Monthly Review*, Vol. 18, No. 4, pp. 17–31.

Frey, B.S. and Eichenberger, R. (1989), 'Should Social Scientists Care About Choice Anomalies?', *Rationality and Society*, Vol. 1, No. 1, pp. 101–22.

Friedgut, T. and Seigelbaum, L. (1990), 'Perestroika from Below', *New Left Review*, No. 181.

Friedman, M. (1953), *Essays in Positive Economics*, University of Chicago Press: Chicago.

Fukuyama, F. (1989), 'The End of History', *National Interest*.

Galbraith, J.K. (1967), *The New Industrial State*, Houghton Mifflin: Boston.

Galbraith, J.K. (1969), *How to Control The Military*, Doubleday: New York.

Gerratana, V. (1977), 'Althusser and Stalinism', *New Left Review*, pp. 101–02.

Gerschenkron (1962), *Economic Backwardness in Historical Perspective*, Harvard University Press: Cambridge.

Giddens, A. (1971), *Capitalism and Modern Social Theory*, Cambridge University Press: Cambridge.

Giddens, A. (ed.) (1974), *Positivism and Sociology*, Heinemann: London.

Gordon, B. (1976), *Political Economy in Parliament 1819–1823*, Macmillan: London.
Gough, I. (1972), 'Marx's Theory of Productive and Unproductive Labour', *New Left Review*, No. 76.
Grampp, W.D. (1960), *The Manchester School of Economics*, Stanford University Press: Stanford.
Hahn, F. (1984), *Equilibrium and Macroeconomics*, Basil Blackwell: Oxford.
Hahn, F. (1985), *Money, Growth and Stability*, Basil Blackwell: Oxford.
Harcourt, G.C. (1969), 'Some Cambridge controversies in the theory of capital', *Journal of Economic Literature*, Vol. 7, pp. 369–405.
Hayek, F.A. (1942–43), 'Scientism and the Study of Society', *Economica*.
Hecht, S. and Cockburn, A. (1989), *Fate of the Forest*, Verso: London.
Hegel, G.W.F. (1956), *Philosophy of History*, Dover: New York.
Heilbroner, R. (1980), *Marxism: For and Against*, W.W. Norton: New York.
Hennipman, P. (1976), 'Pareto Optimality: value judgment or analytical tool?', in Cramer, J.S., Heertje, A. and Venekamp, P. (eds), *Relevance and Precision. From Quantitative Analysis to Economic Policy*, pp. 39–69.
Hicks, J.R. and Weber, W. (eds) (1973), *Carl Menger and the Austrian School of Economics*, Clarendon Press: Oxford.
Hindess, D. and Hirst, P. (1975), *Precapitalist Modes of Production*, Routledge and Kegan Paul: London and Boston.
Hinton, W. (1990), *The Great Reversal*, Monthly Review Press: New York.
Hirschman, A. (1981), *Essays in Trespassing: Economics to Politics and Beyond*, Cambridge University Press: Cambridge.
Hirst, P. (1976), 'Althusser and the Theory of Ideology', *Economy and Society*, Vol. 5, No. 4.
Hobsbawm, E.J. (1962), *The Age of Revolution*, Mentor: New York.
Hobsbawm, E.J. (1968), *Industry and Empire*, Penguin: Harmondsworth.
Hobson, J. (1968), *Imperialism – A Study*, Allen and Unwin: London.
Hollander, J.H. (1910), *David Ricardo: a Centenary Estimate*, Johns Hopkins Press: Baltimore.
Hollander, S. (1977), 'The Reception of Ricardian Economics', *Oxford Economic Papers*, n.s., 29, pp. 221–57.
Hollis, M. and Nell, E.J. (1975), *Rational Economic Man*, Cambridge University Press: Cambridge.
Hoogvelt, A. (1982), *The Third World in Global Development*, Macmillan: London.
Hume, D. (1748), *Essays Moral and Political*, A. Millar, etc.: London.
Hume, D. (1886), *A Treatise on Human Nature*, Clarendon: Oxford.
Hunt, D. (1989), *Economic Theories of Development*, Barnes and Noble Books: Savage, Maryland.
Hunt, E.K. (1983), 'Joan Robinson and the Labour Theory of Value', *Cambridge Journal of Economics*, 7, pp. 331–42.

Hutchinson, T.W. (1956), 'Professor Machlup on Verification in Economics', *Southern Economic Journal*, 22.

Hutchinson, T.W. (1973), 'Some Themes from Investigations into Method', in Hicks, J.R. and Weber, W. (eds).

Illich, I. (1971), *Deschooling Society*, Harper and Row: New York.

Joseph, G.G. (1992), *The Crest of the Peacock*, Penguin: London.

Joseph, G.G., Reddy, V. and Searle-Chatterjee, M. (1990), 'Eurocentrism in the Social Sciences', *Race and Class*, Vol. 31, No. 4, pp. 1–26.

Kanth, R. (1985), 'The Decline of Ricardian Politics: Some Notes on Paradigm-Shift in Economics from the Classical to the NeoClassical Persuasion', *European Journal of Political Economy*, Vol. 1, No. 2, pp. 157–87.

Kanth, R. (1986), *Political Economy and Laissez-Faire: Economics and Ideology in the Ricardian Era*, Rowman and Littlefield: Totowa, New Jersey.

Kanth, R. (1991a), 'Economic Theory and Realism: Outlines of a Reconstruction', *Methodus*, Vol. 3, No. 2, pp. 37–45.

Kanth, R. (ed.) (1991b), *Explorations in Political Economy*, Rowman and Littlefield: Savage, Maryland.

Kanth, R. (1992), *Capitalism and Social Theory*, M.E. Sharpe: Armonk.

Kanth, R. (ed.) (1994), *Paradigms in Economic Development*, M.E. Sharpe: Armonk.

Kanth, R. (forthcoming, 1997), *Breaking With the Enlightenment: The Twilight of History and the Rediscovery of Utopia*, Humanities Press: New Jersey.

Kidron, M. (1968), *Western Capitalism Since the War*, Weidenfeld and Nicolson: London.

Kolokowski, L. (1972), *Positivist Philosophy from Hume to the Vienna Circle*, Penguin Books: Harmondsworth.

Koshimura, S. (1975), *Theory of Capitalist Reproduction and Accumulation*, DPG Publishing Co.: Ontario.

Kuhn, T.S. (1962), *The Structure of Scientific Revolutions*, University of Chicago Press: Chicago.

Kuhn, T.S. (1970), *The Structure of Scientific Revolutions*, 2nd ed., University of Chicago Press: Chicago.

Lakatos, I. and Musgrave, A. (eds) (1970), *Criticism and the Growth of Knowledge*, Cambridge University Press: Cambridge.

Lal, D. (1985), 'Misconceptions of Development Economics', *Finance and Development*, 22, pp. 10–13.

Lange, O. (1945), 'The Scope and Method of Economics', *Review of Economic Studies*.

Latsis, S.J. (1972), 'Situational Determinism in Economics', *British Journal for the Philosophy of Science*, 23, pp. 207–45.

Latsis, S.J. (ed.), (1976), *Method and Appraisal in Economics*, Cambridge University Press: Cambridge.

Lawson, T. (1994), 'A Realist Theory for Economics', in Backhouse, R.E., pp. 257–85.

Lecourt, D. (1975), *Marxism and Epistemology*, Verso: London.

Lenin, V.I. (1939), *Imperialism, the Highest Stage of Capitalism*, International Publishers: New York.

Leontief, W. and Hoffenberg, M. (1961), 'The Economic Effects of Disarmament', *Scientific American*.

Letwin, W. (1964), *The Origins of Scientific Economics*, Doubleday & Co., Inc.: New York.

Lewis, W.A. (1954), 'Economic Development with Unlimited Supplies of Labour', *The Manchester School*, Vol. XXII, No. 2, pp. 139–91.

Lindbeck, A. (1971), *The Political Economy of the New Left: an Outsider's View*, Harper and Row: New York.

Lipietz, A. (1987a), *The Crisis of Global Fordism*, Verso: London.

Lipietz, A. (1987b), *Mirages and Miracles: the Crisis of Global Fordism*, Verso: London.

Lukacs, G. (1971), *History and Class Consciousness*, MIT Press: Cambridge, Mass.

Luxemburg, R. (1968), *The Accumulation of Capital*, Monthly Review Press: New York.

Lyotard, J.F. (1984), *The Post-modern Condition: A Report on Knowledge*, University of Minnesota Press: Minneapolis.

Machlup, F. (1978), *Methodology of Economics and Other Social Sciences*, Academic Press: New York.

Malthus, T.R. (1964), *Principles of Political Economy Considered with a View to Their Practical Application*, 2nd ed. (1836), with an introduction by Morton Paglin, Augustus M. Kelley: New York.

Malthus, T.R. (1982), *An Essay on the Principle of Population and a Summary View of the Principle of Population*, (1970), Flew, A. (ed.), Harmondsworth: Penguin.

Mandel, E. (1968), *Marxian Economic Theory*, Monthly Review Press: New York.

Mandel, E. (1970), *Marxism Economic Theory*, Vol. 1, Monthly Review Press: New York.

Mandel, E. (1971), *The Formulation of the Economic Thought of Karl Marx*, Monthly Review Press: New York.

Mandel, E. (1974), 'Ten Theses on the Social and Economic Laws Governing the Society Transitional between Capitalism and Socialism', *Critique*, 3.

Mandel, E. (1978), *Late Capitalism*, Verso: London.

Mandel, E. (1986), 'In Defence of Socialist Planning', *New Left Review*, No. 159.

Mandel, E. and Freedman, A. (eds) (1984), *Ricardo, Marx, Sraffa: the Langston Memorial Volume*, Verso: London.
Mantoux, P. (1961), *The Industrial Revolution in the 18th Century*, Macmillan: New York.
Marx, K. (1853), 'The Future Results of British Rule in India', *New York Daily Tribune*, 8 August.
Marx, K. (1935), *Value, Price and Profit*, International Publishers: New York.
Marx, K. (1961), *Capital*, Vol. 1, London.
Marx, K. (1965), *Pre-Capitalist Economic Formations*, Hobsbawm, E.J. (ed.), International Publishers: New York.
Marx, K. (1967), *Capital*, International Publishers: New York.
Marx, K. (1969), *Theories of Surplus Value*, Lawrence and Wishart: London.
Marx, K. (1988), 'Theses on Feuerbach', in Engels, F., *Ludwig Feuerbach and the End of Classical German Philosophy*.
Marx, K. and Engels, F. (1964), *The Communist Manifesto*, Sweezy, P. and Huberman, L. (eds), Monthly Review Press: New York.
Marx, K. and Engels, F. (1968), *The Communist Manifesto*, Monthly Review Press: New York.
Marx, K. and Engels, F. (1970), *The German Ideology*, Lawrence and Wishart: New York.
Mattick, P. (1969), *Marx and Keynes*, Porter Sargent: Boston.
Meek, R.I. (1950), 'The Decline of Ricardian Economics in England', *Economica*, n.s., 17, pp. 43–62.
Melman, S. (1970), *Pentagon Capitalism*, McGraw Hill: New York.
Melman, S. (ed.) (1971), *The War Economy of the U.S.*, St. Martin's Press: New York.
Mendes, C. (1989), *Fight for the Forest*, Monthly Review Press: New York.
Mill, J. (1968), *History of British India*, Chelsea House: New York.
Mirowski, P. (1988), *Against Mechanism*, Rowman and Littlefield: Totowa, New Jersey.
Molyneux, M. (1990), 'The "Woman Question" in the Age of Perestroika', *New Left Review*, No. 183.
Myint, H. (1946), 'The Classical View of the Economic Problem', *Economica*, n.s., 13, pp. 199–30.
Myint, H. (1954), 'An Interpretation of Economic Backwardness', *Oxford Economic Papers*, Vol. 6, No. 6, pp. 132–63.
Myrdal, G. (1959), *Value in Social Theory*, Routledge and Kegan Paul: London.
Myrdal, G. (1970), *Objectivity in Social Research*, Gerald Duckworth: London.
Nambroodripad, E.M.S. (1952), *The National Question in Kerala*, Bombay.
Neurath, O. (1973), *Empiricism and Sociology*, D. Reidel: Dordrecht.

Nurkse, R. (1952), 'Some International Aspects of the Problem of Economic Development', *American Economic Review*, Vol. XLII, No. 2, pp. 571–83.

O'Brien, D.P. (1970), *J.P. McCulloch: A Study in Classical Economics*, Barnes and Noble Inc.: New York.

O'Brien, D.P. (1975), *The Classical Economists*, Clarendon Press: Oxford.

Okishio, N. (1961), 'Technical Changes and the Rate of Profit', *Kobe University Economic Review*, No. 7, pp. 85–99.

Oswald, A.J. (ed.) (1991), *Surveys in Economics*, 2 vols, Basil Blackwell: Oxford.

Outhewaite, W. (1977), *Understanding Social Life*, George Allen and Unwin: London.

Pasinetti, L. (1974), *Growth and Income Distribution*, Cambridge University Press: Cambridge.

Pasinetti, L. (1977), *Lectures on the Theory of Production*, Columbia University Press: New York.

Peach, T. (1984), 'David Ricardo's Early Treatment of Profitability: A New Interpretation', *Economic Journal*, 94, pp. 733–51.

Peach, T. (1987), 'David Ricardo and the Invariable Standard', unpublished paper presented to the 1987 History of Economics Conference, Boston.

Peek, M. and Scherer, F. (1962), *The Weapons Acquisition Process*, Division of Research, Graduate School of Business Administration: Boston.

Pigou, A. (1933), *The Theory of Unemployment*, Macmillan: London.

Plekhanov, G.V. (1972), *In Defense of Materialism*, International Publishers: New York.

Popper, K.R. (1962), *The Open Society and its Enemies*, Routledge and Kegan Paul: London.

Popper, K.R. (1972), *Conjectures and Refutations: the Growth of Scientific Knowledge*, Routledge and Kegan Paul: London.

Prebisch, R. (1950), 'The Latin American Periphery in the Global System of Capitalism', *CEPAL Review*, No. 13, pp. 143–50.

Reich, M. (1980), 'Empirical and Ideological Elements in the Decline of Ricardian Economics', *Review of Radical Political Economics*, 12, pp. 1–14.

Ricardo, D. (1951–73), *The Works and Correspondence of David Ricardo*, 11 vols, Sraffa, P. (ed.), Cambridge University Press: Cambridge.

Ricardo, D. (1974), *Principles of Political Economy and Taxation*, Winch, D. (ed.), Dent: London.

Robbins, L. (1935), *An Essay on the Nature and Significance of Economic Science*, 2nd ed., Macmillan: London.

Robbins, L. (1953), *The Theory of Economic Policy*, Macmillan: London.

Robinson, J. (1962), *Economic Philosophy*, C.A. Watts: London.

Robinson, J. (1966), *Economic Philosophy*, Penguin: London.

Rogin, L. (1971), *Meaning and Validity of Economic Theory*, Books for Libraries Press: New York.

Rostow, W.W. (1960), *The Stages of Economic Growth*, Monthly Review Press: New York.

Rowthorn, R. (1974), 'Neo-Classicism, Neo-Ricardianism, and Marxism', *New Left Review*, 86, pp. 63–87.

Rubin, I.I. (1979), *A History of Economic Thought*, Ink Links: London.

Samuels, W. (ed.) (1988), *Institutional Economics*, Edward Elgar: Aldershot.

Samuelson, P.A. (1966), *The Collected Scientific Papers of Paul A. Samuelson*, Vols. 1 and 2, MIT Press: Cambridge, Mass.

Samuelson, P.A. (1971), 'Understanding the Marxian Notion of Exploitation: A Summary of the So-Called Transformation Problem between Marxian Values and Competitive Prices', *Journal of Economic Literature*, 9, pp. 399–432.

Schumpeter, J.A. (1954a), *History of Economic Analysis*, Oxford University Press: New York.

Schumpeter, J.A. (1954b), *Economic Doctrine and Method*, Oxford University Press: New York.

Schumpeter, J. A. (1976), *Capitalism, Socialism and Democracy*, George Allen and Unwin: London.

Sen, A.K. (1983), 'Development: Which Way Now?', *Economic Journal*, 93, pp. 745–62.

Senior, N. (1928), *Industrial Efficiency and Social Economy*, Vol. 1, Henry Holt and Co.: New York.

Shiva, V. (1989), *Staying Alive*, Zed Books: London.

Shiva, V. (1991), *The Violence of the Green Revolution*, Zed Books: London.

Shove, G.F. (1942), 'The Place of Marshall's Principles in the Development of Economic Theory', *The Economic Journal*, 52, pp. 294–329.

Simon, H. (1957), *Models of Man*, Wiley and Sons: New York.

Smith, A. (1970), *Wealth of Nations*, London.

Sraffa, P. (ed.) (1951–73), *The Works and Correspondence of David Ricardo*, Cambridge University Press: Cambridge.

Sraffa, P. (1960), *Production of Commodities by Means of Commodities*, Cambridge University Press: Cambridge.

Stedman-Jones, G. (1971), 'The Marxism of the Early Lukacs', *New Left Review*, 70.

Stigler, G.J. (1950), 'The Development of Utility Theory', *Journal of Political Economy*, 58, pp. 307–96.

Stigler, G.J. (1952), 'The Ricardian Theory of Value and Distribution', *Journal of Political Economy*, 60, pp. 187–207.

Sweezy, P. (1970), *Theory of Capitalist Development*, Monthly Review Press: New York.

Sweezy, P. (1971), 'The Transition to Socialism', in Sweezy, P. and Bettelheim, C. (eds), *On the Transition to Socialism*, Monthly Review Press: New York.

Sweezy, P. (1984), personal communication, 2 June.

Thomson, D. (1978), *England in the 19th Century*, Penguin Books: Harmondsworth.

Thurow, L.C. (1975), *Generating Inequality*, Macmillan Press: London.

Toynbee, A. (1920), *Lectures on the Industrial Revolution of the 18th Century*, Longmans, Green and Co.: London.

Toynbee, A. (1928), *Lectures on the Industrial Revolution of the 18th Century*, Longmans, Green and Co.: London.

Tribe, K. (1978), *Land, Labour and Economic Discourse*, Routledge and Kegan Paul: London.

Udis, B. (1973), *The Economic Consequences of Reduced Military Spending*, Lexington Books: Lexington.

Union for Radical Political Economists (1975), *Radical Perspectives on the Economic Crisis of Monopoly Capitalism*, URPE: New York.

US Government (1982), *Economic Report of the President*, Washington.

Walsh, V. and Gram, H. (1980), *Classical and Neo-Classical Theories of General Equilibrium*, Oxford University Press: New York.

Warren, B. (1980), *Imperialism: Pioneer of Capitalism*, Verso: London.

Watts, M. (1983), *Silent Violence*, University of California Press: Berkeley.

Weber, M. (1949), *The Methodology of the Social Sciences*, Shils, E.A. and Finch, H.A. (eds), The Free Press: Glencoe.

Weidenbaum, M. (1968), 'Arms and the American Economy', *American Economic Review*

Winch, P. (1958), *The Idea of a Social Science*, Routledge and Kegan Paul. London.

Wittfogel, K. (1957), *Oriental Despotism*, Yale University Press: New Haven.

Wood, J.C. (ed.) (1991), *David Ricardo: Critical Assessments*, 4 vols, Routledge: London.

DATE DUE

~~NOV 19 2001~~	~~DEC 10 2001~~	
~~SEP 0 8 2003~~		
~~APR 1~~		
~~NOV 0 7 2005~~		

Printed in USA

HIGHSMITH #45230